THE DEATH OF THE BIG MEN
AND THE RISE OF THE BIG SHOTS

ASAO Studies in Pacific Anthropology

General Editor: Rupert Stasch, Department of Anthropology, University of California, San Diego

The Association for Social Anthropology in Oceania (ASAO) is an international organization dedicated to studies of Pacific cultures, societies, and histories. This series publishes monographs and thematic collections on topics of global and comparative significance, grounded in anthropological fieldwork in Pacific locations.

Volume 1
The Anthropology of Empathy: Experiencing the Lives of Others in Pacific Societies
Edited by Douglas W. Hollan and C. Jason Throop

Volume 2
Christian Politics in Oceania
Edited by Matt Tomlinson and Debra McDougall

Volume 3
The Death of the Big Men and the Rise of the Big Shots: Custom and Conflict in East New Britain
Keir Martin

Volume 4
Creating a Nation with Cloth: Women, Wealth, and Tradition in the Tongan Diaspora
Ping-Ann Addo

The Death of the Big Men and the Rise of the Big Shots

Custom and Conflict in East New Britain

Keir Martin

berghahn
NEW YORK · OXFORD
www.berghahnbooks.com

First published in 2013 by

Berghahn Books

www.berghahnbooks.com

© 2013 Keir Martin

Library of Congress Cataloging-in-Publication Data
Martin, Keir.
The death of the big men and the rise of the big shots : custom and
conflict in East New Britain / Keir Martin.
   p. cm.
   Includes bibliographical references and index.
   ISBN 978-0-85745-872-8 (hardback : alk. paper) --
   ISBN 978-0-85745-873-5 (e-book)
1. Ethnology--Papua New Guinea--New Britain Island. 2. Big man
(Melanesia)--Papua New Guinea--New Britain Island. 3. Reciprocity
(Commerce)--Papua New Guinea--New Britain Island. 4. Social conflict--
Papua New Guinea--New Britain Island. 5. Natural disasters--Papua New
Guinea--New Britain Island. 6. New Britain Island (Papua New Guinea)--
Social life and customs. I. Title.
   GN671.N5M36 2012
   306.09958'5--dc23

                                                      2012025596

British Library Cataloguing in Publication Data
A catalogue record for this book is available from the British Library
Printed in the United States on acid-free paper.

ISBN: 978-0-85745-872-8 Hardback
ISBN: 978-0-85745-873-5 Ebook

Dedication

I would like to dedicate this book to two friends from Papua New Guinea, who died between the completion of my fieldwork and the completion of this work. Both Anton Daniels and Joap ToMong provided great assistance and, most importantly, great times and great friendship during my time in East New Britain. Without them this book would not have taken the form that it did and without them I would have missed out on many wonderful times. They were both truly great men and it is with a mixture of great pleasure and great sadness that I dedicate this book to them both.

Contents 🏵

List of Illustrations

Photographs

All photographs were taken by the author, in December 2009 and January 2010

Diagrams

Acknowledgements

There are a number of people and organisations that I feel the need to thank for their help over the years in making this book a possibility. Fieldwork between 2002 and 2004 was supported by grants from the Economic and Social Research Council (ESRC) in the UK and the Wenner Gren Foundation. The ESRC also supported a visit to the Melanesian archives at the University of California San Diego. This visit was also supported in part by the Friends of the UCSD library, whom I should also like to thank. Finally the Danish Council for Independent Research Humanities supported a return visit to my field site in 2009 and provided support during some of the time that I was completing this manuscript. In Papua New Guinea, the National Research Institute and National Cultural Commission provided valuable help in facilitating my research and I should like to thank their officers for that assistance.

As a postgraduate student at the University of Manchester, I received intellectual stimulation from a number of my peers. I should like to especially thank Emily Walmsley, Richard Sherrington, Mattia Fumanti, Lorenzo Cana-Botos, Paul Strauss, Carlo Cubero, Lucy Pickering, Tom Wormald, Tom Grisaffi, Tiffany McComsey, Pablo Jaramillo, Penny Moore, Rosie Read and Will Rollason. I should like to thank a number of members of staff (some of whom are now colleagues) for their support, including Don Kulick, John Gledhill, Maia Green, Sarah Green, Richard Werbner, Peter Wade, Stewart Muir, Michelle Obeid, Jack Taylor and Penny Harvey. Special thanks should go to Lynn Dignan without whom this book would have had no chance of appearing. During my time at San Diego I benefitted from conversations with a number of graduate students including Candler Hallman, Nicole Petersen, Ryan Schram and in particular Nicole Barger. I also benefitted from conversations with Joel Robbins, whose support I am particularly grateful for, and from the late Don Tuzin. Perhaps my greatest regret regarding the publication of this book is that I will not be able to discuss its shortcomings with Don, who, as a true friend and a serious scholar, would not have insulted me by hiding them from me. Nonetheless, I am grateful for the feedback that Don was able to give me and his influence is present in Chapter Four in particular. Particular thanks should also go to Kathy Creely and to the staff of the Special Collections section at UCSD. In Denmark, I am grateful for conversations that I have had with members of staff there including Ton Otto, Nils Bubandt, Maria Louw, Poul Pedersen and Lotte Meinert. In particular, however, I should like to thank the exceptional community of Ph.D. scholars who were gathered at Aarhus University at the time of my stay there: Anders Sybrandt Hansen,

Bjarke Nielsen, Bagga Bjerge, Christian Suhr Nielsen, Henrik Hvenegaard, Maj Nygaard-Christensen, Marie Hojlund Braemer, Martin Demant Frederiksen, Mette-Louise Johansen, Nina Holm Vohnsen, Peter Bjerregaard, Yasna Singh, Thomas Sogaard Jensen and Thomas Fibiger. I should like to extend a particularly strong 'thank you' to Anders Emil Rasmussen and Steffen Dalsgaard who provided many useful insights. During my visits to Australia I benefitted from conversations with Colin Filer, Michael Lowe, Borut Telban, Jadran Mimica, Neil Maclean, Andrew Moutu and Holly High. In visits to the Max Planck Institute in Halle I was grateful for the chance to consult with Holger Jebens, Joachim Otto Habeck and Ludek Broz. This list in no way exhausts those to whom I have an intellectual debt and I hope that those that I have had to exclude understand that I am still deeply grateful for their contributions.

Preparing a book manuscript is an often frustrating process. I am deeply grateful for the patient support provided by the editor of this book series, Rupert Stasch, without whom, it is safe to say, I would never have completed this process. Rupert invested a great amount of time and energy in helping me past all of the intellectual and technical barriers that I had placed in my own path in the course of writing this book and I should like to extend a heartfelt thanks to him. I should also like to thank the staff at Berghahn Books and the anonymous reviewers for their input. Particular thanks should also go to my Ph.D. thesis examiners, Rane Willerslev and Chris Gregory, both of whom provided useful comments and insights. Rane has provided continuous intellectual engagement over the years as has Chris, whose intellectual influence on the development of the ideas in this book should be apparent.

Earlier versions of certain passages and arguments in this book have appeared in other forms before. Parts of Chapter Three appeared as 'Land, Customary and Non-Customary in East New Britain' in J. Weiner and K. Glaskin (eds.), *Customary Land Tenure and Registration in Australia and Papua New Guinea*, published in 2006 in Canberra by the Australian National University Press. Parts of Chapter Four appeared as 'Names as Markers and Makers of Contested Identity: On Social Groups in the New Guinea Islands', published in 2009 in *Oceania* 79(2):162–76. Parts of Chapter Eight appeared in 'A Fish Trap for Custom: How Nets Work at Matupit', published in 2006 in *Paideuma* 52:73–90. Parts of Chapter Nine appeared in 'The Death of the Big Men: Depreciation of Elites in New Guinea', published in 2010 in *Ethnos* 75(1):1–22. Parts of Chapter Ten appeared in 'Your Own *Buai* You Must Buy: The Contested Ideology of Possessive Individualism in East New Britain', published in 2007 in *Anthropological Forum* 17(3):285–98. I should like to thank the publishers of these pieces for making it possible for me to reproduce or rework elements of them for inclusion in this book.

A special 'thank you' must go to T.S. (Scarlett) Epstein whose work among Tolai villagers at Rapitok is well known to scholars of the South Pacific.

Scarlett was very generous in offering me advice before I began fieldwork and has also been kind enough to allow the use of extracts from her late husband's (A.L. Epstein) fieldnotes taken at Matupit in the late 1950s and 1960s. The perspective taken in this book differs in some respects from that taken by the Epsteins and other previous ethnographers of the region, but what I have done here would have been impossible without the previous groundbreaking work of Scarlett and others whose work has stood the test of time as demanding an intellectual engagement.

The biggest intellectual 'thank you' must go to my Ph.D. supervisor, Karen Sykes, who has been a part of this project from the very beginning. Supervision and collaboration should always be a process of intellectual challenge, and Karen has provided that in abundance. Although I know that Karen does not agree with every argument or formulation in this book, the influence of her input and our discussions marks and shapes every chapter. Without that influence, this book, if it existed at all, would be a far poorer piece of work.

A great debt of thanks must go to the many people who helped me conduct fieldwork in Papua New Guinea. Many members of the expatriate community in Rabaul provided friendship and support, amongst whom I must thank Gerry and Joyce McGrade, Bruce Alexander, Suzie Alexander, Guy and Catherine Cameron, Steve Saunders and Andrew Avenell. Particular thanks must go to Andy Holding for hospitality and anthropological decompression. Thanks also go to David Loh who has sadly passed away in the years since I completed fieldwork. Most of all I should like to thank the people who hosted me and took the time to help me and hang out with me at the villages of Matupit and Matupit-Sikut. I cannot thank all of the individuals who helped me here and I hope that a few names of those that I was closest to will suffice to express my gratitude to everyone. Donald Bakut, Casi Buabua, Harrison Ereman, Peter Gumla and Pisa Lambert all gave generously of their time. Peni Dokta in particular became a close friend whose day-to-day company was one of the great pleasures of fieldwork. Eliab Wuat and Helen and their entire family very graciously looked after me at Matupit for which I am deeply grateful. ToMesak spent many days at Matupit helping me to work out the changing patterns of social life and provided many hours of fruitful conversation. Thanks must also go to Dr Jacob Simet, both in his capacity as director of the National Cultural Commission, and in his capacity as home-grown anthropologist of Matupit, for his help, both practical and intellectual, in making sense of Tolai social life. Particular thanks must also go to ToDi Turagil, his wife Margaret and their entire family for the assistance that they gave me at Sikut and their companionship. Again, I can only apologise for the many others that I do not have space to recognise here.

On a personal note, I should like to thank my parents, both of whom encouraged me in writing and academic endeavours from an early age. I should also like to thank Ruth James for her support in starting this project and friends of mine in Manchester, such as Sue Hawkins, Nick Donlon and Sid Baxter, for hanging out with me during the years it has taken to complete it. Most of all, I should like to thank Anne Kehlet Bavngaard for her support and assistance during the completion of this book. Anne's contribution to this book has been immense. She has given a great amount of time to helping me sort out technical problems. Most importantly, she has been there to offer support throughout this process. Anne has given me the confidence and resolve to complete this process at times when I felt like throwing all my work out of the window and I should like to express my thanks to her for putting up with me during this period.

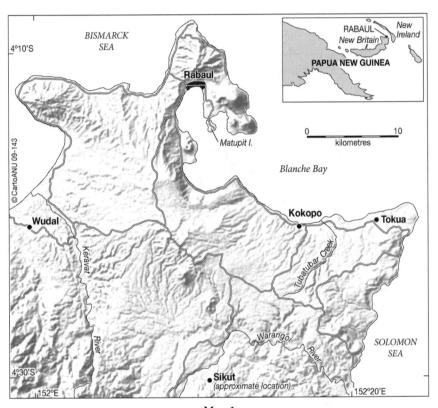

Map 1

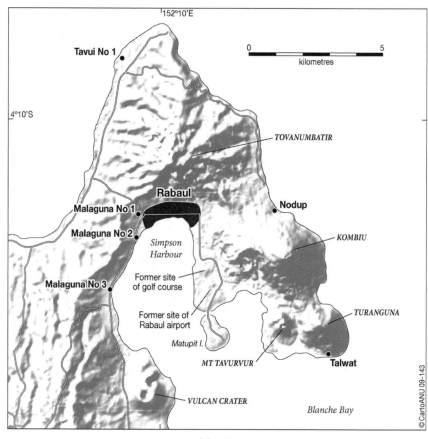

Map 2

Note on Language 🏵

Three languages are routinely used by Tolai people in the Gazelle Peninsula, and were routine languages of my field research: English, the Papua New Guinean lingua franca Tok Pisin, and the Tolai vernacular Kuanua. Because language and cross-language processes are central to this book's subject, it is often important to be clear about which words are from which languages. Throughout this book, Kuanua words and expressions are given in *italics*, while Tok Pisin words are given in combined *italics and underlining*. At certain points, for extra clarity I also indicate the language of key terms using the abbreviations 'E.', 'TP.', and 'K.'.

Introduction

Land Politics and Postcolonial Sociality in the Wake of Environmental Disaster

On 14 September 1994, the twin volcanoes of Tarvurvur and Vulcan erupted, devastating Rabaul, the provincial capital of East New Britain, as well as many surrounding villages predominantly inhabited by members of the ethnic group known as the Tolai (see Map 1). The destroyed Tolai villages included Matupit, the community that is at the heart of this study (see Map 2). The volcanic eruption is what first drew the attention of many, including myself, to this area of the South Pacific, a part of the independent country of Papua New Guinea (PNG). After the volcano, the residents of Matupit, who are called 'Matupi', fled in all directions, many to stay with relatives in other villages across the wider surrounding region. Some Matupi began returning to their home village within months of the eruption, and most were back at Matupit at the time of my fieldwork from 2002 until 2004. Others have permanently resettled in other areas. For all of them life has changed forever. Permanent homes that had cost the equivalent of thousands of pounds sterling to construct, representing the major investment of a lifetime, had been destroyed.[1] Agricultural land, from which many Matupi had made a good living through cash cropping, had been rendered barren. The town of Rabaul, a major source of income for the large number of Matupi who worked or sold produce there, had been almost totally devastated, not just by the volcano itself, but also by the waves of looters that swept through in the weeks following the eruption. People with previously steady incomes and comfortable standards of living are now living hand to mouth in the shattered ruins of their former homes.

Once stable lives have been thrown into a state of uncertainty that the Matupi are only now beginning to accept as permanent. In 2002, shortly after I arrived in East New Britain to conduct fieldwork, one man described to me how when his family left Matupit they thought that they would be returning in a few days, as had happened after a mini-tsunami in the early 1970s. This man had lived in a permanent-materials house with a Yamaha keyboard and large amplifiers that he had imported from the U.S.A., along with other consumer durables such as a large refrigerator and an electric sewing machine for his wife. His family did return to the village a few days after the eruption, but

1. View of Rabaul Town and Simpson Harbour

only to collect some belongings. He then thought that they would be back for good a few weeks later and that life would be back to 'normal' in a manner of months. He told me retrospectively that his biggest regret was that he was not 'sad enough' when he went back to Matupit that first time and stood in the wreckage of his former home. 'If I had known that we were not going to get it back again, I would have been more sad.'

Beyond 'Before and After': A History of Contest and Change

Such an event of radical rupture has parallels in processes of cultural and historical change that are a major focus of attention in much contemporary Melanesian ethnography. Seeking to break away from a stereotype in which Melanesian peoples are described as the essentially unchanging opposite of Western society, some contemporary scholars are keen to stress moments of radical change. A typical case of this is the experience of religious conversion and subsequent rejection of former customs (Tuzin 1997, Robbins 2004). Other examples include dealing with the impact of mining projects, or the increasing role of the state in regulating social relations through institutions such as schools or village courts. In studies of these topics, the reader is presented, as the title of one recent ethnography put it, with 'a world of before and after' (Knauft 2002).[2]

In East New Britain, the volcanic eruption of 1994 was indeed a cataclysmic event that disrupted every aspect of social life. It would be tempting to treat this as a unique watershed that pushed the Matupit social world into a state of complete chaos and novelty, in which utterly new kinds of social relations and conceptualisations of social relations seemed to emerge. One new figure of this era, for example, is the figure of the 'Big Shot'. This is a derogatory label applied to Tolai who are considered to have forgotten their moral obligations to others in their eagerness to join the ranks of an emergent socio-economic elite. (Besides the English language expression 'Big Shot', Tolai also use the Tok Pisin word *biksot* to talk about this figure.) However, even highly novel contemporary conceptualisations such as this only make sense in the context of a history of concern about the appropriate limits of reciprocal interdependence, and as a conscious contrast to older categories such as the 'Big Man'. Rather than looking at concepts that have been radically changed, created or destroyed by the cataclysm of the volcano, this study is concerned with the ways in which core concepts of Tolai social life have in fact been evolving in the context of changing patterns of integration with a global political economy for decades.

But the processes of disruption, relocation and reconstruction that unfolded after the volcano's eruption did lay bare many emerging social trends and tensions. In the wake of the volcano, there were frequent disputes over the degree of responsibility of elected political leaders or successful local entrepreneurs for helping their less fortunate kin and fellow villagers to reconstruct their lives. These disputes cast into relief how much 'grassroots' villagers felt ignored and belittled by their more fortunate cousins, the aforementioned 'Big Shots'. (The term 'grassroots' is commonly used throughout Papua New Guinea in English and Tok Pisin to describe ordinary villagers who make up the majority of the country's population.) Debates over management of new land granted to the Matupit community after the eruption similarly put under harsh new light ongoing tensions over land rights and the often fraught relationship between nuclear families and extended kinship obligations based on 'clans'.[3]

In this book, I will examine how these social controversies precipitated by the eruption are indicative of a fundamental tension in Tolai society: namely an ongoing multifaceted contest over the appropriate limits of reciprocal interdependence and obligation. The increasingly important distinction and conflict between grassroots villagers and Big Shots can to a large extent be understood as a battle of different perspectives over the contexts in which it is appropriate to make claims based on a history of previous interdependence and when it is possible to assert independence from such interlocking obligations. Attempts to claim independence from reciprocal obligations are at the heart of the increasingly important assertions of individualism in different contexts. Such individualism takes many forms. Indeed the same person or set of persons can be viewed or presented as an entity that is constituted by its relations with others in one context, and as an entity that exists independently prior to its relations with others in another context.

In this book, I examine how growing social divisions and diverse emergent forms of individuality are produced by battles to fix the ever shifting boundaries of reciprocal interdependence. In the first four chapters, for example, I outline the changing politics of land in Tolai villages such as Matupit. Discussions of land tenure in Papua New Guinea are often dominated by assertions of the virtues and drawbacks of collective customary land tenure. This customary tenure is contrasted with attempts to introduce individual land ownership, which some people hope will promote greater economic development. In the Gazelle Peninsula, where Tolai live, this discussion often comes down to a dispute over the desirability of continuing to organise access to land around matrilineal clan membership versus switching towards patrilineal inheritance, which is commonly understood to involve prioritising individual or family-based interests. I argue in this book that the assumption that patrilineal inheritance is more 'individualistic', while shared by opposing sides in the debates, actually misses the complexity of the different ways in which individuality is asserted and constructed in different social contexts. In some contexts, an individual property holder can be the individual person or family unit attempting to assert claims of independence against the overlapping claims of relatives within a clan. In other contexts, the clan can attempt to constitute itself as a collective individual property holder, against others that it has a history of relation to, and who may themselves claim overlapping interests in the land by virtue of that history of relationship.

At this point it would probably be useful to briefly clarify my use of the term reciprocity. As Rio (2007:450) observes, the history of anthropology as a discipline has left us with 'a problem with the terminology' regarding the meaning of the term. Gregory (1994:911) observes that in anthropological use, the term has a more specific meaning than it does in non-anthropological discourse. For anthropologists, reciprocity is a 'non-market principle', tied to gift exchange that is 'at the heart of theoretical debates concerning the distinction between market and non-market forms of valuation' (ibid.). Gift exchange implies links of ongoing reciprocal interdependence, as opposed to commodity exchange which is characterised by reciprocal independence, or what Marx (1976:182) describes as 'reciprocal isolation'. Although commodity exchange is reciprocal in the commonsense understanding that one receives in return for what one gives, it is a transaction conducted as if in a stand-alone moment, with no prior or resultant ongoing moral obligations between participants, and hence does not help to constitute the transactors as persons whose existence is reliant upon ongoing ties of reciprocal interdependence. My use of the term 'reciprocity' in this book follows this common anthropological usage, to describe transactions embedded in relations of ongoing reciprocal interdependence. Persons advocating 'reciprocity' as a value stand in contrast to persons who attempt to lessen the importance of ongoing ties and to instead present events of material transaction more as stand-alone moments with no ongoing obligations and interdependency attached. These I describe by contrast as perspectives that stress 'non-reciprocal independence'.[4]

Of course all exchanges and transactions are embedded in social relations, and only possible by virtue of a history of previous transactions, and all transactions only make sense in the context of future outcomes and relationships that they are attempts to shape. Ethnographic analysis shows that this is as true for the seemingly archetypal commodity transactions conducted on Wall Street (e.g. Ho 2009) as it is for the archetypal gift traders of the *kula* ring (Malinowski 1922). For some scholars, this makes an absolute distinction between different types of exchanges, such as the classic Gift/Commodity distinction problematic. Following Appadurai's (1986:11) critique of what he saw as a tendency towards the 'exaggeration and reification of the contrast between gift and commodity in anthropological writing', disavowal of such supposedly outdated binary oppositions has been widespread. Yet people the world over, including the Tolai whom I conducted fieldwork with, often seem to be stubbornly attached to drawing stark distinctions between different types of exchange and to disputing how to characterise particular moments of exchange or particular ongoing exchange relationships. Among Tolai, too, it is clear enough that all transactions are embedded within ongoing histories of other transactions. But what I will also argue is that attempts to stress or lessen the importance of particular kinds of histories in order to define the nature of a specific exchange remain as important to Tolai at the start of the twenty-first century as they did the Trobriand Islanders of the early twentieth century, whom Malinowski describes as debating whether their fellows were truly engaged in *kula* or *gimwali*. The extent to which people are able to assert that their actions or the actions of others only make sense within ongoing histories of reciprocal obligation or the extent to which they can claim they stand free of such obligations relies upon their ability to rhetorically assert and contest differing claims as to the type and nature of the transactions that they are engaged in: claims that in East New Britain are often at the heart of disputes as to the meaning of 'custom'.

Hence, for example, the distinction between customary and non-customary land in New Guinea should not be taken as an absolute empirical distinction. Ethnographic inquiry reveals that often legally customary land is a focus of partial commodification through attempts to constitute the landholder (be that a single person or collective individual such as a clan) as more of a discrete individual (at least in the context of relations with other parties who may have an interest in that piece of land). Conversely, legally non-customary land, which is supposed to be held by individual tenure, often is surrounded by acknowledgement of claims made on the basis of customary relations. Instead of claiming that either a customary relational ethic continues to dominate the relationships that Papua New Guineans have to land, or that idioms of individual property ownership are making fundamental inroads, our starting point should be an analysis of how claims made on the basis of these opposed conceptions are made in different contexts. The distinction between customary and non-customary land, as it is played out at a village level, is best seen not as a distinction between two types of land, but rather a distinction between two ways of evaluating what kinds of claims it is appropriate to accept or reject in different contexts.

Among Tolai, this use of the concept of 'custom' as a means of evaluating claims made on the basis of reciprocal interdependence or non-reciprocal independence goes far beyond claims to land. In the second half of this book, I analyse the contested uses of the Tok Pisin term *kastom* ('custom') on the Gazelle Peninsula at the start of the twenty-first century, particularly the ways in which it is used as a term of moral evaluation. The concept of *kastom* is well known across the South Pacific, and is often presented in the anthropological literature as an expression of an underlying cultural substrate that is resistant to the impact of external forces such as colonialism, globalisation and commodification, or sometimes even as the mechanism by which such forces are tamed and indigenised (e.g. Gregory 1997:55–56, Strathern 1988:80–81). Whether understood as a form of resistance to colonialism, as an invented tradition of postcolonial nation-building or as a sign of the emergence of distinct cultural, economic and political spheres of sociality, the emergence of the concept of *kastom* can be seen as evidence of a distinctly Melanesian modernity. But uses of the term *kastom* at a village level are complicated. People dispute whether or not a particular person's actions were *kastom* or whether or not *kastom* is the correct way to adjudicate the appropriateness of a particular action. Contested uses of the word *kastom* mark the unstable boundaries between moral perspectives of reciprocal interdependence and non-reciprocal independence. Claims to customary legitimacy involve acknowledging or denying claims and obligations built on a history of reciprocal interdependence in some contexts but not in others. By recognising this, it is possible to trace the boundaries of the emergence of a variety of contested forms of individualism in East New Britain at the start of the twenty-first century.

The emergence of claims of individuality is intrinsically linked to claims to property rights over things such as land. Individualism is ultimately a claim to self-proprietorship, or ownership of oneself. This 'possessive individual' is of course an ideal type, who does not exist in pure form in contemporary Melanesia anymore than in contemporary Britain: absolute self-reliance and therefore absolute self-proprietorship is an unrealisable fantasy. Nonetheless, viewing the person as a discrete self-contained, self-possessing entity constituted prior to the relations that they enter into is a powerful dream. It underlies not only a great deal of social theory but is also a conception of great political and everyday importance. What is important is the contexts in which a person can claim proprietorship of the self and the ways in which they accept or reject claims made on their person on the basis of a history of interdependence. The importance of such claims is not in any way lessened by our knowledge that the ideal of absolute personal individuality is an ideal that can always be demonstrated to be false by pointing to the moments when a person acknowledges their intrinsic entanglement with others. This book is an ethnographic account of a variety of ways in which Tolai at the start of the twenty-first century asserted and rejected claims to individual autonomy through contests over the limits of reciprocal interdependence in different contexts: a contest to which competing uses of the concept of *kastom* are often central.

The extent to which one person can make claims on another on the basis of a history of reciprocal interdependence, or conversely the extent to which a person can attempt to constitute oneself as a person who stands outside such a history, have been fundamental to the ways in which Tolai people have attempted to rebuild shattered lives in the aftermath of the volcano. A tension between these alternative perspectives is not new and is not specific to East New Britain. I hope to demonstrate the long history of this tension in Matupit throughout the twentieth century. As Mauss (1970:63–82) observed, this tension is as central to the problems and moral dilemmas of modern European societies as it is to societies of the South Pacific. The most important conceptual issue is not to draw a major typological distinction between societies allegedly built on one ethic or the other, but to recognise (the often uneasy) co-existence of different rhetorically opposed perspectives. An ethnographic account of the ways in which people contest and rhetorically assert the appropriateness of different idioms of obligation and interdependence can provide us with a powerful illustration of the ways in which people in one part of the world are making their own history at the start of the twenty-first century.

Reconstruction in a Neo–Liberal World

The reconstruction process following the eruption of 1994 took place in a unique historical context. The volcano's last big eruption had occurred in 1937 when the region was under Australian colonial administration, but now in 1994 Papua New Guinea was an independent state. The political economy of the more recent reconstruction also reflected a particular moment in global economic history. Neo-liberal assumptions mandated prioritisation of large-scale reconstruction initiatives. Money was to be spent not on individual assistance to those most affected, but on infrastructure projects that would help to revive the local economy. These projects were to be undertaken by private contractors chosen by competitive tendering. The volcano provided at least in part a blank slate with which to push forward with processes of liberal political economic restructuring that might otherwise have been more difficult to impose.[5]

But at a local level things are more complex. If a contrast between societies based on reciprocal interdependence and those based on non-reciprocal independence is not the most helpful contrast upon which to base our analysis, then it follows that we should not restrict our theoretical options to seeing neo-liberal globalisation as a tidal wave of individualising commodification, or focusing on the resilience of indigenous collective or relational cultures (see also Knauft (2002:7)). Rather, the key to understanding the interaction of local agency and global neo-liberal economic culture is to focus on the moral contestability of transactions and their definition. For example, rather than seeing gift and commodity as categories that empirically describe transactions, I take as my focus in this study transactions that can be viewed from either perspective, depending on the position of the person describing them. Ethnographic study of such contests over value makes visible the processes by which Matupi describe and constitute new kinds of sociality. In particular, it makes visible the fraught and prominent emergence of an indigenous elite.

In focusing in this study on contests over value as a key to understanding social change in the South Pacific, I place particular emphasis on sociolinguistic struggles over the meaning of key terms as both an index and motor of changing social relations. Following Volosinov's (1973) critique of structuralist models of language that fail to emphasise the importance of contest between different persons and social groups in producing shifts of language, my concern is to present an analysis of contemporary Tolai society in which change, the contest of multiple perspectives and the uneasy coexistence of mutually contradictory values is the norm (see also Keane (2007:5)). The battles over what a term such as _kastom_ might mean in different contexts, or when it is appropriate to refer to someone with contempt as a 'Big Shot' are, as Volosinov would agree, among the most powerful indicators available as to where the limits of reciprocal interdependence and obligation are being contested in this particular historical moment.

This does not only apply to new concepts like the Big Shot, but also to older well-established ones, such as the _vunatarai,_ a Kuanua (Tolai vernacular) term often translated as 'clan'. A.L. Epstein (1969:164) long ago pointed out the systematic ambiguity of this term as Tolai use it, a theme to which I will return. The meaning of concepts like these is fought over. People try to use them to put forward or to reject claims about appropriate behaviour. As people create new kinds of social relations, these concepts inevitably reflect those changes, and become part of the process of creating new ones.

The history of Matupit is very different from that of many of the places described in the 'before and after' ethnographies. Often these ethnographies describe out of the way villages, that until recently had had little contact without outsiders. Here the ethnographer can present the pre-contact or pre-cataclysm state of affairs as still within living memory (perhaps he or she was lucky enough to have seen it themselves during their first fieldwork), and then contrast it with the current state of affairs. Matupit by contrast has a very long history of engagement with Christian Missions, state powers, and a global commodity economy. By the late 1950s when many villages elsewhere in PNG were still recovering from the shock of their first contact with a colonial patrol officer, the Matupi had already been running their own cash cropping enterprises for half a century, and had been largely Christian for nearly seventy years. Hence also by this period, a history of social change was a taken for granted backdrop to any discussion of Tolai society by outsiders (such as in the anthropological research initiated by A.L. Epstein, discussed below). Social relations and the ways in which they were conceptualised had for decades been being constantly contested and renegotiated in the context of a changing global political economy.

The volcano and its aftermath has been another episode in that process, not a stand-alone moment of transformation. Its significance and effects can only be understood when it is placed in the context of longer-term trajectories. Many Matupi do refer to the eruption as the day that the world changed for them, and to the days before the eruption as 'the good time before'. But in other conversations they acknowledge other changes and problems that were emerging in the years leading up to the eruption, and that shaped how the volcano impacted their lives.[6] Even to the extent that the eruption was a moment of total transformation for Matupit villagers, this was not purely a result of the volcano's natural effects. The town had been comprehensively destroyed in the eruption of 1937. It was then rebuilt, and remained the regional administrative centre. It also suffered extensive damage during the Second World War. Following the 1994 eruption, the decision was made to move the administrative centre, and this was just as important to the restructuring of the political economy of the Gazelle as the physical damage caused by the eruption. Not only did the government refuse to rebuild Rabaul, but it also banned private owners and businesses from rebuilding in large areas of the town on health and safety grounds. The extent to which these fears were rooted in actual dangers was bitterly disputed by those who had not made the move to the new administrative centre of Kokopo, but had stayed behind in Rabaul.

Matupit and the Gazelle Peninsula

Matupit is located on the Gazelle Peninsula in the north-east of East New Britain. Tolai people across the Gazelle region share a common language called Kuanua, and there are similarities between most Tolai villages with regard to customary practices and kinship organisation. During my field-work, I was told by local civil servants that there are currently estimated to be 120,000 Tolai, making them the second largest ethnolinguistic group in PNG. Many of the country's approximately 800 vernacular languages are spoken only in single isolated villages with less than a hundred inhabitants, so the size of the Tolai population is exceptional. With respect to anthropological and historical scholarship in particular, the Tolai region, and Matupit in particular, is notable both in the quantity and quality of researchers who have previously worked in the region.[7] Tolai people's history of engagement with colonialism and global capitalism is thus a story that has been told in detail elsewhere (Salisbury 1970:17–64, T.S. Epstein 1968:1–53, A.L. Epstein 1969:8–34, Neumann 1992, A.L. Epstein 1992:29–52). The history of Matupit in particular is discussed in the work of A.L. Epstein (1969:35–39) and Simet (1991:26–31). The Tolai rapidly became viewed throughout the territory of New Guinea as something of an indigenous elite. They were richer and better educated then other groups of New Guineans, and they came to view themselves as more sophisticated than other New Guineans too. The Tolai villages around Rabaul underwent the fastest change. Matupit in particular became emblematic of this change. Wherever I traveled in Papua New Guinea, I was struck by the fact that everyone knew the name of Matupit, even though it was 'only' a village. Its status was secured by it being, as one resident of New Ireland put it to me, 'the village that was not a village'. My Matupi friends would not have known the name of his village, but to him as to many other Papua New Guineans, Matupit was a noteworthy place.

Many Melanesian villages are a collection of geographically separate hamlets, each containing a handful of temporary bush material houses, loosely affiliated with each other on the basis of kinship ties or under the patronage of a Big Man.[8] Matupit was originally an island of about half a square kilometre. It is now linked to the mainland by a narrow causeway. At the end of the nineteenth century, the island consisted of three separate hamlets. However, population growth led the character of the village to change rapidly. Although the names of the three original hamlets are still used to describe different locations in the village, any sense of physical distinctness has long since been wiped away by the fact that almost every available piece of land on the island has now been built on. A.L. Epstein (1969:199) wrote of the Matupit that he observed in the late 1950s, at a time when many areas of the Highlands were only just out of their 'first contact' experience:

Of all Tolai communities, Matupit comes closest to resembling a true village in the sense of a discrete physical and residential group. However, given the limitations of space, the dense population, and the large number of its people who work in Rabaul, the island has taken on increasingly the appearance of a peri-urban settlement or suburban dormitory.[9]

In 1960 38.7 per cent of Tolai males were in regular wage employment, including 61.3 per cent of 20–29-year-olds (op cit.:58). Across most of the colonial period, the only wage-earning options open to most New Guineans were as indentured labourers on plantations such that the young men in employment left their villages for years at a time. The Matupi, by contrast were largely uninterested in such work and mainly undertook semi-skilled work in or around Rabaul (ibid.). In contrast to the Sepiks and Highlanders doing unskilled plantation work, and who were looked down on by the Tolai, fully 33 per cent of Epstein's total were teachers or clerks (op cit.:60).

The Tolai had another advantage that made unskilled manual labour less attractive to them, namely their land. Successful indigenous cash cropping is a comparatively recent phenomenon in most of PNG. The Highlands coffee boom only really took off in the 1970s, and it is only at the start of the twenty-first century that the 'green gold' of vanilla has generated significant income for customary landholders in the Sepik region. Most cash cropping up till now has been on large foreign owned plantations, including in the early colonial period ones run on indentured labour. By contrast, the Tolai have been cash cropping for themselves since the start of the twentieth century.

2. A new settlement of five households on the edge of Matupit and Rabaul

The northern areas of New Guinea were initially colonised by the Germans, who planted their first flag at Matupit in 1884, and who then established their new colonial capital at Rabaul in 1910. After the First World War, the territory was given to Australia to run by a League of Nations mandate. The Australians governed it jointly with the Territory of Papua (the south-east section of the overall island of New Guinea that had previously been a British possession), until independence in 1975. Under the Germans a large number of plantations had been established. Fully 40 per cent of land in the Gazelle has been alienated from customary ownership, compared to an average of 3 per cent of land across the whole of PNG. Nearly all of this was land that was alienated from Tolai to make way for plantations under the Germans.[10] This area was attractive because volcanic activity gave the soil a unique fertility, and because Simpson Harbour (upon which the town of Rabaul would be built) provided a fine natural harbour. The Germans built a large network of roads across the Gazelle using native labour, making movement across the area easier than in any other part of the Territory. As a consequence of this network of roads and proximity to the port at Rabaul, Tolai whose land had not been alienated could easily grow cash crops for the export market. Production with the intention of commodity exchange on the global market has been central to Tolai social life for generations, very much in contrast with the experience of many other Papua New Guineans.[11] By the 1950s, Matupit Island itself was so full of houses that there was very little room left for cash crops. But many Matupi had claims to land stretching down to Rabaul Town, and on the other side of Matupit harbour at the base of Tarvurvur. The primary cash crop was coconuts that were processed to make copra. After the war there were attempts to grow cocoa, but climatic conditions made this crop more suitable for inland Tolai villages.

The widespread alienation of land that earlier fuelled the plantation economy of the Gazelle was one major cause of the political discontent that rocked the region in the late 1960s and early 1970s. As the most educated and wealthiest indigenous group of Papua and New Guinea, many Tolai had become increasingly frustrated with the limits of advancement presented to them by the colonial regime. Bitter debates emerged pitting radicalised Tolai against those who preached caution and a more conciliatory attitude towards the Australians. The immediate cause of the protests was the proposed establishment of a 'Multi Racial Council' (MRC) to govern the area around Rabaul. Many Tolai saw this move as designed to buttress the dominance of economically powerful expatriates. A major underlying cause of the discontent, however, was the perceived historical injustice of the widespread alienation of Tolai land (see Simet 1991:22–24). The Tolai had experienced a population boom in the course of the twentieth century that was only temporarily interrupted by the Second World War. At the end of the nineteenth century

3. Houses at Matupit

there are estimated to have been between 15,000 and 20,000 of the people now known as Tolai (Fingleton 1985:42). By the 1960s this had risen to 40,000 (A.L. Epstein 1969:195), and by 1991 the figure was around 100,000 (Simet 1991:11). Only in the years since independence in 1975 has most of the rest of PNG experienced a similar boom. In addition, the increased reliance on the cash economy meant that access to land for cash cropping was becoming ever more important. In this context it is understandable that expatriates' ownership of huge swathes of land as plantations became a source of increasing resentment.

At Matupit, although no customary land had been taken over by plantations, much land had become part of Rabaul Town itself. This meant that, unlike the more rural villages whose land had been taken for plantations, Matupi were still subject to pressures for further expropriation. Matupit customary land between the causeway and Rabaul was the only place that the town, ringed by volcanic peaks, could be expanded. Initiatives such as the building of a town rubbish dump or the expansion of the Rabaul airport at Lakunai provided flashpoints between the Matupi and the Administration from the 1930s onwards (see A.L. Epstein 1969:48–56). In addition Matupit had undergone a population explosion that was remarkable even by the standards of the Gazelle Peninsula, further intensifying land pressure at the village. The population of Matupit had risen from around 800 in 1900 (A.L. Epstein 1969:35), to 1,190 in 1953, notwithstanding the widespread loss of life that resulted from the Japanese occupation of the area in The Second World War.[12] By the early 1960s it had risen to 1,400 (A.L. Epstein 1964:5), and by 1980 the population was 2,139 (PNG National Census, cited in Simet 1991:37). Although rapid population growth and subsequent land pressure have affected the whole Tolai region, Matupit experienced a particularly intense version of this phenomenon, and started to feel its effects earlier than most other Tolai villages. A.L. Epstein (1969:195) estimated the population density for the Tolai in 1961 as being around 130 per square mile, or 213 per square mile once the large areas of alienated land had been taken into the equation. Although these figures would still be high in most parts of PNG forty five years later, they pale in comparison with the figures for Matupit in 1961, namely 350 per square mile. T.S. Epstein (1968:111) reports that at the inland Tolai village of Rapitok, the population were just beginning to become aware of land pressure as a potential future problem. She contrasts this situation with the coastal villages (such as Matupit) where they were already an acknowledged phenomenon. By the early 1960s, 'on contemporary Matupit . . . all available land has now been taken up . . .' (A.L. Epstein 1969:126).

Given the intensity of these problems at Matupit, and given the village's status as one of the most developed and educated Tolai villages (which by definition made it one of the most developed and educated villages in the Territory), it is no surprise that the political unrest of the late 1960s and early 1970s largely centred on Matupit. At the centre of this unrest was the rise of an organisation known as the Tolai Mataungan Association.[13] Most of the Association's meetings were held at Matupit, and most of its leaders were Matupit-based. In the national elections held by the Australians in 1972 to constitute a House of Assembly that was the precursor for an independent PNG's parliament, three Mataungan Association-backed candidates were elected, from the Gazelle's four constituencies. Of these, two were from Matupit, including John Kaputin, who was to be Member for the Rabaul Open constituency for the next thirty years, and who went on to become one of postcolonial PNG's most prominent statesmen.

After PNG achieved independence in 1975, conflict over land continued between the Matupi and the state. Matupit remained one of the most prosperous and economically advanced villages in PNG. Simet (1991:16–17) sums up the situation in the early 1980s:

> Matupit, being only a small island is mostly a residential place. The islanders' traditional gardening areas were on the mainland. Today most of this traditional land has been planted with copra and cocoa. The Matupit no longer do any 'serious gardening' . . . . The shortage of land makes it difficult for the Matupit to maintain some aspects of their traditional life. For instance, much of their diet today consists of imported foods, such as rice, bread, biscuits, tinned-meat, tinned-fish. For more traditional foods such as bananas, taro and <u>aibika</u> (spinach), the Matupit have to depend very heavily on the town market.

The Matupit are very much tied to the town for their livelihood. They engage in village-based economic activities such as fishing, collecting megapode eggs, and preparing food for sale in town. The fish, the eggs and the food, all have to be sold in town for money.

By the early 1990s, Matupit was home to a number of nightclubs, and some houses even had satellite TV supplied by a local entrepreneur. Such developments may seem unexceptional to students of villages in other parts of the developing world such as South Asia, but in PNG, it is still a remarkable picture. The Gazelle itself was a unique area of PNG. Almost every area of bush had been cultivated, and the whole region was criss-crossed with roads joining together settlements of permanent houses, rather than forest tracks joining together small hamlets of bush material dwellings. And within that environment Matupit stood out as the most 'urban' of the region's villages. Michael Lowe, who was working as a human geographer at the Tolai village of Rapitok at the time of the eruption, reports that inland Tolai viewed the travails of the Matupi with not only sympathy, but also a sense of satisfaction. They remarked that people who had deserted their roots so spectacularly, almost totally abandoning subsistence agriculture for the cash economy, somehow almost deserved what had happened (Lowe: personal communication).[14]

The story of the Matupi in the aftermath of the eruption is told in Neumann (1996:129–36). Neumann's book is a short account of the aftermath of the 1994 eruption written for a non-academic audience that covers the experience of the inhabitants of Matupit in some detail. The Matupi were offered a resettlement scheme at Sikut, a rainforest location a long distance from Rabaul, where many of them were given agricultural blocks. Many Matupit families have settled at Sikut. More have returned to Matupit, and many families spend time keeping up houses and interests at both locations. The reallocation of land to the Matupi was partly a response to the disaster, but was also an opportunity for the Provincial Government to address the longer-term problem of overpopulation and land pressure at villages near Rabaul. And land pressure was not the only issue that the Provincial Government had to address in the aftermath of the eruption. Most crucially the controversial decision was made to relocate the provincial capital from Rabaul to Kokopo. The government claimed that this decision was scientifically based, and that no one would have chosen to build from scratch at Rabaul if they had known the ongoing risk posed by the volcanoes. Opponents claimed that Kokopo was also at risk, from tsunamis in particular. Darker motives were also hinted at. Some claimed that senior officials had investments in land at Kokopo that stood to rapidly increase in value. Many Matupi told me that they believed that Tolai from less 'developed' villages who were now coming into positions of authority in the Provincial bureaucracy resented the pre-eminence of the Rabaul area, and were using the volcano to do them down. The authorities were able to retort that major funding authorities, such as the World Bank, had insisted on the relocation of most services from Rabaul, as a precondition of financial assistance. The relocation from Rabaul to Kokopo was cynically summed up to me by one of its expatriate opponents as a move from an economy in which East New Britain produced goods (primarily copra) exported through Rabaul port, to an economy dominated by government bureaucrats flying in and out of the new airport at Tokua, near Kokopo, holding cheques and pieces of paper. The shift away from the copra economy perhaps predates the eruption, but the disaster provided the catalyst for geographic changes that made the shift more visible. For the Matupi, the relocation was an added disaster on top of the destruction of their cash crops. It removed much of the other main source of their economic well-being: wage labour in town.

Prior to 1994, Rabaul was a major administrative centre and port with a population of around 20,000. Only five people died as a direct result of the eruption, but the entire area was evacuated. Over two thirds of buildings were destroyed, either by volcanic activity, or by looting. Direct losses totalled 280 million Australian dollars. In the aftermath of the eruption the Gazelle Restoration Authority (GRA) was established by an Act of Parliament to channel 117.7m K (PNG Kina), approximately thirty million pounds sterling, of aid. The major sources of this aid were: Papua New Guinea's national government (K14.5m), Australia (K34m), Japan (K26.6m), European Union (K6.2m), the World Bank (K33.3m), Germany (K2.4m) and the Asian Development Bank (K700,000).

By 1999 the population of Rabaul had returned to 3,000, and by the time of my fieldwork, local government officers quoted a figure of around 5,000 to me. Many of these were squatters living in the patched up ruins of town houses. The majority were not Tolai, but first or second generation immigrants from other provinces. In the years preceding the eruption Rabaul had been attracting a growing semi-recognised squatter population, many of whom 'rented' land from Matupit *vunatarai* who claimed customary land rights on the edge of the part of Rabaul that had come to be known as Malay Town. The state had recognised the claims of some of the Matupit *vunatarai* in some of the peripheral areas of town, leading to some confusion as to the exact legal status of these arrangements. The arrangements certainly led to tension. Many Tolai were keen to see the squatters removed. The biggest protest to take place in Rabaul in the years between the Mataugan movement and the eruption was an 'anti-crime' Tolai demonstration in 1987 directed against the squatter population (see Neumann 1992:223). In the aftermath of the eruption, some squatters moved into deserted properties in the heart of the ruined town, and a few Tolai now joined them. A few people based at Matupit were squatters during the time of my fieldwork.

4. Ruins of former PNG Prime Minister Sir Julius Chan's Rabaul residence

This is not the only example of the eruption being a catalyst for some Tolai to start behaving in ways that many had previously looked down upon as the manner of immigrant outsiders (*waira*, 'strangers'). Some Matupi who had settled on land at Ulagunan offered to them by a local matrilineage now worked on the nearby plantation. At Matupit, some people now gained a living scavenging on the new town rubbish dump. People differed as to whether Matupi had earned money in this manner in the past. Some said never and others told me that it was done only on rare occasions when people knew that a load containing much valuable material had been dumped. What people were fairly unanimous about was that it had not been a main source of income for a section of the population in the way that it had become in the years after the eruption.

A precondition for most of the aid was that it was to be spent on resettlement areas such as Sikut, or the redevelopment at Kokopo.[15] Rabaul was seen as having a future only as a port and a minor regional centre. Comparatively small amounts of money were earmarked for it. The villages surrounding Rabaul, such as Matupit, were allocated no money at all. Consequently a village that had previously had electric street lighting on the main road circling the island was now plunged back into darkness, with no immediate prospect of the lights ever being turned back on again. Whereas Sikut has a primary school, the Gazelle Restoration Authority is clear that they cannot provide funds for the school at Matupit to be reopened, despite Matupit now having a bigger population. This is a source of great resentment; Matupit was one of the first villages in the country to have its own school, and its pre-eminence was based on education as much as copra, as the careers of men like Kaputin and Simet illustrate. A second precondition was that the money be spent on infrastructural redevelopment (transport, power supplies, drainage etc.), rather than individual assistance. The GRA commissioned Snowy Mountain Engineering Consultants to plan the 'reoccupation and resettlement' of Rabaul. Their report devotes only two paragraphs to the city's residential areas, and less still is given to villages such as Matupit.

Conducting Research at Matupit at the Start of the Twenty-First Century

The contemporary situation of the Matupi is unique, and presents specific problems for an anthropologist attempting to analyse the ongoing reconstruction of social relations and material interest in the post eruption era. My intention as a fieldworker was to examine how people mobilised resources for reconstruction and through this to understand the processes by which people constituted a distinctively Melanesian postcolonial and neo-liberal sociality. Access to raw materials for building a house, or the labour necessary to clear an agricultural block were clearly important. Perhaps most important of all, however, was access to land. But if the eruption had helped to make access to land problematic for the Matupi, it also complicated my attempts to analyse the social relations constituted through the land. It should be clear from the description outlined above that to understand how people gain access to land, and to understand the social relationships that are constituted through its use, requires an understanding of how relations have been negotiated over several generations. While an anthropologist cannot stay in the field for several generations in order to directly observe this process, some of these relations might be expected to become apparent in the course of observing who gardens in what places, or listening to disputes about who should be allowed to build on which pieces of land. Yet for the Matupi this situation is at the moment largely not the case.

At the new resettlement location of Sikut, people's length of residence is not long enough to be able to trace such relations. The Matupi have been there for less than a decade, and it is impossible to tell what patterns of transmission will predominate. People do speculate and argue as to how the land at Sikut should be handled in the coming years, and I deal with that situation in more depth in Chapter Two. But, as Jacob Simet (personal communication) pointed out to me on my arrival in East New Britain, to get the same kind of data regarding land at Sikut, as A.L. Epstein did for Matupit in the early 1960s, would probably involve having to return to Sikut at around the year 2050.

At Matupit all of the agricultural land was destroyed. As we have seen, the majority of gardening land had already been turned over to cash crop production, making Matupit almost unique amongst Papua New Guinean villages. There is good reason to believe that this change affected social relations conducted through land. Certainly the ways people that I spoke to described agricultural land tenure at Matupit contrasted significantly with the existing descriptions of nearby matrilineal communities in the province of New Ireland, to whom the Tolai are close in terms of language and many customary practices. In particular, it seems safe to point to a trend towards less fluidity in the negotiation of access to land, and the growing prioritisation of the claims of the matrilineages (*vunatarai*) most closely associated with the land, who increasingly came to be referred to as 'landholders'. In 1992 it would have been possible to conduct fieldwork on how people negotiated access to coconut plantations or on disputes over coconut grove ownership, and this kind of fieldwork would likely have turned up contested relations negotiated through land stretching back over several generations. Other pieces of land that were economically valuable, such as those on the outskirts of town where the cement works, golf club, or airport had been built would have revealed the same processes. At that time, the Matupi customary claim to these lands had recently been legally recognised, and Matupit *vunatarai* had begun receiving compensation payments for them.

In 2002, when I arrived in the Tolai area, this kind of research was no longer possible. Most of the land was arid desert, covered with volcanic ash. People simply did not discuss the land anymore. Coconut plantations that had been the subject of ongoing dispute for decades ceased to be of importance. The ongoing dispute between two of Matupit's best known *vunatarai* over the ownership of (and therefore rights to payment for use of) the Rabaul Town rubbish dump at Rapidik, went into abeyance. Towards the end of my fieldwork I had another conversation with Jacob Simet in which he told me that the one thing he most noticed on arriving back at Matupit from Port Moresby was the disappearance of the local spirits (K. *kaia*). The land around Matupit upon which the Matupi had made their coconut plantations was thought to be densely populated with such *kaia*. Yet after the eruption, he noticed that he never heard them mentioned again. I too had rarely heard stories of *kaia*, and those that I had heard were nearly always stories from many decades earlier. It was as if, Simet said, the eruption had destroyed their habitat, and wiped them clear from the land. It struck me that these were not the only stories that the volcano had wiped from the land surrounding Matupit. There was a parallel with the stories and genealogies that I would have collected had the land still been in use but that had instead been wiped away. Maybe one day the disputes and stories of who was related to whom through the land will also return: perhaps if the land becomes fertile again, or if Rabaul Town is somehow rebuilt, or if the Matupi find some other use for it.

So too, the stories of the land of Matupit Island itself had been obscured by the volcano. In the years preceding the eruption the main way in which these stories had become visible was through disputes in which competing histories of land use, purchases, and genealogies would be presented in public. The bulk of the information about land in A.L. Epstein's (1969) *Matupit* monograph comes from these public hearings. Indeed the longest and most important chapter of the book is a description of these hearings and their relevance. As we have seen, in the years running up to the eruption, as the population grew and people became ever more reliant on cash incomes, the number of disputes increased. I was told that if I had arrived in the early 1990s I would have had hearings about land disputes to attend every week. Instead I only learned of about a half a dozen disputes that became public during my two years of fieldwork at Matupit. People explained to me that the pressure on land at Matupit Island had largely been relieved by the relocation to Sikut, such that very nearly half the pre-eruption population was no longer resident. By 2000, the population of Matupit had fallen back to 1,600, but 928 people lived at Sikut. On top of this there were 167 people living at the unofficial Matupit resettlement camp at Ulaveao, known as 'Ulamatis', and between 100 and 200 Seventh Day Adventists (SDA) living at a settlement known as 'Sunny Bird' on land that they had bought in the mid-1980s following denominational conflict and a previous volcanic scare in 1984.[16] This meant that the total population of the Matupit community in East New Britain had risen from 2,139 in 1980 to between 2,800 and 2,900 in 2000, but the actual population resident at Matupit had fallen back to late 1960s levels as a result of the volcano.

In addition many of the permanent houses Matupit that prior to the eruption were valuable and contested assets had been destroyed or severely damaged. The construction of new permanent houses in the past was often the catalyst for a public dispute (see for example A.L. Epstein, op cit.:147–48). At my time at Matupit, there seemed to be no expensive permanent houses in the process of being built. Most house building was occurring at Sikut. Matupit was not awash with money anymore. In addition, the volcanic ash still issuing forth from Tarvurvur in huge clouds almost hourly would rapidly corrode new iron roofs, so building a permanent house would be an unwise invest-ment. Most of the people who returned to Matupit made makeshift repairs to their old houses, or cobbled together temporary ones out of scraps. People expected that old disputes would arise again and new ones would emerge, if the population rose, the volcano stopped expelling clouds of sulphur, and house building recommenced. I was told that in the years immediately after the eruption there had been no overt disputes at Matupit at all, but that the handful that had emerged in the years that I had been present presaged a return to more familiarly high levels of disputes in the future.[17]

Under these circumstances, much of the information that one would expect to collect in two years of fieldwork in a Papua New Guinean village was not available. I gathered information on land use on some of the new blocks at Sikut to see to what extent they remained under the control of the individual nuclear families that had been allocated the land by the Provincial Government, or whether their use was influenced by other obligations that were the result of histories of reciprocal interdependence stretching back to before the eruption. Such information is useful as a snapshot of what kinds of obligations were recognised with regard to land in the immediate aftermath of the eruption. But it is as well to be wary of presuming that current patterns predict a radical break from the past as of assuming that previous patterns will automatically reappear. I also collected information on the small number of land disputes that did emerge at Matupit during my fieldwork. It was possible to track some of the history of disputes on economically valuable land around Rabaul Town through interviews. However, these stories seemed to be temporarily frozen at 1994. People did not give up their competing claims, but claims were no longer pursued with great vigour. The materials I collected felt more like the oral histories collected by a social historian than the ethnographic participant observation of an anthropologist. They were stories of how the Matupi were in the past, rather than how they were at the time that I lived with them. Likewise, I could have focused my research on old disputes that were likely to re-emerge and interviewed around them. Such an approach, however, would have been likely to stir up animosities that were currently dormant. In addition it would again have been an example of prioritising a preconceived idea of the ethnographic information that an anthropologist of Melanesia should be collecting over the reality of the unique situation that I found at Matupit during my stay. All of the information mentioned above is of value, and I use much of it in the chapters that follow, but it does not occupy the central part in my research that I expected it to before I arrived at Matupit.

I arrived in East New Britain in February 2002 and stayed until February 2004. I also returned for two follow-up visits of six weeks each in December 2004 to January 2005 and in December 2009 to January 2010. I spent nearly all my time resident at either Sikut or Matupit. At Sikut I lived in an unoccupied government residence, and at Matupit I lived with a family who were willing to accommodate me. Although I was engaged in various 'data collecting' routines throughout my stay, the vast majority of the useful insights that I gained came via the classic anthropological technique of happening to be in the right place at the right time, or suddenly noticing what was going on whilst hanging around waiting for a meeting to happen. The information that was gathered from more structured or deliberate research routines was also important, and much of it is contained in this book. But often throwaway comments such as 'that's not real *kastom*' or 'we don't call those people Big Men' provided the context within which information gathered in more structured ways made any sense. Often the importance of these fleeting comments only sunk in several days or weeks after I heard them.

Upon first arriving at Sikut, I conducted a survey of the entire village with a pre-prepared questionnaire about house building. I asked questions such as how access to land was acquired, who had helped build the house and clear the block of trees, who the householders had helped in a similar fashion, what payments (if any) were made and so on. In doing so, I hoped to start to build a map of the nature and extent of interlocking obligations created in the process of post-disaster reconstruction. I personally collected all of this information during my first six weeks at Sikut, walking up and down steep hills in the blazing sun, and entering the information into a tiny Psion palm top computer. Unfortunately I was unable to back the information up on my laptop, which had been lost in Singapore in transit by British Airways. By the time the larger computer arrived with me in New Britain several months later, one of my new friends had spilt water onto my palm top, wiping out my first two months of fieldwork. It would be nice to report that, undaunted, I leapt back into the fray and continued my research. Instead I spent a week contemplating quitting or throwing myself into the volcano as a kind of sacrificial offering. I could not face doing the whole thing all over again, so eventually I hit upon the idea of printing out copies of the survey, and paying a few local residents to go around Sikut re-collecting the information for me. Following this, I applied the same technique at Matupit using a modified questionnaire. I collected information from over 90 per cent of the households at both locations. Although I have not used the statistical information gathered in this questionnaire in this book or my other publications, these inquiries were immensely useful in giving me a sense of how people began to rebuild their lives after the eruption and what kinds of social networks they saw as help and hindrance in that process. I sat down with my research assistants each evening to go over the information collected and elicited their glosses on what they thought various answers really meant. This experience in particular was one of the key first steps in my growing understanding of the importance of contested interpretations of morally ambiguous relationships and transactions for Tolai sociality at the start of the twenty-first century.

Following this, I spent much of my fieldwork time conducting other semi-structured routines alongside keeping a journal recording day-to-day observations and overheard remarks. In particular, I built up a series of case studies of people who were in the middle of building a new house (mainly at Sikut). Again, the plan was to develop a more in-depth understanding of how people viewed the web of relationships they were entangled within, through a focus on the mobilisation of resources needed to build a house. And again, not much of that material has made it directly into this book or my other writings, which deal only in passing with the practicalities of building a house. But as before, this work helped me better understand the tensions and contests that, in different ways, underlaid every household at Matupit and Sikut. Many of the lengthier quotes that I use to illustrate certain perspectives held at Matupit and Sikut come from these conversations. And over time, my day-to-day experiences in these two locations have left me feeling certain that these statements are far from unrepresentative.

In addition, I attended village meetings, meetings of social movements (Martin 2007a), land dispute hearings (when they actually occurred) and *kastom* events, making detailed notes on the activities and arguments that occurred. I watched people gardening and fishing. I went with them to work and rode shotgun with them as they drove buses. All of this, I hope gave me a rounded insight into what was going on in people's lives. Most important of all, however, was what I learnt as we gossiped in the evening, sitting around a fire under the stars, smoking cigarettes and drinking endless cups of sugary tea.

At first fieldwork was conducted mainly in Tok Pisin, the main lingua franca of PNG that I had taught myself prior to starting fieldwork. Many Tolai, particularly those who are middle-aged or older and were educated in the colonial period, speak fluent English, and some conversations were carried out in English. On arrival, I also tried to teach myself Kuanua, the local vernacular of Tolai people. My progress was frustratingly slow until I hit upon the idea of borrowing books that were used to teach English to small children at the local primary school, and spending an hour a day translating the English sentences into Kuanua, to then have them corrected by a local woman who used to work herself as an English teacher. This led to much quicker progress in my language abilities. During my second year of fieldwork, most of the interviews and conversations that I was involved in took place in Kuanua. I was also now able to follow the gist of what was going on at meetings and disputes, although I still needed details explained to me afterwards, and sometimes when people became angry or emotional and started shouting at each other I often did not know exactly what was going on. Over the course of my fieldwork, I switched between all three languages commonly used on the Gazelle: Kuanua, Tok Pisin and English.

I have decided to use pseudonyms in this book to try to lessen the possibility that the expression of controversial opinions could re-ignite old animosities. On some occasions, I have not identified speakers, even with pseudonyms, when I have considered this risk to be most acute. Some characters that I describe may be identifiable to some people who are familiar with Matupit, but even here, I have decided to keep to the policy of using pseudonyms in the interests of consistency. In all cases, I have gained the permission of the people involved to repeat their opinions. The only cases where I have not used pseudonyms is with reference to public figures, such as politicians like Sir John Kaputin, the Member of Parliament for Rabaul at the time of my arrival for fieldwork in 2002.

I have also made a decision to write this book using the writing style that has come to be known as the 'ethnographic present'. Anyone who has been schooled in social or cultural anthropology in recent years will have been made repeatedly aware of the critique of the ethnographic present, and in particular its alleged tendency to place people and cultures outside of history in an unchanging reified trap. It might seem particularly odd to maintain this much-criticised convention in an ethnography of socio-cultural change over a long period of time, and that is explicitly outside of a prevalent tradition in Melanesian research of emphasising the ahistorical radical alterity of Melanesian societies. But following Smith (1994:18), I feel that the stylistic clarity of this way of writing outweighs the disadvantages. I should make it clear that the ethnographic present that I am writing about is Tolai society as I witnessed it between 2002 and 2004, with a few updates from my last fieldwork visit from 2009 to 2010. In no way do I imagine that what I have described is an unchanging social reality that is in all respects going to reflect what might be the situation at Matupit and Sikut at the time of publication or at whatever time the reader finds themselves reading these lines.

I also want to mention an important element of Tolai life with which this book does not explicitly deal: namely gender. Gender is, of course, of immense importance to how Tolai negotiate social relations, as demonstrated by the ongoing debates over the relative merit of patrilineal versus matrilineal transmission of rights in land, to give just one example. As a male researcher, most of my close interlocutors tended to be men. It is often not easy for an outside man to forge close relationships with Tolai women without attracting suspicion. Over the course of my fieldwork, however, I was able to gain increasing access to women's point of view on many of the issues dealt with in this book. Although gender was often an important factor in shaping people's opinions and actions, the fundamental problems dealt with in this book – the problem of the appropriate boundaries of reciprocity, and of the moral dilemmas thrown up by increasing socio-economic differentiation – are faced by men and women alike. For example, the specific issue of how Big Shots allegedly used their money to philander and corrupt young women was often seen differently by grassroots men and women. Hence gender is undoubtedly an important part of how increasing economic divisions are constituted and appraised. However, both male and female grassroots Tolai tended to share many attitudes towards the emerging elite, just as both male and female Big Shots tended to share many similar attitudes toward to the grassroots. Bradley (1982) rightly takes previous Tolai ethnographies to task for their gender blindness. Her thesis with its emphasis on how gender shapes social relations provides a valuable addition to the literature on this location. But there are other issues that have also until recently not received the attention that they deserve in Melanesian ethnography, such as the ongoing moral dilemma over the appropriate limits of reciprocity and how this intersects with emerging economic divisions. In emphasising this issue in this book, I have based my description of Tolai attitudes on both male and female interlocutors. But reasons of space have not allowed me to go into the details of how gender shapes such attitudes. I hope one day to have the opportunity to examine this particular issue in more detail.

One would expect to encounter transactions regarding land, and creating social relationships through it, on a regular basis in a Melanesian village. Many of the archetypal ongoing relationships of reciprocal interdependence of this type had perhaps already been disturbed at Matupit long before the eruption. At Sikut, where there is more reconstruction occurring than at Matupit, it is possible to observe such processes more closely, but even here the view that emerges is a snapshot of a particularly exceptional moment, on land that is, to all current intents and purposes, without history. Such a snapshot is valuable, but its true value is perhaps only likely to become fully apparent many years in the future when both the metaphorical and literal dust from the volcano has settled. One would expect discussions about land also to be highly concrete. However, the comparative paucity of actual land disputes does not mean that land per se has ceased to be a topic of active interest, and in fact the discussions about land that do now occur tend to be arguments as to how land tenure should look in general: what kinds of obligations one should acknowledge towards others with regard to land. As a consequence these discussions usually centre on very abstract concepts. I examine one of these concepts _kastom_ in detail throughout the book. Such concepts are not only used in abstract discussion of course. People appeal to _kastom_ in order to back up or discredit a particular argument in the course of a dispute, for example. But it is striking how many discussions are of a seemingly abstract nature. It is almost as if with the disappearance of the plethora of transactions, debates and disputes involving land that characterised much of Tolai social life in the years before the eruption, abstract theorising now flourished. Even the most common of concrete discussions about what will happen to a piece of land over the next few years tend to have an abstract feel. Such discussions may be tied to a concrete example, but imagined futures are largely justified with reference to abstract concepts, such as an assertion that a certain piece of land should be 'customary' or 'non-customary'.

As a consequence, this ethnography places a great deal of emphasis on the analysis of how Matupi use language. Language is of course central to human existence, and there is a long history in anthropology and social theory more generally that prioritises analyses of language as the key to understanding human sociality (for overviews see Silverstein 1976, 2004 or Salzmann 1993). The central focus on language in this book, however, is not simply the result of a theoretical choice, but instead largely follows from the kinds of discussions that Matupi were having about land in the absence of the previous plethora of specific land disputes. At the moment Matupi social life is a state of seeming flux and it is the language that people use to discuss their hopes for the future that made the most striking impression upon me. In this new social landscape old terms and concepts are tried out to advance different interests in different contexts. It is primarily through the creation of new concepts and battles over the meanings and relevance of old ones that moral dispositions towards an imagined future are negotiated.

In the next chapter I examine in detail battles over the future of land use among the Matupi, paying particular attention to contests over the use of the key concept of *kastom*. In doing so I aim to illustrate how these kinds of linguistic contest are central to a process of limiting the scope of claims based on reciprocal interdependence with regard to land tenure. In subsequent chapters, I describe the way in which the same processes are central to other instances of partial possessive individuation and social differentiation, including those that underpin the emergence of the new indigenous elite, the Big Shots.

Notes

1. A.L. Epstein (1988:32) reports that in the mid-1980s, Tolai told him that building a house cost 8,000 to 10,000 PNG Kina, at a time when the Kina was in parity with the U.S. dollar.
2. This parallels an earlier trend in Melanesian ethnography during the 1950s and 1960s when the passing of Melanesian culture under the impact of Westernisation was thought to be imminent. The ways in which this trend played itself out and was then countered by analyses that claimed a fundamental continuity of Melanesian cultural forms are well summarised in Carrier and Carrier (1989:5–7).
3. The English term 'clan' and cognate Tok Pisin word *klan* are used in PNG to refer to a variety of different kinds of extended kinship groups joined together on the basis of a wide range of histories of exchange or genealogy. Although the use of the term is problematic in many respects, particularly as the boundaries of where a 'clan' legitimately lie are often fiercely contested, it does act as a kind of easily recognised shorthand for a kind of social grouping that is immediately recognisable to most people living in PNG. The problems of defining a 'clan' are developed in more detail in the discussion of landholding below in Chapters One to Four.
4. In using this phrase 'non-reciprocal independence' I do not wish to suggest that an asserted state of independence exists only for one party in a relationship. Rather, I use the phrase as a conceptual opposition to perspectives stressing reciprocal interdependence. If we were limited to the common sense meaning of the term reciprocity, then it would be more accurate to describe this state as 'non-reciprocity and

independence' or even, as Marx (see above) describes it, as '*reciprocal* independence' (my emphasis).

5. As such the post-disaster reconstruction of the area around Rabaul could be seen as a small example of the 'Shock Doctrine' of using disasters to impose neo-liberal policies, described by Klein (2007).

6. This situation parallels something that Lindstrom (2008:162) notes in a discussion of Robert Tonkinson's earlier analysis of the development of the concept of *kastom* in Vanuatu: that the volcanic eruptions of 1991 in Ambrym were a context in which 'volcanic flows and ash falls increased the traffic of people, goods and practices within that Pacific archipelago; such mobility is the chief feature of creeping "globalization", although few then used this word'. Lindstrom further comments on how Tonkinson was able to gain 'a useful perspective on the mysteries of . . . cultural stability and social change' through the experience of the volcano's refugees (ibid.). See also op cit.:163.

7. I have made most use of the work of A.L. (Bill) Epstein, who conducted his main research between 1959 and 1961, and made frequent return visits to Matupit up until his death in 1999. Bill Epstein was a student of Max Gluckman's and was a leading member of the so-called Manchester School of anthropology. Epstein shared Gluckman and other Manchester School theorists' interest in issues of urbanisation and social change, and he conducted his first fieldwork in East Africa's 'Copper Belt' in the 1950s. Bill Epstein then took this interest to New Guinea, and in particular to the study of Tolai villages near Rabaul, with their long history of interaction with colonial authority and commercial activities, as a counterpoint to the many studies being then conducted at the time on only recently contacted villages in the New Guinea Highlands. Bill Epstein's was one of the first anthropological studies of Melanesia to focus on urbanisation and social change. His monograph *Matupit* remains one of the most detailed and nuanced ethnographies of these issues in the region. Epstein was accompanied by his wife T.S. (Scarlett) Epstein. Scarlett Epstein had an interest in rural economic development that followed on from her original fieldwork in India. She produced an ethnography of a less economically 'developed' Tolai village called Rapitok, around twenty miles inland from Rabaul. Her main argument was that pre-contact Tolai habits of trade and accumulation culturally pre-disposed Tolai to succeed in a modern cash exchange economy, a perspective reflected in the title of her monograph *Capitalism: Primitive and Modern*. The other major ethnographer of the Tolai region in the 1960s was Richard Salisbury, who was already well known in New Guinea ethnographic circles for his monograph from the Highlands region *From Stone to Steel*, which argued that the introduction of new Western derived tools and technologies could have a radically transformative effect on pre-contact cultures. Salisbury moved to the Tolai region in order to follow up his study of a recently contacted Melanesian society with an in-depth study of the effects of a history of socio-economic change occurring in the context of colonialism. In particular, in the context of the debate that raged within economic anthropology of the 1960s between formalists and substantivists, Salisbury sought to use the material that he gathered from the village of Vunamami to support the formalist position. Christine Bradley conducted fieldwork in the late 1970s near Rabaul with a particular focus on the relationship between economic development and changing gender relations among Tolai people. In the 1980s, further research was carried out

by James Fingleton, who had a particular interest in land tenure, both in Tolai villages and in government sponsored resettlement schemes. Fingleton was keen to stress the usefulness of the flexibility of customary land tenure in opposition to those who viewed customary tenure as an impediment to economic development. Twenty five years after his fieldwork, he remains an active participant in policy debates on this issue. New research at Matupit was also carried out by Jacob Simet, a Tolai who was himself from Matupit. Simet's main concern was to detail the circulation and uses of *tabu* and its cultural importance for Tolai people. Simet has gone on to be a major figure in PNG national cultural politics and at the time of my fieldwork and writing was the director of the PNG government's National Cultural Commission. Research around the Gazelle Peninsula was also conducted by Klaus Neumann in the late 1980s. Neumann's interest was in constructions of Tolai history, and his main theoretical concern was a post-structuralist inspired desire to deconstruct what he saw as attempts to construct a unitary and hegemonic version of Tolai history, as reflected in the title of his monograph, *Not The Way It Really Was*.

8.   See for example A.L. Epstein (1964:4), with regard to the contact-era Gazelle.

9.   Elsewhere, A.L. Epstein, (1999:210) was keen to stress that the different hamlets still kept separate identities. But even here he contrasts the archetypal Tolai village as collection of distinct hamlets with the appearance of Matupit: '. . . Matupit appears to diverge from this pattern, the tiny island seeming to constitute a single, unbroken and heavily settled area of settlement.' In my travels to other parts of PNG, I was always struck by the extent to which social organisation seemed to be written in the geography for the outsider to read, in contrast with the situation in Matupit, with its 'peri-urban' feel. And although the names of different areas such as Kikila and Rainatun were still used, in my experience this was largely for practical directional purposes. If asked where they came from, the first response of any Matupi would be 'Matupit'.

10.   A.L. Epstein, (1969:24) reports that the Tolai had lost 39 per cent of their land by the outbreak of the First World War.

11.   The argument of T.S. Epstein (1968:19–33) that Tolai were culturally predisposed to economic success due to a tendency towards 'primitive capitalism' predating colonialism has been criticised theoretically by Gregory (1980:627) and challenged historically by Neumann (1992:275–76). This argument is discussed further in Chapter Six.

12.   These figures are taken from census records of Australian Patrol Officers held in Melanesian Archives, University of California San Diego.

13.   For contemporary anthropological accounts of the rise of the Mataugnan, see A.L. Epstein (1970) and T.S. Epstein (1970).

14.   Analysing the relation between newspaper advertisements and emergent middle class consumption patterns in PNG, Foster (1995:171) notes that an ad for Ramu Sugar contains a recipe for sago cake that imagines certain ingredients, like milk and margarine, that probably not 'be a popular item of bush consumption' because 'they presume access to a supermarket'. From this Foster goes on to ask the rhetorical question, 'To what extent, then, is this recipe an index of an emergent set of urban, middle-class consumption practices?' A village like Matupit, though, throws into question the implicit distinction between 'bush' life and 'urban middle-class' life. The inhabitants of Matupit, both before and after the eruption could not all be unproblematically classified as 'urban middle-class'. But before the eruption many of them would have

been able to refrigerate milk, and cake baking (and eating) continued to be a popular pastime after the eruption as well.

15. The World Bank in particular was said by many East New Britain civil servants to have promoted this stipulation. See for example World Bank (2001:15–16).

16. All of these are National Census Figures, contained in East New Britain Census Reports, available from ENB Provincial Administration, except for Sunny Bird for which I was unable to gain precise figures.

17. I was also told that a spate of deaths of older people demonstrated an increase in sorcery. This in turn was taken as a sign that a number of dormant land disputes simmering under the surface were about to re-emerge. Given that many of these deaths seemed to be linked to some kind of respiratory failure and that they coincided with a period when Tarvurvur had begun expelling clouds of sulphuric ash over the village after several years of peace, I was inclined towards a more 'Western' medical explanation of the deaths. Nonetheless this interpretation in and of itself demonstrates a keen sense that problems that had been put into abeyance by the particular circumstances of the immediate post-eruption situation were now in the process of reappearing.

An Orientation to the Shifting Patterns of Tolai Land Tenure

Land has probably always been central to Tolai social life. Salisbury (1970:67) reports his informants routinely saying that land 'is the most basic element of life'. A.L. Epstein (1969:2) likewise states that on his very first visit to Matupit, 'I was at once made acutely aware of the importance the Matupi attached to land, and of the tensions that could be generated when any question arose that seemed to touch on it'.

Descriptions of the ways in which Tolai organise access to land have most commonly emphasised the role of the *vunatarai* in negotiating such access. The Kuanua term *vunatarai* is used to refer to different types of descent groups, ranging from each of the two moieties into which the Tolai of the Gazelle Peninsula divide themselves, down to village-based lineage sections. These local lineage sections are commonly of the most relevance in discussing land rights (A.L. Epstein 1992:50–51). A man would acquire rights to land by virtue of his membership of a matrilineage, often involving him moving to his mother's brother's hamlet upon marriage or his father's death (T.S. Epstein 1968:6). This has never operated as a simple stable descent system however. There have always been a variety of different claims for both rights of access to land generally, and membership of *vunatarai* specifically (A.L. Epstein 1992:51, T.S. Epstein 1968:6–7). This chapter examines the different principles by which people make claims on land and group membership. In particular, I examine how some claims come to be increasingly prioritised over others across time, and what the contests over such conflicting claims can tell us about how Tolai are reconstituting sociality in an era of postcolonial neo-liberalism.

Matrilineal Groups and the Claims of Their Children

The Tolai pattern that is commonly described as 'matrilineal inheritance' has been considered to be a problem by many, both analytically and practically, for a long time. Tolai themselves have apparently been discussing the advantages of a shift to patrilineal inheritance for a century (Pullen-Burry 1909:225). Firth reports his surprise at being told in the 1950s that the 'community should change their structure from matrilineal to patrilineal' because 'it was not fair that a child should not inherit from his father and that another man's child should' (Firth foreword to T.S. Epstein 1968:viii). T.S. Epstein (1968:83) reports that in the early 1960s, '. . . many native councillors suggest a change from their traditional system of landholding vested in the matrilineage to one of individual ownership, so as to enable a man to leave his perennial crops and other assets to his own son rather than to his brother or sister's son'.

In this quotation we see a number of theoretical propositions that surface again and again in anthropological reflections on Tolai culture. First, that there is a 'traditional system of landholding vested in the matrilineage'. Second that such a system can be conceptually opposed to one of 'individual ownership', and by implication that to replace matrilineality by patrilineality would be to move away from a communal landholding system to one of individual property. Thirdly, changes in the material uses of land as a result of global economic integration are what spur people to look for new ways of organising access to land. These changes include the stewarding of cash-generating 'perennial crops', like cocoa, as well as investment in other 'assets' like permanent houses (rather than temporary bush material homes), that also further made land something to be fought over (A.L. Epstein 1969:147–48).

I broadly agree with the last of the three outlined propositions. Tolai people's involvement in an ever changing global political economy, including their appropriation and trading of new material artifacts such as cocoa trees or permanent houses, has clearly created new conditions within which to recreate social relations, as both A.L. and T.S. Epstein demonstrated for the Tolai many decades ago. The first two propositions are more problematic. By critically examining these two propositions, we can begin to appreciate the existence of a longstanding and deep tension between moments of assertion of individual ownership rights unencumbered by relations and obligations to others and assertions of overlapping rights rooted in relations of ongoing interdependence. This tension, however, does not simply oppose the individual person or nuclear family to the *vunatarai*. The *vunatarai* can itself in some contexts be the discrete individual unit that seeks to strengthen its position vis-a-vis other groups. The battleground over where one draws a line around claims that can be made on a basis of ongoing reciprocal interdependence changes from year to year, and from context to context. Indeed one could argue that the battle over defining these limits is the only constant.

The first proposition, to the effect that there is (in T.S. Epstein's way of putting it) a 'traditional system of landholding vested in the matrilineage' is complicated by the existence of other means of acquiring access to land besides membership of the matrilineal *vunatarai* as corporate descent group. These include the common expectation that a man's children would be able to continue to live on or use his *vunatarai* land, even after his death. This expectation would be even harder to refuse if the children had been attentive to their customary obligations towards the father's clan, above all by distributing large amounts of *tabu* at mortuary feasts (A.L. Epstein 1969:136). I examine some of these other means of acquiring access to land in more detail in the course of this chapter.

Although it is possible to describe Tolai land tenure as anchored in a principle of matrilineal descent around which all exceptions to the rule are organised, I argue in this chapter that another way of conceptualising land tenure better enables us to grasp the changing ways in which access to land has been contested and negotiated across the twentieth century. Matrilineal descent through *vunatarai* is one of the principles by which Tolai have negotiated access to land, and it is clearly an extremely important one that has as a consequence been prioritised as the underlying standard against which all other principles should be measured, both by Tolai explaining their land tenure system to outsiders, and by ethnographers. There is nothing wrong with describing a situation with a multiplicity of different claims in such terms, as long as we remain aware of what is lost in such explication. A model of 'structure' or 'system' as a means of describing how a set of unfamiliar social relations 'works' has similar dangers to those identified by Volosinov (1973:82) with regard to the task of describing language as a 'system' in order to make sense of the unfamiliar speech of unfamiliar peoples:

5. *Tabu* being stored in a spare room of a house in Sikut

Language as a system of normatively identical forms is an abstraction justifiable in theory and practice only from the standpoint of deciphering and teaching . . . alien language. This system cannot serve as a basis for understanding and explaining linguistic facts as they really exist and come into being. On the contrary, this system leads us away from the living, dynamic reality of language and its social functions, notwithstanding the fact that adherents of abstract objectivism claim sociological significance for their point of view . . . . These presuppositions are least capable of furnishing the grounds for a proper understanding of history – and language, after all, is a purely historical phenomenon.

Volosinov does not deny that systematisation of speech is ever useful or necessary. Rather, he argues that we need to beware of the tendency to reify such systematisations at the expense of acknowledging the 'living, dynamic reality of language'. This is a tendency that Volosinov characterises as 'abstract objectivism'. The same risk inheres in attempts to systematise land tenure in terms of an underlying structural principle such as matrilineality. It is in this same vein that Wagner (1974:119) said of sociological and anthropological concepts such as 'society' or 'groups' that while they are sometimes a necessary shorthand for describing certain social processes, we should not mistake the concepts for the full depth of the process that exceeds them.

As Volosinov notes, the dangers of abstract objectivism are particularly acute with regard to the historical development of human interactions, be these the exchange of linguistic signs, or the transactions and relations by which Tolai negotiate access to land. For example, T.S. Epstein in her already-quoted expression describes matrilineality as underpinning a *'traditional* system of landholding' (emphasis added). Or as A.L. Epstein (1999:64) puts it: 'The basic principle of Tolai land tenure can be stated very simply: *a pia kai ra vunatarai* – "ownership" of the land vests in perpetuity in the *vunatarai* or matrilineal descent group'.

However, the situation observed by the Epsteins and Salisbury in the early 1960s was one in which Tolai had already been for eighty years renegotiating relations of access to land in the context of integration into a global colonial political economy. As we shall see, there is evidence to suggest that prioritisation of the matrilineal principle over other ways of claiming access to land had in fact increased in the course of that engagement, rather than simply having been the 'traditional' principle that was now under threat from trends towards patrilineal individuation. The scare quotes around the word 'ownership' in A.L. Epstein's above cited statement of the matrilineal principle register a desire to qualify that claim. Elsewhere he describes the relationship between *vunatarai* and land as being not one of 'ownership', but of a claim (A.L.

Epstein 1969:126). This claim (K. *kakalei*) differs significantly from Western legal notions of property. For example the holders of the *kakalei* are often expected to acknowledge wider inclusiveness of social participation than is typical of a 'property' idea, such as the strong claims that can be made by children of the *vunatarai*. The term 'children of the clan' (TP. *blut*, literally 'blood [of the clan]', K. *a warwarngala na vunatarai*) refers to those people whose fathers were considered to be members of the clan in question. The barriers to the complete alienation or transfer of rights to land mark another significant difference between many ideal-typic descriptions of land as individual property. These are the types of issues that led A.L. Epstein (op cit.:110) to claim that, 'In the Tolai vernacular there is indeed no term which corresponds to or otherwise adequately translates our own concepts of property and ownership'.

This leads us to the problem of the second proposition that I outlined above, namely that the ever-changing nature of Tolai land tenure should be seen primarily as a contest between a traditional system of matrilineality and a modern patrilineal system threatening to displace it. It is abundantly clear that the principle of matrilineal descent is important in negotiating access to land. But so are other principles, including those already mentioned based on ties of patrilineal descent, and as best can be determined this has always been the case. What has changed over time is the contexts in which different principles apply as people contest their applicability in changing circumstances. In the 1960s T.S. Epstein (1968:67) reported of one Tolai that he 'is typical . . . in his attitudes to landholding. He bought land in his sons' names and planted it with cocoa and coconuts so that they alone will inherit his perennial crops. At the same time he continues to support matrilineage interests by associating in . . . joint matrilineal land'. Likewise Fingleton (personal communication) observes that: 'My recollection from the 1980s was that a Tolai man did two things at once: i) he fought to prevent his clan brothers from claiming *vunatarai* land that he had "bought out" for his children. ii) he tried to prevent his clan brothers from "buying out" *vunatarai* land for their children. He tries, of course, to have the best of both worlds'.

The situation viewed historically is perhaps best seen as one in which both matrilineality and patrilineality have been strengthened in different contexts. Matrilineality has been strengthened at the expense of patrilineality as part of the strengthening of the *vunatarai*'s claim on land relative to other claims. The qualifying quotation marks that A.L. Epstein puts around the word 'ownership' in the extract above consequently become perhaps a little less essential. Conversely, the increasing tendency of Tolai men to buy land in order to secure the rights of their children to inherit it, above all land upon which they have made expensive investments, strengthens patrilineal claims in other contexts. Customary land that is purchased by a man can be passed on to his children. Hence, in the first generation the transmission of land rights is patrilineal. It is widely acknowledged, however, that only his daughter's children are able to access those rights in the next generation. This could be analysed as the operation of an underlying structural matrilineality that is reverted to after the anomaly of the first generation. Yet this does not change the fact that land passes from the control of one matrilineal descent line to another, and most importantly, that at the time of this first generation patrilineality is strengthened as a means of securing access to land, and becomes central to determining how matrilineality will operate over coming generations. I discuss the implications of land purchase more fully later in this chapter. The introduction of individual family blocks at resettlements such as Sikut may also be another example of such a tendency to strengthen patrilineal over matrilineal claims, although it is currently too early to tell.

Explaining Changing Land Tenure

These tendencies for matrilineality or patrilineality to be strengthened at different points are best seen as manifestations of a wider trend towards prioritising claims made on the basis of exclusive individual ownership over inclusive overlapping claims. Inclusive overlapping claims are often acknowledgements of the reciprocal interdependence of different persons and groups. Lea (1997:12) observes that, '[T]he modern understanding of private property right . . . is an exclusive rather than an inclusive right'. He contrasts this situation with the tendency in Melanesian land tenure to concentrate on inclusive rights. Lea is concerned that there are processes at work, such as mining projects, in contemporary Melanesian society that are replacing inclusive rights with exclusive rights of individual ownership. I suggest that this contradiction takes a number of different forms, in addition to the expected one of individual or family excluding the clan. The clan equally can construct itself as a unitary individual owner that begins to exclude others, such as children of the clan, from inclusive rights of access, rights those others might previously have expected to enjoy by virtue of a relationship of reciprocal interdependence.

In the rest of this chapter I sketch ethnographically some of the processes by which Tolai increasingly prioritise these kinds of claims. In doing so, they increasingly construct themselves as discrete individuals, be these the singular individual head of a household who relates to land that he holds as a singular owner, or the collective individual of a *vunatarai* whose exclusive rights of 'ownership' are stressed over interlocking reciprocal claims. If ownership in its most abstract ideal sense relies on a discrete individual owner, then a shift towards relations that can more readily be described as exclusive ownership are a way of increasingly constituting persons and groups as individuals.[1]

The best example of the kinds of overlapping inclusive claims that cause quotation marks to be placed around the word 'ownership' in most descriptions of 'traditional' Melanesian land tenure is the previously mentioned relationship between a *vunatarai* and its 'children'. Land has long been central to that relationship. For example there have always been expectations that children of a clan that had *kakalei* ('claims') to a particular piece of land would be granted rights of access to that land. A.L. Epstein (1969:133) reports that Tolai recognise that a man:

> . . . is entitled to 'eat' of his father's land. Strictly speaking, this is a privilege, a matter of grace, rather than an enforceable right, and it lapses on the death of the father. Very often, however, particularly where relations between the two groups have been good, the matrilineage of the deceased father will acquiesce in his sons continuing to work the land or taking its profits . . . . It frequently happens too, if a vunatarai is rich in land, that the matrilineage is willing to grant a permanent interest in the land to the sons.

These are examples of the kinds of 'inclusive' claims to land that Lea contrasts with Western property concepts stressing 'exclusive' rights. The quoted passage clearly implies, however, that such claims have long been tied to the recognition of the obligations that the children of the clan have to the clan that 'fathered' them ('where relations between the two groups have been good'). In particular it is important for the children of the clan to honour deceased members of the father's clan with *tabu* distribution at mortuary feasts (an issue that I describe in more detail in Chapter Six). Hence the relationship between a *vunatarai* and its 'children' is ideally one of reciprocal interdependence (see for example Simet 1991:279–80).

The quoted passage also makes clear that the dynamics of reciprocal interdependence in any given context are shaped by concrete circumstances. A clan's willingness to allow more permanent rights of access is, amongst other things, tied to the amount of land that it has a claim to. The conditions within which Tolai negotiated their relationships to land altered massively over the course of the twentieth century. Changes such as a rising population, increasing pressure on land due to cash cropping, and the increasing use of land for long-term investments such as cash crops and permanent houses have made the acknowledgement of intertwined reciprocal obligations that play out over generations increasingly problematic. T.S. Epstein reports in this vein that:

> According to informants, patri-virilocal settlement gave rise to few problems during pre-contact days. There was then ample land and no perennial cash crops and the matrilineage of the father was obliged to

provide land for the sons' food gardens. These cultivation rights also served to keep alive matrilineage claims to land, since rights tended to lapse where the land itself was not cultivated for a lengthy period. (T.S. Epstein 1968:7; see also A.L. Epstein 1969:147–48)

Allowing children of the clan to use clan land has gone from being welcomed as means of keeping claims alive, to being guarded against so that even when they are acknowledged, these claims are carefully delimited.

The overall historical trend has thus been towards trying to constitute the *vunatarai* as a local land-based descent group, standing as a discrete owner of land and thereby to minimise claims made on the basis of reciprocal interdependence that threaten to undermine that discrete identity. This is not to say that absolute reciprocal interdependence is suddenly replaced with absolute independence. At certain points reciprocity is still stressed. Members of a clan might still be mindful of customary obligations to their children, and might still be upset if children of the clan failed to meet their own obligations. But increasingly an attempt is made to say that these ongoing reciprocal obligations are not an appropriate way of negotiating land rights.

As we shall see, this attempt by clans to limit the extent of customary reciprocity by clans with regard to land is paralleled by the attempts of Big Shots to limit customary reciprocity in order to protect their business and financial assets. Both are attempts to constitute a particular kind of individual, one who acknowledges reciprocal interdependence in some social contexts such as customary ritual, but who also claims in other contexts that their individual capacities, such as ownership of assets, are ontologically prior to such reciprocal interdependence. This individual is constituted through the deliberate rejection of reciprocal interdependence. Such a constitution is, again, necessarily an incomplete process; the bourgeois individual with no inherent claims on his or her own person is ultimately a fantasy even in Western capitalist societies.

With regard to land, sometimes the fault line is between a clan and its children, which in the Tolai context means prioritising matrilineal claims over patrilineal ones. At other points a *vunatarai* will draw limits around the relations of reciprocal interdependence that it has with another *vunatarai*. Or at other points an individual family head will draw limits around his children's involvement with his wife's relatives, in order to protect them from the emergence of clan-based claims on what he considers to be non-customary land. The points at which increasing degrees of individuality are claimed and contested, the kind of ties of reciprocal interdependence that one has to partially reject, and the singular or collective person claiming the individuality may vary, but it is this process of attempting to defend individually exclusive claims against inclusive claims based on ties of interlocking reciprocal interdependence that best allows us to trace the changing patterns of Tolai land tenure.

In the next several chapters I shall examine this process by means of three different examples that illustrate the partial loosening of ties of reciprocal interdependence. I begin with an examination of the contemporary situation at Sikut at the time of my main fieldwork. I explore how people talk about their blocks at Sikut, and in particular how they attempt to draw a line around family-owned blocks to the exclusion of matrilineal *vunatarai* interests. I then describe and analyse the partial commodification of the customary transaction called *kulia* at Matupit. Finally I examine in detail a specific land dispute that highlights the question of the relationship between different sections of *vunatarai*, and ways in which a section of a *vunatarai* describes itself as ontologically prior to its ties of reciprocal interdependence with other sections, at least as far as land is concerned. My discussion of all three of these examples will pay particular attention to the concept of 'customary' land. Whether expressed via the Tok Pisin word <u>kastom</u> or the English one 'custom', this concept is consistently at the forefront of disputes over land use. This is as true of face to face land disputes at the village level as it is of policy debates amongst politicians, lawyers and bureaucrats. In policy debates over the reform of customary land tenure in Melanesia, the definition of 'custom' is often left unclear (see Fingleton 2005). But even a brief overview of patterns of land disputes at Matupit demonstrates the number of different ways that the category of 'custom' is used at a grassroots level, something that requires scholars also to pay attention to the uses we make of key concepts in the course of trying to understand what is at stake in such debates.

Note

1. This process has parallels in Anglo-American capitalist societies. These societies' most powerful institutions – corporations – are legally defined as 'persons' and 'free individuals' (Bakan 2004:16). See Foster (2002:6) for a discussion of the nation of Papua New Guinea as a kind of emergent 'collective individual', and how this 'resonates well with the commodity form', a resonance he sees as being tied to 'the expansion of practices and discourses of possessive individualism through capitalist markets' (op cit.:6–7). See also Foster (1995:18–19, 154).

🏵 2
Land at Sikut

Freedom from _Kastom_ and Economic Development

In the immediate wake of the volcanic eruption of 1994, the residents of Matupit fled to many different locations, but today most Matupi live either at the resettlement camp of Matupit-Sikut or have returned to Matupit. Land at Sikut provides a challenge to the legalistic distinction between 'customary' and 'non-customary' land. Legally the land at Sikut is supposed to be 'non-customary', but many residents fear (or in a few cases hope for) the gradual re-emergence of customary land tenure practices over time. Some people even claim to have detected the first signs of their re-emergence only a few years after the establishment of the settlement. Yet despite this the distinction between the two land tenure regimes is vital to any understanding of how access to land is secured and social relations are transacted through land. It is through the rhetorical distinction between the customary and non-customary land rights that Matupi negotiate and contest the legitimacy of claims made to the land at Sikut. The ways in which _kastom_ is used to assert and deny such claims can be seen as part of the wider pattern by which individual rights of property in land are rhetorically asserted or denied in particular contexts. This is done by attempting to extend or limit the contexts in which it is considered legitimate to make claims on others by virtue of a history of reciprocal interdependence. In this chapter I explore the ways in which _kastom_ as a concept is rhetorically deployed by Matupi resident at Sikut to legitimise or delitimise claims made on land on the basis of such disputed histories. _Kastom_ is revealed in this discussion to be a shifting signifier whose meaning is always dependent upon the context of its use. Uses of the term to attempt to delitimise certain kinds of claims to land at Sikut will be the first of several examples encounted in this book of ways in which _kastom_ acts as both a marker and maker of the ever-shifting limits of social claims grounded in a morality of reciprocal interdependence.

Householding and Landholding at Sikut

Many families maintain houses at both Sikut and Matupit. Thus any census or village survey runs the danger of conveying an inaccurately static picture of residential patterns. Nonetheless, along with a group of research assistants, I conducted a survey of both sites between March and April 2002. We surveyed 111 households at Sikut, and 175 households at Matupit. At the time of the survey, there were 299 blocks allocated at Matupit-Sikut, according to Provincial Government records. However, the majority of these blocks were not yet inhabited. Many were totally undeveloped, and others were going through the initial stages of development, such as cutting down of trees and undergrowth. Normally this was done before block holders moved onto the block. For example, many people lived at Matupit and commuted for a few days at a time, staying overnight with friends or relatives. Other families who had recently been allocated blocks stayed at the temporary care centre at the middle of the settlement and went up to their blocks to begin work on them during the day.

Of the 111 households surveyed at Sikut, 23 were staying at the care centre rather than directly on blocks. About half of these families also had access to a block, in most cases by virtue of their own title, and in a few others because a relative who had been given a block and was living elsewhere had given them access (often with the expectation that they would sign the block over to them later). Most blocks that were inhabited had one house on them. In half a dozen cases, there were several houses on the same block. One man had five houses on his block: his own, and one for each of his four married daughters and their families. But while I did come across a few other similar cases during my time at Sikut, this kind of subdivision was the exception rather than the rule. In general, people did not want to let such permanent interests be established on their blocks. I came across two cases in which such an arrangement had led to a dispute. In each case the block holder wished to remove a relative that they previously had allowed to stay, and the relative was holding out for compensation for their house and the work that they had put into the block. A further, slightly different case involved two women of identical name who both heard that the block had been given in their name. They each built houses at opposite ends of the block. At the time of fieldwork, neither was prepared to budge, and they were awaiting official adjudication as to which of them was the official block holder.

For those not wishing to return to the ruins of Rabaul and Matupit, Sikut has many advantages. At Sikut settlers have been given provisional license for the land by the government, with the promise of permanent title once surveying and legal technicalities have been completed. Other Tolai who have resettled after the eruption have to make do with small plots of land.

6. ToDi Turagil, my main research assistant and friend at Matupit and Sikut

At the resettlement camp of Gelagela where Tolai from many other villages near Rabaul have been given land, each household has around one-fourth of a hectare of land, barely enough to provide food for most families. At Sikut each person who has been allocated a block has around three hectares, enough to feed a family and potentially to provide a large income through cash cropping. These advantages are for many enough to outweigh the major disadvantage of life at Siku, its distance from towns. The East New Britain Provincial Government does not have enough money to maintain the roads, and these suffer extensive damage during the rainy season. As a consequence, Sikut is about an hour's journey from the new Provincial Capital and com-mercial centre of Kokopo (see Map 1). In addition, the poor state of the roads means that cars need frequent and expensive repairs. The result is that very few people can afford to run their own cars, and running a bus (known as PMV: Passenger Motorised Vehicle) is not a profitable business. During my time at Sikut, there was always a shortage of PMVs. Thus on top of the hour that it took to get into town, one could often anticipate an additional three or four hours sitting around waiting until a vehicle with room to board arrived. Additionally, travelling all the way to Rabaul requires a change of PMV at Kokopo and a second hour of travel, while going on to Matupit requires a further change of vehicle and a twenty minute ride, with the possibility of equally long waits for vehicles at both interchanges. Given that people often have to return 'home' to Matupit for burials and other family and customary occasions, the travel difficulties are a real concern. The amount of time some-times required to wait for the three buses needed to travel between Matupit and Sikut means that the journey can take more than a whole day. People are sometimes left stranded overnight in Kokopo, having to stay with relatives, or having to sleep on the streets. The cost of transport is also significant. The combined fare to travel from Sikut to Matupit at the time of my fieldwork was around 10 Kina one way, while the average fortnightly wage for a Tolai working in town as a shop assistant or clerk was likely to be between 150 and 300K. If someone had to transport a family with three or four children from Sikut to Matupit and back again for a customary event, the costs could be severe indeed.

And people with jobs are the lucky ones. Many households at Sikut do not have a member working in town. Persons who could find such jobs often forego doing so, since the cost of the daily commute makes the work barely worthwhile. And most Sikut residents do not yet have a steady income from cash cropping. Thus to fulfil monetary obligations, many people depend on irregular and uncertain sources of income, such as the occasional sale of garden vegetables at Kokopo market, or the largesse of wealthier relatives.

Most families at Sikut now live on their blocks. A few have completed large-scale permanent houses, similar to what they would have had at

Matupit prior to the volcano. These houses are made of modern building materials such as masonite, fibro, and tin iron roofing, and also have amenities such as a water tank. A few families still inhabit temporary shacks, made out of cast off permanent materials and scraps of wood. Most families are somewhere between these poles, moving between temporary housing and their semi-completed permanent house. The process of construction is a long one. Most block holders have been building for several years, and are still some way from final completion. A few lucky block holders who were allocated their blocks early received pre-fabricated kit houses from the Provincial Government or from church charities. In some cases, these houses still stand. Often parts of the kit were taken by friends or relatives in greater immediate need, and kit components are complemented with cast off material. Much of the material that makes up the semi-permanent structures at Tolai villages such as Sikut and Matupit was looted from buildings that were still standing in Rabaul in the days following the eruption. People who have not developed their blocks often cite the fact that earlier settlers received kit houses while later settlers like themselves did not, putting them at a disadvantage. This pattern has played into the debate about block forfeits that I detail below.

As noted above, just over twenty households in Sikut remain in what is referred to as the 'care centre'. Unlike the care centres set up in places such as Kokopo High School in the immediate aftermath of the eruption, there is no 'care' as such provided here. The families clustered together in this area are still waiting for a block and have each been allocated about one hectare of land on a temporary basis. This land is earmarked for future development, such as the construction of permanent churches, cemetery, a high school and shops. It is envisioned that at some point in the future when Sikut is electrified that it will become a township, but for now Sikut retains a frontier settlement feel. Those families who have temporary blocks have been instructed to only plant garden vegetables. Permanent cash crops such as cocoa would inevitably lead to compensation claims and disputes, when the time came to remove them for community developments. So these care centre residents currently live in a kind of limbo. They are able to feed themselves, but unable to plan any kind of economic development.

A few families in the care centre already have blocks, but have decided not to move on to them yet. Not all of the roads that were supposed to link all the blocks in Sikut to the centre of the settlement and to the main road to Kokopo have been completed. Most block holders living at the care centre have blocks that would be hard to access. Absence of other people in neighbouring blocks reinforces reluctance to start settling these areas. People are afraid that isolation will leave them easy prey to criminals (TP. _raskols_), or worse, bush spirits. So for the time being they travel up the hills to their blocks for a few hours or

7. House in process of being built at a block in Sikut

a few days a week to garden. There are other uninhabited blocks at Sikut that were allocated to people who have since moved back to Matupit. The future of these blocks is a source of great controversy, as I shall describe in greater detail later.

During my residence at Sikut, I lived in a house at the edge of the care centre. The house was built by the government for the appointed care centre resettlement coordinator, who at the time had other duties to perform for the Provincial Government at offices in Gelagela, such that it was easier for him to live in his wife's village. Thus he was looking for someone to look after and maintain the house. This location was central to the settlement and meant that I was more readily integrated into the care centre community than if I had lived on a block located far away from the centre.

The Daily Cycle in Sikut

Because New Britain lies only a few degrees south of the equator, the sun rises at almost exactly six a.m. all year round, and it is already starting to get light at around a quarter past five. By half past five the peace of the night is disturbed, first by the cockerels, and then by the children running from door to door, selling pre-cooked bread rolls or deep fried flour balls for breakfast. Many families make a little extra money by preparing such food, which will be bought by those who are in a hurry to get to Kokopo for work or marketing, or perhaps by those who want to make an early start to work in their own gardens. This small-scale buying and selling is an ever-present part of daily life at both Sikut and Matupit, with almost all households being involved in marketing of baked foodstuffs, cigarettes bought wholesale in town, or betel nut. Most dip in and out of this kind of trading depending on how much they need money at the time. Very few participate in it as a permanent and important part of their household economy. The further step of running a trade store selling items bought wholesale in town such as rice, tinned meat and batteries requires a special kind of person, able to resist the demands for credit of friends and kin. Most trade stores only last a few months or a couple of years at most, because they either go bust or the owner tires of the battle and quits while still ahead. On my arrival in February 2002 there were three trade stores in Sikut: two in the care centre, and one on a nearby block bordering one of the settlement's main roads. By the time I left in February 2004, all three had closed. Most people go into town themselves to pick up trade store items or rely on others going into town to collect them on their behalf, or they head to the two stores located about two miles from the care centre at the Warangoi bridge, a distance of four to five (very hilly) miles for those living on some of the more isolated blocks.

8. Small business selling mobile phone top-up cards in Sikut

After breakfast the PMVs start running to Kokopo between six and seven a.m. People with no business in town head towards their blocks or their gardens if they are planning on working, as it is best to get as much work done as possible before the heat becomes unbearable. Others, claiming to be tired from too much work the day before, will hang around. Perhaps they will do odd jobs on their house, re-fixing a piece of corrugated iron to the roof that last night's wind removed. Or failing that they will find others in the same predicament to gossip, and smoke and chew betel nut with. If they have no work to do, there is always a good chance that someone else will find work to rope them into. Perhaps someone needs help clearing bush before making a new garden. There are a few attempts to organise such assistance on a constant basis. For example the Catholic women in the care centre arrange one morning a week where they take turns to help on each other's blocks. On the whole, however, such arrangements are ad-hoc. The extent to which payment is expected in exchange for such assistance, or the extent to which it should be expected as the result of a close relationship or as the return of previous assistance, being an often unspoken, yet nonetheless keenly felt potential bone of contention, of which everyone is aware. Garden work is mostly carried out by all members of a household who are present and physically capable of doing so; men, women and children. Both men and women will attend to gardens. Although in my experience women were more likely to have the job of harvesting, whereas men were more likely to organise clearing a new garden, and to cultivate cocoa, this was no hard and fast rule.

By around eleven o'clock it grows very hot, and most people decide to relax (TP. *malolo*) for a few hours. Maybe that will be it for the day, or maybe

9. Food market next to the bridge over the Warangoi River

they will start again at around three o'clock with a few hours more work before it gets dark at around half past five. Young people often congregate to play sports as it gets darker and cooler. Volleyball is particularly popular. The other time-consuming task that is often carried out in the evening is collection of water. During the rainy season, this is not a problem, as there are a number of water tanks at the community centre next to the care centre, and many households have their own water tanks, such that even at the most distant blocks it is possible to find water relatively easily. In addition some of the blocks have natural springs or wells. But while the water tanks are supposed to be large enough to supply the settlement with drinking water throughout the dry season (which lasts for almost half of the year), in reality a few months into that season the water is exhausted, because people ignore repeated requests not to use the tap water for washing bodies and clothes. They are reluctant to use the often muddy streams for washing, especially as they are considered to carry a great risk of catching water-borne parasites. In addition the tanks are often vandalised by youths. So during the dry season people have to travel several miles to the river Warangoi. There they wash themselves and their clothes, before filling up containers with water, and waiting, perhaps for hours, for what is referred to as a 'chance car' that will take them back to their homes. The water, although a lot cleaner than the muddy streams that pass through Sikut, is of course still affected by the bathing and washing that takes place in it. Even with boiling, stomach upsets are not unknown. Donald, an old man that I was close to and who ran one of the trade stores, died of dysentery during my time in the field, almost certainly as a result of the Warangoi water.

In the evenings, as people come back from gardens or town to the care centre or to their houses, they begin to socialise. Stories, betel nut and cigarettes are exchanged around open fires whose smoke is intended to repel the mosquitoes that thrive at Sikut. The high incidence of malaria is one of the common reasons people give for preferring to move back to the ash-covered ruins of Matupit. During fieldwork, my own evening would be spent copying up scratch notes by the light of a battery powered lamp. Perhaps, if I had forgotten to buy enough batteries on my last trip to town, or if I simply could not be bothered, I would wander down to the care centre where young men were gathered playing darts. We would pool our money for kerosene to power the lamp, stock up on tobacco, and be set for the evening. For those uninterested in such pursuits, there is always a church event to prepare for. Among families living on the blocks there is less communal activity of this kind in the evenings. Families tend to stay together, or visit friends and relatives on a nearby block. On some evenings the whole care centre and many people from other blocks gather to watch the television belonging to Karlo, who works for the Provincial Government in Kokopo as an engineer. Friday nights are Australian rugby night, when PNG's sole terrestrial channel, EMTV, carries the big game live from Brisbane or Sydney. Karl runs the TV off of his car battery, and between 60 and 100 of us might gather to watch. On other occasions people show video CDs, on another TV run off a generator, often as a fund raiser, maybe for a church event or to help a family with school fees. Action movies are most popular. Films are chosen largely by whether the star of the film is well-remembered from a previous outing. Stallone, Schwarzenegger and Jackie Chan are big hits. On weekends, much of the settlement will attend church. Matupit has three main congregations. The two largest are the United Church and the Roman Catholic Church which each comprise around 40 per cent of the community. The other established church is the SDA who make up most of the remainder. Smaller evangelical and charismatic churches that have recently gained many converts in PNG have yet to make much of an impact among the Matupi. Two or three families have converted to the Church of Christ (CoC), and they conduct a Sunday service at the house of one of their converts about three quarters of a mile from the care centre. The enthusiastic strumming of guitars and the joyful shouts of 'Hallelujah!' that can sometimes be heard as far away as the care centre provoke much rolling of eyeballs and shaking of heads from those who prefer their Christianity a little more sedate.

On Wednesdays the community is supposed to gather for communal work, such as cutting back the overgrowing grass at the road sides. However, this is not too strictly enforced, and many people are conspicuously absent more often than they are present. There is often talk of fining persistent non-attenders, but most people realise that it is talk that will never be acted on. Work sessions are often followed by a community meeting held in the community centre, a large open walled structure with a cement floor and iron roof built with Japanese aid money. Sikut is relatively well-equipped with such amenities, also having a primary school and medical Aid Post. These facilities were built in the years immediately after the eruption, and the Provincial Government does not have the money for their maintenance, so although still functional, they are run down, with broken fly wire and damaged water tanks. Meetings are called by the resettlement committee. Once a year the community meets and elects a committee chairman, and he appoints members to this committee. Matupit councillors are also on the committee or able to nominate members to it. Rather than being divided into new wards, Sikut residents still vote for a councillor representing the ward in which they lived 'at home'. This means a lot of extra work for councillors moving back and forth between the two sites, and also means that many people are represented by a councillor living a day's journey away, whom they hardly ever get the chance to see. Sikut residents still vote as members of the Rabaul Open constituency at national elections, even though they are now geographically located within the Gazelle Open. Meetings often go on for hours, discussing issues of concern to the community such as the running of the school, or thefts of cocoa from people's blocks.

Fieldwork at Sikut

A working day at Sikut for me, as anthropologist, could involve a lot of walking. If I was interviewing people outside the care centre, I would take care to leave early enough to avoid traipsing up the hills in the blazing midday sun. Travelling to and from interviews was often the most relaxing part of the day. On the roads I could go several minutes without bumping into anyone. If I was interviewing on one of the blocks off the road, then passing through the walking tracks that connect these blocks provided rare moments of solitude that were a welcome contrast to the hustle and bustle of Matupit. These walks also gave an overview of the state of development at Sikut. The further one went from the roads the less developed a block was likely to be. Cocoa plantations and cleared ground ready for planting tended to be replaced by increasing amounts of virgin rainforest.

Much of my time at Sikut was spent with seven families whose housebuilding activities I followed closely over the course of nearly two years. I conducted more rudimentary studies with several other families and a survey of the village. But it is with these particular sets of people that I spent the most time, in addition to some of the young men living in and around the care centre with whom I became friendly. Some of these people will be introduced at later points in the book.

One family in particular that it is important to mention is the family of the man ToAtun, who became my main research assistant during my fieldwork. He often travelled with me around Sikut or to Kokopo, Rabaul or Matupit. ToAtun was a grassroots villager, around forty years old, living in Sikut at the time of my arrival. He was born in the Rainatun area of Matupit in the early 1960s. His mother was from the village of Malaguna Number Two on the other side of Rabaul, and ToAtun spent his childhood moving to and fro between the two locations. After leaving school, ToAtun had worked a little with his father on his coconut plantations near Matupit producing copra. Then he worked in town at a variety of jobs 'when times were still good', during the 1980s. Most of these jobs were gained through kinship connections. ToAtun worked as a storeroom attendant or night security guard for one very close relative of Sir John Kaputin, to whom ToAtun was also related. As a youth ToAtun had spent much time with Sir John's father, Daniel Kaputin, who was perhaps the most respected and important of Matupit Big Men during the 1960s, and who was the leader of ToAtun's *vunatarai*. He was also notable amongst his age group for the strength and depth of his involvement in customary activities. While most men of his age were involved in customary activities to some extent or other, ToAtun was at the most active end of the spectrum. Often he was called upon to help with the preparations for customary rituals. Owing to the relative depth of his ritual knowledge, he was seen as one of the few people of his generation who were capable of taking over some of the leadership of customary events in the future. However, his lack of money meant that he could never be a customary leader in the early twenty-first century, in a manner that someone like Daniel Kaputin had managed to be without much money forty years earlier.

Following the eruption in 1994, ToAtun had stayed at a variety of care centres living on government supplies. In the middle of 1995, he and his family moved to the unofficial resettlement camp at Ulagunan. They stayed there for two years before the lack of government assistance and disputes within the community led them to move to Sikut (the Provincial Government did not recognise the Ulagunan resettlement). ToAtun lived in the care centre at Sikut with his wife and twelve children. He was normally unemployed, but occasionally picked up casual employment as a semi-skilled carpenter. Eventually, a land block at Sikut was given to ToAtun by a sibling with a well-paid clerical job who lived in his wife's village many miles away from the block itself. But it was difficult for ToAtun to fully relocate to the block with limited financial resources. At the time of my return visit to East New Britain around Christmas 2009, he was still only half way towards building a permanent house on the block for his family, although he did have several hundred cocoa trees that were now almost ready to bear fruit.

When we were working together, ToAtun accompanied me to make introductions to villagers who might be useful to talk with, to translate and perhaps most crucially to give his explanation about what had happened at meetings or what the person that we had been talking to really meant and why he or she had said what they had said. As I stayed longer at Sikut and Matupit, I had less need either of introductions or translations. But ToAtun kept accompanying me, and not just, I think, for the daily stipend that I gave him for his assistance. ToAtun became increasingly fascinated by my work and by the end had perhaps become as interested in the strange interpretations that I made of what we had observed during the day as I was in his. His interpretations of the day's events as we drove or walked back towards Sikut care centre were amongst the most valuable and illuminating parts of my field research, and not just for the information they provided. After a while I was able increasingly to predict ToAtun's interpretation of events, and how it might differ from the interpretations of other people that I was close to. The fact that I now felt that I intuitively understood why specific positions would be held by persons in specific social positions and with particular world views, gave me confidence that I was making progress in my fieldwork, at times when day-to-day events seemed to conspire against me completing any of the routines that I had carefully detailed in my pre-fieldwork plan.

When we were not together, ToAtun's average day could take a variety of courses. Most commonly, he would rise early, have a small breakfast and then take off to work on his block for a few hours, either cleaning ground for planting, planting new garden foods or cocoa trees, or harvesting food to eat. Sometimes he would have paid work for a wealthier relative, such as Isaac ToLanger, a senior public servant living in Port Moresby who rented a nine hectare block from the government near the Sikut resettlement camp and who often hired ToAtun to cut timber on his block or harvest cocoa. Such arrangements inevitably involved a large amount of sitting around waiting and miscommunication. In the days before mobile phones reached the Gazelle changes in plan were impossible to communicate.[1] Something nearly always goes wrong when trying to co-ordinate such activities: ToLanger's aeroplane might be delayed due to volcanic ash, or his car might get yet another flat tyre or broken axle due to the mass of potholes on the roads. As a consequence, it is most uncommon for ToAtun to be picked up on the first date that was set for him to be picked up to work for men such as ToLanger. This would often impede his plans to develop his block, as he had to delay planting new cocoa trees for example, only to find that by the time he could get around to planting them a heavy rain might have made it impossible. Often after a full day's paid work in the tropical heat, ToAtun would be unable to do much the next day and would sit around relaxing, drinking tea, smoking and chewing betel nut. Still ToAtun considered himself fairly fortunate, as he now had access to land. This meant that whatever happened, his family would have enough food, and the little amount of money that he occasionally earned could be spent on those essential luxuries of tea, sugar, tobacco, betel nut, batteries and so on. Sometimes they might go to town to buy a box of cigarettes wholesale to sell for a profit, though this was never a regular activity, and two weeks later they might be buying from the same neighbours that they had been selling to a fortnight previously.

As a man who was active both in customary activities and in the United Church, ToAtun was often away from the house for whole days at a time, either at church committee meetings, choir practices or in preparations for customary rituals and events. His wife Mary's average day was probably less varied. In the dry season it would begin with her and the eldest children walking with a variety of plastic containers to pick up water. At the start of the dry season, the journey was not too arduous, because she could walk to my house about half a mile from their block, before returning uphill, laden with water. One morning, in an attempt to be helpful, I tried carrying water for her up to her home. I carried about half the amount that she normally carried, and at the end of it felt in such pain and exhaustion that I had to lie on the ground in front of their fire for almost an hour as my breath returned to normal, much to the delight of her children. Later in the dry season when all the water had been drained from my tank, life was more difficult, and along with other villagers Mary, sometimes accompanied by ToAtun and various children, might have to wait hours for a car along with dozens of other families to get to the river Warangoi to collect water. There the whole family would wash their bodies and their clothes, before filling the plastic containers and waiting for a car to take them home again. The rest of the day would be taken up with garden work and the preparation of food, normally baked tubers such as taro or sweet potato, and the cooking of green vegetables in coconut milk.

Freedom from *Kastom*: The Hopes and Fears Attached to Non-Customary Land at Sikut

The government's adamant position that Sikut land is not 'customary' land was constantly repeated to me in my discussions and interviews with administrative officials (often conducted in English). By this they meant that it is to be owned by individual families, not by clans, and that it will be inherited as property by the children of the title holder (in most cases the husband of a nuclear family unit). This position is, on the surface, supported by the majority of those Matupi who have relocated to Sikut. I was struck by the number of occasions on which Sikut residents told me that the land at Sikut was 'better' than Matupit land, not because it was more productive or plentiful, but because it was not 'customary'. They described themselves as being 'free' from customary ground and all of its problems. Here they could work hard and pass on the benefits to their children.

However, just because the land at Sikut is not 'customary' does not mean that it is free from dispute. Rather most disputes have a new character, pitting some block holders against those still waiting for blocks. The existence of many undeveloped blocks held by families who have returned to live at Matupit, coupled with the number of years that those at the care centre have had to wait to get on with their lives, has led to increasingly vocal demands for undeveloped blocks to be forfeited and given to those still waiting in the care centre.

In my experience a majority of the Sikut community supported the forfeit policy, as did in theory the provincial government Lands Department. Towards the end of my time in Sikut a concerted effort was made by the resettlement committee to get the Lands Division to authorise a mass forfeit of around forty of the undeveloped blocks. These blocks were allocated to all families living in the care centre. This led to a series of stormy meetings at Sikut which block holders and their supporters living at Matupit would attend en masse. Block holders who had been threatened with forfeit by the resettlement committee turned up to 'work' on the block for a few weeks, as a warning to the person to whom the block was to be allocated, before returning to Matupit. It had been hoped by many that the official backing of the Lands Division would make this tactic unsuccessful. However, political leadership at all levels was divided. The elected members of the resettlement committee were largely in favour of the forfeit. However, they were opposed by most of the councillors, who went to the Rabaul District Government to declare the resettlement committee null and void. No one knew whether the Rabaul District Government or the Provincial Government's Land Division held authority over the land. Thus any forfeit policy was likely to be held up by several years of legal wrangling.

An additional problem was that no-one yet has title to the Sikut blocks. Most of the blocks were allocated in early 1995, with the expectation that title would be issued to individual title holders within a year. Yet at the start of 2004, title had yet to be issued, because the Provincial Government and the Gazelle Restoration Authority (GRA) have not had the money to complete the necessary surveys. According to the GRA this is because World Bank regulations have consistently led to delays in funding. The result is that the forfeits issued by the Lands Division would not stand up in court, as one lawyer who was sympathetic to the forfeit policy informed a Sikut meeting shortly before I left. In 1995 every block holder had been issued with a one year temporary title, but this title had not been renewed. Consequently, every block holder at Sikut, whether resident or not, is in legal terms a squatter remaining on government land with tacit approval. Only when title was issued would the government be able to attach conditions such as block development to the continuation of that title. The resettlement committee went ahead with the forfeits anyway and started moving people onto the blocks. In my last week of fieldwork in East New Britain in February 2004, the inevitable fights were breaking out as the original block holders arrived to remove the newcomers.

On the surface, the current situation at Sikut may not appear to be a dispute over *kastom*. Both sides accept that Sikut is 'non-customary' land. But the debate over forfeits has in fact become, at least in part, a debate over the role of *kastom* in structuring landownership. Often in debates over the appropriate use of land at Sikut the phrase 'it's not customary ground' would be thrown at opponents. Supporters of the forfeits argued that their opponents (deliberately) failed to understand the difference between land that was given by state license, whose continued ownership was contingent upon development of that land, and customary land that was tied to clans by virtue of an inalienable right, or *kakalei* (see A.L. Epstein 1969:131). In these arguments the word *kastom* is used in an entirely negative sense as the alleged recourse of those who are too 'lazy' to develop their state land. The opponents of the forfeit policy never claimed to consider Sikut to be 'customary' land, but some of their counter-arguments did draw on practices that would be considered to be customary by most. Part of the rationale of the resettlement programme was anticipation that blocks would be developed in the bush at Sikut so that in the event of another eruption, the displaced people of Matupit would be able to go stay on blocks at Sikut that they had developed, or with kin who had developed blocks. This was because it was 'custom' among the Tolai to go stay with kin and seek assistance from them in times of need. The original distribution of Sikut blocks had followed the division of Matupit into different council wards. Consequently there was a tendency for members of the same *vunatarai* or people who had other close customary kinship relations to be situated near to each other. According to some, this pattern was put at risk by forfeits that gave priority to residents of the care centre. Opponents of the forfeit argued that this breaking up of spatial closeness jeopardised customary networks of assistance in case of emergency. They argued that if forfeits were truly necessary then the blocks should be given to relatives of the original block holders to preserve these networks. Although it is accepted that the land is not 'customary', according to this argument it is still important to take *kastom* into account in the governance of this land.

This kind of argument is not limited to opponents of the forfeits. The wave of forfeits that occurred towards the end of my first fieldwork period was spearheaded by ToParam, the chair of the resettlement committee. ToParam was a Seventh Day Adventist man in his late forties who took over as the chair of the resettlement committee following the resignation of his controversial predecessor, Tony Dannett, in 2003. ToParam was initially popular as he was expected to have a less confrontational style than Tony. But it did not take long for disputes to emerge. At the meeting in Sikut at which he announced that the forfeits were going ahead, ToParam raised another issue. He wanted to correct the imbalance that meant that in some families large numbers of brothers had each been given blocks, but none of their sisters had. Later ToParam told me that the purpose of trying to ensure that sisters also received blocks was to keep clans together. He was scared of anger arising among young men of the clan if there were no road open to them to inherit land as well. More important, however, was his concern to keep the clan together, as a kind of social security network. He acknowledged that some people at Sikut said that the clan should become a thing of the past, and that individual families should be self-sufficient. However, he believed that this kind of 'Western' self-sufficiency would never be an option for most Papua New Guineans, and that even those people who had told me that they would not help their nephews, would feel obliged to if pushed.[2] ToParam felt that the continuation of this kind of *kastom* was still going to be essential for years to come, and he saw managing the land tenure system in such a manner as a means of encouraging its survival. ToParam argued that this would ensure that people lived close to at least some members of not just their own clan, but also people who had been 'fathered' by their clan, ensuring that these relationships were of a day-to-day importance to them, and strengthening bonds of reciprocal assistance. Again, while the 'non-customary' nature of the land is asserted, this is combined with a concern that this 'non-customary' land be administered in a way that helps preserve at least elements of what is considered to be 'customary'.

Individual Land Ownership and Economic Development

Some people in government point to the widespread enthusiasm of Sikut residents for the new land as 'freeing' them from the obligations, constraints and disputes inherent in customary landownership as evidence that a more general reform of customary tenure would be a spur to development. There has been significant investment and development in some blocks. Some block holders have planted thousands of cocoa trees and are now beginning to enjoy an income of as much as several thousand Kina a month (subject to contingencies of price fluctuations and crop success). Yet there are some qualifications to this development success story. Individual tenure requires the state to have the resources and intention to back it up, if tenure is to be more than a piece of paper. The inability of the state in East New Britain to even provide title after ten years, and lack of clarity about which of the competing arms of government has jurisdiction at Sikut, has directly led to the under-utilisation of large amounts of Sikut land. Those people who have been allocated new blocks are often wary of putting too much effort into the land, because they have seen others lose their blocks back to the original landholders before.

One example illustrates the shaky basis of government jurisdiction. One of the two main roads leading up to the blocks at Sikut is only sealed half way. This is because in 1995, despite warnings to the contrary, one of the block holders planted cocoa seedlings close to the edge of his block. When the time came for the road to be sealed, he demanded several hundred Kina compensation if the Division of Works was going to remove his seedlings to seal the road. Exasperated by the prospect of wasting years and thousands of Kina on legal action, the Provincial Government re-allocated the money to another resettlement scheme. Now all of the blocks further away from the centre of Sikut are served by a dirt track. Buses refuse to run past this block holder's house, as the cost in spare parts if they go on the dirt track is prohibitive. For a similar reason it is hard for these block holders to hire cars or trucks to take their cocoa to selling points. As a result these blocks are among the least developed in the resettlement area. In theory, because this was government land rather than customary land, the government could have taken action to remove his cocoa seedlings and press on with the road development. In reality they could not afford the legal costs, or the cost of the police action. They were as unable to enforce development projects on land to which they had title as they often are on customary land, leaving their ability to enforce tenure reform on customary ground in serious doubt.

It is also worth bearing in mind that individual title in and of itself does not free one from the demands of kin and customary obligations that many see as a disincentive to development. While large amounts of development have occurred at Sikut, no-one has yet planted their entire three hectares with cash crops and food. The maximum level seems to be two out of three hectares.[3] One reason that is frequently raised is the desire not to be the target of constant appeals for assistance, and not to be the target of jealousy. People would know exactly how much you were selling, and once you reached a certain amount, you would not keep much over that for yourself. One of the Sikut block holders, called Philip, told me that 'if they see me harvesting all the time and I don't give to some people they can do some things to my block and my cocoa won't bear fruit'. Or worse, as Philip and others also told me, people who consistently refused such requests could end up dead or injured because of sorcery, nearly always inflicted by jealous siblings or cousins (although the problem was apparently not as bad as it had been twenty or thirty years ago).[4] The chair of the resettlement committee before ToParam, Tony Dannet was one of the few who consistently attacked this fear, yet his credibility in the village in this respect was undermined by chronic arthritis in his left leg, seen by many as being caused by the jealousy of someone having magical power.

Most important of all, the granting of individual title does not guarantee that tenure practices that many would describe as 'customary' will not re-emerge on the land. There is a precedent for this in East New Britain. In the 1950s, the Australian administration released several large blocks of land for lease to individuals from Tolai villages near Rabaul. These leases came with the guarantee of individual title, and a policy that the land was to be inherited by the next of kin, ideally the children of the block holder. However, in most cases the land has stayed within the block holder's clan, often passing on to his sisters' sons, as would be the case with customary land. Although the majority of Tolai are adamant that this is 'new land', and it is morally right for the children of the block holder who had put in all of the hard work of development to inherit it, the strength of kinship ties makes it hard to refuse nephews of one's own clan when they arrive asking to be allowed to help out on the block and plant a section of it for their own cash crops. Once they are on the land in numbers, it is even harder to remove them. In most cases they have ended up in possession of the block after the death of the original block holder. In theory they could be removed legally. Practically though, such a process could take decades, and cost thousands of Kina, which is not a realistic option for most Tolai. A plaintiff would probably have to wait several years before the case was heard by a local land court, and any case heard in a local land court would be liable to appeal in a higher court. There are three blocks at Wudal that were given to Matupi. Of these, two are now inhabited by nephews of the same clan as the block holder. In only one case have the children managed to assert their legal right to inherit the title.[5]

However, many Sikut residents argue that Tolai society has changed from the 1960s. They assert that the nuclear family is today stronger, and that the large number of people at Sikut as opposed to Wudal will make it easier for a situation to emerge in which demands by clan nephews will be easier to resist. Unlike the older resettlements, Sikut is envisaged as a new community that is capable of establishing new rules. Although people never refused to recognise their nephews, I observed many occasions on which clear boundaries were drawn around the relationship and in particular the nephews' rights to come and stay for extended periods on the block.[6] Men like Philip and the former chair of the resettlement committee, Tony Dannet, were far from alone in asserting the importance of drawing this distinction. Traditionally the relationship between a boy and his maternal uncle was seen as being in many contexts more important than a boy's relationship to his father, and uncles and nephews were expected to spend as much time as possible together. Now fear of land grabbing means that uncles try to limit this relationship and limit the amount of time that nephews spend on their blocks. This was put strongly to me by many, including Philip, whom I quoted above on fears of sorcery. Although Philip was apprehensive of the threats posed by jealous relatives, he was still adamant that he was part of a new wave of people who were renegotiating the relationship between individual families and wider kinship networks.

I spent many afternoons with Philip, tracking the progress of the large house that he was building on his block at Sikut. He was in his late forties at the time of my fieldwork, and was working as an engineering supervisor at a large foreign owned mining project in another part of PNG, which gave him a cash income far higher than the vast majority of other Sikut residents. Philip's opinions, although characteristically blunt in expression, were representative of wider opinion. One afternoon, as we were talking in Tok Pisin, he told me that:

> Now *kastom* is fading away. What happened at Vudal won't happen here. Sometimes the nephews do just take over. But that can't happen now. You've got no right to come and just grab the land from my family. Why do I have to grow my kids? Why do I have to settle someplace? This *kastom* from the past is no good. Our ground is clan ground, but my ground is my ground automatically. I will never

give it to the clan, no way. This kind of thinking is just for the old or the ancestors, now we've been to school we've got better ideas. If I develop this ground with my children? With my sweat? I'm just going to come and let the nephews kick them off?! No way. Not now! Why should I bother getting married? This kind of thinking is bloody rubbish and bullshit from before . . . The nephews won't be able to put demands on the kids just because the father was the same clan. It's different now. The kids will be able to get a bush knife and chase them away! My kids haven't seen a cousin come and help, and if they come and ask, I'll tell them no way. If the nephews take over, the people today see it's no good. You're making the man's family suffer. If I behaved like this on clan land, of course there would be talk, and yes at Vudal it happened, but this generation we've seen it's not good. Because the father raised the children. The father planted the cocoa. It's not the nephews'. It's not the clan's.

Philip did not qualify as a 'Big Shot' businessman or government bureaucrat. Nonetheless his comparatively high income and financial independence perhaps helped to explain the particular strength of his disdain for the idea of *kastom* and the *wantok* system as a kind of grassroots mutual aid and social security system (discussed in Chapter Five). But although the strength and consistency with which Philip expressed his position might have been extreme, he was not alone in these views. I was continually struck by the strength with which these feelings were expressed at Sikut. Although there were some who felt that customary tenure would re-establish itself as it seemed to have done at Vudal, these people were a minority. Although it is early days, in the majority of cases where blocks have been transferred as a result of death or choice, the land has gone to the original holders' children or other relatives outside the clan. Perhaps the most vitriolic dispute that I encountered at Sikut was a conflict between a sister and brother over possession of a block. The block was in the name of the mother who initially allowed her daughter to live on it. Several years later she decided to remove the daughter and replace her with a son. This action was believed to be motivated by an intense dislike of her daughter's husband. The daughter and her husband had already planted hundreds of cocoa seedlings and erected a permanent house, so the removal effort led to a very heated dispute. What was commented on by many Sikut residents was that the mother's original arrangement would have ensured that the land stayed in her clan for the next two generations. By attempting to remove her daughter and replace her with a son, she was, in one person's words, 'giving the land away'. Many Sikut residents saw her actions as evidence of a new attitude developing towards kinship and land tenure on state land.

The above examples illustrate that the situation at Sikut is not one in which the land can be easily described as 'customary' or 'non-customary'. Indeed they illustrate that we have to be careful in making any assumptions that we know what it is for land to be 'customary' or not in the first place. Although Sikut is supposed to be 'non-customary' land, patterns of social relations are emerging that can be construed by some as heralding a re-emergence of 'customary' land tenure practices. These include initiatives towards reinvigorated performance of some forms of customary ritual that involve the mobilisation of clan-based kinship networks. However, the position is not as simple as the resilience of traditional Melanesian *kastom*. Rather *kastom* itself is a kind of shifting signifier whose meaning is fought over and whose changes in use and meaning reflect many of the changes in the ways in which social relations are being made amongst the dispersed Matupit community. In particular, the contextually shifting use of the term *kastom* in such disputes and discussions itself is a way in which the shifting boundaries of reciprocal interdependence and individual autonomy are marked. As such this term's use also acts as a marker of the shifting terrain and battle lines along which such contests are played out. As we shall see in the next chapter, land at Matupit is defined in the eyes of the state as 'customary'. Yet the status of this land is complicated by the emergence over recent years of new patterns of relating to land that similarly throw common understandings of *kastom* into question.

Notes

1. Perhaps the most immediately striking change when I returned to East New Britain in 2009 after a five year absence was the explosion of mobile phone use. In 2004 there had been no mobile phone coverage, and hence no mobile phones in East New Britain. In 2009, I only met one adult without one, and even he was planning to buy one in the following year.
2. The English origin word 'Western' would often be used in conversations to do with custom and social change in conversations held in any of the three major languages in which I conducted fieldwork: English, Tok Pisin and Kuanua.
3. The households at Sikut with whom I conducted in-depth case studies had cleared between half a hectare at one extreme and two hectares at the other.
4. For an earlier description of how fear of sorcery can act as a disincentive to the development of cash-cropping, see Moulik (1973). See also Martin 2009.
5. Fingleton (1985) gives a fuller discussion of the emergence of this tendency in the resettlements of the 1960s.
6. The increasing importance of the nuclear family in Tolai social life is discussed in more depth in Chapter Six.

Kulia

An Ambiguous Transaction

> Paulus explains the great Roman debate on whether or not *permutatio* was a sale. The whole passage is of interest – even the mistake which the legal scholar makes in his interpretation of Homer.
>
> (Mauss 1970:129)

While the allegedly individual, discrete nature of block holdings at Sikut is complicated by the tendency of customary ways of thinking and acting to creep back in, so too the tenure of customary land back at Matupit has been complicated by Tolai responses to new economic circumstances. Debates around land tenure in this part of East New Britain have long centred on the issue of patrilineal versus matrilineal transfer of rights, with patrilineality being associated by many with a positive move towards more 'modern' land tenure systems. What is often at stake in these debates is an argument about the alleged economic advantages of removing interests in land from cycles of ongoing customary obligation and reciprocal social relations, thereby making land the alienable property of individual persons or household units (see for example Hughes 2003). While in most of PNG anthropologists have described people as having 'patrilineal' customary land tenure, in the matrilineal Gazelle by contrast the distinction between matrilineal and patrilineal inheritance has understandably often come to stand for the choice between customary obligation and individualism. A shift to patrilineality can represent the removal of clan-based reciprocal obligations. However, the ways in which Matupi negotiate these tensions today illustrates how characterising land as 'customary' or 'non-customary' is a far from simple matter. The distinction between customary and non-customary land is one that is often made rhetorically by Matupi to distinguish between appropriate and inappropriate claims that could be made on other persons or pieces of land in different contexts. And because the distinction is made differently in different contexts, so too knowing what is meant by 'customary' and 'non-customary' requires an in-depth understanding of those contexts. The distinction is a way of attempting to draw appropriate boundaries of reciprocal interdependence in a particular context.

But because those boundaries are so fluid and contestable at different times and places, the value of *kastom* as a term cannot be fixed. The power of this category, both for the Matupi and for the ethnographer, lies in the way its contextually shifting contested meaning both marks and makes the boundaries of reciprocity.

Ambiguities of Alienation

This chapter explores the shifting meaning at Matupit of a transaction known as *kulia*. This transaction involves the transfer of land from one party to another, yet in a manner that often differs significantly from the ideal of alienable commodity exchange underpinning much Western economic theory. In this respect, *kulia* could be taken as a transaction that embodies a radically different cultural logic that would be in danger of being misrecognised in Western economic terms without the benefit of ethnographic expertise in which Melanesian anthropology has specialised since the days of Malinowski. Like *kastom*, however, *kulia* is also in danger of being misrecognised as designating a fixed cultural logic. What *kulia* legitimately describes or allows is a matter of contention and can change over the years or when described from different social perspectives. Whilst it would be too simplistic to replace the model of unchanging cultural alterity with one of fixed teleological cultural evolution (in which *kulia* had simply been converted into an ideal type commodity transaction), an analysis of *kulia* at Matupit in the early 2000s demonstrates that the kinds of ambiguities contained within the meaning of *kulia* itself are constantly shifting. *Kulia* is an inherently ambiguous and contestable transaction, sharing that characteristic in common with all transactions perhaps. But the grounds of that contest are themselves shaped by the outcomes of previous contests, and in the early 2000s there appeared to be more scope to assert claims of ownership based on absolute alienability than in previous decades.

Throughout this chapter the shifting meanings of *kulia* will be discussed. In particular *kulia* as a transaction occurring on 'customary' land at Matupit will be contrasted with social relations concerning land at 'non-customary' Tolai settlements, both the Wudal settlement established in the 1950s and 1960s and the more recent resettlement camp established at Sikut in the 1990s. Amongst residents of the two settlements, claims as to whether the land is supposed to be customary or not are often central to disputes over what kind of claims on the land or on other persons can be legitimately considered. But in both settlements there are also ambiguities. Just as we have seen the expectation that customary practices of extended reciprocal obligation can creep into the allegedly non-customary resettlement land, conversely we also see the assertion that *kulia*, a customary transaction dependent on continuing customary ties, can be transformed into a transaction that weakens the ongoing hold of claims based on such relationships.

Purchasing Land at Matupit

At Matupit today a large proportion of houses are built on purchased land. It is particularly common for fathers to buy land from their own clan to overcome the problems that will arise between their children and their nephews if they build permanent houses on their own clan land. The buying and selling of customary ground is in theory illegal in Papua New Guinea, unless such buying and selling can be shown to be a customary practice. The custom of 'buying' ground is known among the Tolai as *kulia*. However, A.L. Epstein stressed that *kulia* does not neatly equate with the Western idea of buying and selling as an alienable commodity transaction, noting that '[t]he indigenous concept of *kul* then is translated by the term purchase only at the risk of serious misrepresentation' (A.L. Epstein 1969:132). He further outlines the differences between Tolai customary land tenure and Western property regimes in the following terms:

> In the indigenous system land was not a commodity. Transfers of land were not conducted according to the principles of the market; rather they were effected between parties who saw themselves as already linked by social bonds, and when land was exchanged in return for *tambu* it was usually in recognition of the obligations of kinship or other customary claims ... the payment demanded in *tambu* was also small. This remains the position today in regard to 'sales' of land within the village, where the sums involved in cash and *tambu* fall very far short of the market value. (A.L. Epstein 1969:132)

Two reasons are given here by Epstein why *kulia* should not be considered equivalent to Western commodity transactions. First there is the nature of the bonds preceding the transaction, implying that *kulia* should be seen as a part of an ongoing cycle of customary obligation rather than as a stand-alone purchase of alienable property. Second the low level of payment, 'short of the market value', is provided as evidence that the payment was 'in recognition of ... customary claims' rather than outright purchase. These same two reasons are reported by Fingleton in his study of land tenure at the nearby Tolai village of Rakunat during the mid-1980s (Fingleton 1985).

The conclusion that A.L. Epstein draws from this state of affairs is that the *kakalei* or 'claim' to the land 'remains vested in the vendor lineage' (A.L. Epstein 1969:104). This non-alienability of claims in the land is a key

difference distinguishing Tolai customary land from Western land as property.[1] Tolai told me that in the past there would often be expectations that the
land might return to the vendors at some point after the buyer's death, that the
vendors would be considered to have an ongoing relationship with the piece
of ground, and that if the 'purchasers' failed to be suitably attentive to their
ongoing customary obligations to the vendors then it would be normal for the
vendors to find a way to reclaim the land. However, even by the early 1960s,
A.L. Epstein had identified trends that were moving *kulia* away from this
customary ideal. First, the increasing number of land deals with the colonial
Administration and the large amounts of money involved meant that the clan
elders who controlled the land were 'now encouraged to think of land increasingly as a commodity' (A.L. Epstein 1969:132). Young men who protested at
many of these deals meanwhile were in effect claiming that the elders 'had
no power to dispose of the land so as to remove it from the sphere of Tolai
social relationships and customary obligations' (ibid.). Secondly, cash cropping meant that 'many Tolai are beginning to find it necessary to think of land
as a commodity even in transactions among themselves' (ibid.). A.L. Epstein
cites the example of a young man who bought a plot of customary land in the
village of Napapar to plant cocoa. When his cocoa was ready to bear fruit, they
reclaimed the land. A.L. Epstein (1969:133) concludes that, '[f]or him, as for
many Tolai, the traditional system of land tenure was beginning to reveal its
limitations in meeting the needs of contemporary situations'.

Today, although *kulia* retains features that distinguish it from the purest
ideal of commodity transaction, it has continued to change. Radin (1996)
suggests that what is referred to as 'commodification' is necessarily an incomplete process, and whether a thing, transaction, or relationship should be
viewed as a commodity is therefore a matter of degree, rather than an 'either/
or' distinction. Changes to *kulia* over the past forty years can be usefully
looked at in these terms. Parties to a *kulia* transaction tend to be involved in
ongoing customary relationships, as almost everyone at Matupit is involved
in customary relations with everyone else anyway. Fingleton notes that the
flexibility of relations in the village makes it easy to construct customary ties
that legitimise a *kulia* transaction. '[N]o land transaction may be mounted
without a pre-existing link between the parties, but the relativity of Tolai
concepts of group corporateness and kinship facilitates the establishment of
a connection between willing people' (Fingleton 1985:211). This means that
even outsiders with no history of relationship to the community can buy
land in the village through the creation of 'customary' ties. Although I was
unable to observe the lead up to and the purchase of any land during my time
at Matupit, I was told that it was not hard to give an acceptable face to a land
transaction between any parties whatsoever. For example, as far back as the
1960s a number of settlers from the Sepik area had bought land on the edge

of Matupit, and their descendants were still living there when I was doing fieldwork. Fingleton makes a convincing case that the inherent flexibility of customary tenure makes it better adapted to rapidly changing social relations than fixed Western property law.[2]

Yet if custom is so flexible that it can encompass any kind of relationship then it has the danger of becoming a tautological concept that excludes nothing and can legitimise any kind of transaction. In this vein, Simet (1991:215) writes that: 'In any land purchase, it is important that the parties to the transfer be socially or politically related. Socially, there is a limited number of relationships only through which land purchase is possible'. However, immediately after this Simet adds that, '[I]n the absence of a "real" social relationship, a putative one is emphasised in order to facilitate a purchase'. In other words one needs a certain kind of pre-existing relationship in order to make a purchase; but if one does not have the relationship then one can be made.[3] Thus people from other provinces have bought land at Matupit on the basis of 'adoption' by a family from the village.

Disputes over how 'customary' some manifestations of 'custom' really are commonly occur. The most frequent type is criticism of the involvement of economically powerful 'big-shots' in custom. I was often told that they had 'commercialised' custom. 'Custom' is at least partly judged by whether or not one's actions are considered to be embedded in and constitutive of the kind of customary reciprocal relations of the kind that at the time of A.L. Epstein's fieldwork, young men accused the elders of abandoning by selling land to the Australians. Even if one performs 'custom' as a set of rules perfectly, one's actions can be considered to be fundamentally non-customary when judged on this basis. A contrast between *kastom* based on ongoing reciprocal obligations, and Western social life as being based on business transaction, although far from exhausting the multivalent possibilities of the word 'custom' or *kastom*, was frequently repeated to me by Tolai. If Radin is correct to say that commodification is a necessarily incomplete process, and Gregory (1982:23), drawing on Sahlins, is correct in arguing that 'the distinction between gift exchange and commodity exchange should not be seen as a bipolar opposition but rather as the extreme points of a continuum', then perhaps we are best examining ambiguous situations such as this as being cases where the networks of social relations that go into making up a transaction can be viewed from more than one angle.[4] Indeed they are often are viewed and evaluated as part of a process of assessing the morality of these transactions.[5] The negative attitude of grassroots people towards the big-shots' commercialisation of customary ritual is one example.

The danger with simply describing the ease with which 'customary' relations can be created to make *kulia* possible is that it can assume that which it seeks to demonstrate, namely the fundamental difference of *kulia* as a customary practice from standard Western property transactions. Just as it is possible for Matupi to view the involvement of Big Shots in custom from an angle that declares it to be non-reciprocal and therefore not truly 'customary', it is also possible that 'customary' links that are so easily and flexibly contracted can begin to be viewed and morally evaluated as merely a kind of window dressing that is done in preparation for a *kulia* transaction that now looks more like an out and out purchase. *Kulia* may be formally the same as before, but its increasing importance and degree of finality can make it appear, in certain indigenous descriptions at least, more like a commodity transaction that the preceding transactions are the preparatory work for, rather than part of an ongoing cycle of customary reciprocity. Certainly cases of how <u>kastom</u> can 'hide' the true value of a transaction (see below) suggest that this is one possible indigenous perspective from which *kulia* can be described today. Some transactions sit so clearly towards one or the other of Gregory's two poles that the scope for different perspectives to be taken on them is severely limited. Others however are more ambiguous.

My argument is not that *kulia* is a commodity transaction and that therefore Tolai think of land in the same way as Australians. Rather I suggest that *kulia* is not *simply* the uncomplicated 'customary' transaction that it is sometimes presented as. It can also be viewed as embodying other, less customary, more commodity-oriented ethics, and changes over the past forty years, while not totally 'commodifying' the transaction and by implication Tolai attitudes towards land more generally, have moved this transaction further towards that pole by creating more situations in which Tolai find it fruitful to describe land in property/commodity terms. This is perhaps precisely the process by which partial commodification occurs.

A.L. Epstein and Fingleton each stress the importance of not only the establishment and existence of customary links prior to *kulia*, but also the maintenance and continued recognition of these links after the transaction. For example, after noting the flexibility with which customary connections legitimising *kulia* may be created, Fingleton adds that: 'the connection . . . whether direct or indirect, forms the basis of the land transaction. It characterises the tenure thereby gained, so that its security remains indefinitely dependent upon maintenance of the formative connection' (Fingleton 1985:211). Although there is still a tendency for *kulia* to be transacted between persons or groups who were already strongly linked, such as a man buying from his own clan on behalf of his children, I found no evidence that *kulia* transactions tend to imply a consequently stronger link. And in some cases there is little or no ongoing relationship. One of my closest friends built his house on land that he bought from the last male representative at Matupit of one of Matupit's major landholding clans. This purchase was made in 1983. To my knowledge the purchaser has had no ongoing customary relationship with the seller, and would give the seller little consideration if he came to ask for favours or gifts on the basis of his ancestral links with the land upon which the purchaser has built his house. Most people say that requests such as this are dishonest attempts to get money twice for land that you have already sold. In many contexts in contemporary PNG, such as negotiations with a mining company, landowners demand the establishment of an ongoing and more 'customary' relationship that goes beyond single payments, on the basis of their long-term presence on the land. Amongst Matupi, however, the idea that a transfer of land can be part of legitimising such demands as part of an ongoing customary relationship is treated with near universal incomprehension or repulsion. Papua New Guineans do not view land transfers as undergoing a historical process of inexorable commodification, nor as following an unchanging cultural logic of inalienability. Instead, people of this world region are as capable as any other group of people of judging that different kinds of transactions are morally appropriate in different contexts, and disputing about which transactions are appropriate in which contexts.

Documenting Transactions

Also interesting is people's response to my queries to them about A.L. Epstein's statement that *kakalei* remains with the vendor clan even after *kulia* transactions. From 2002 to 2004, the response to this was universally one of incredulity, and assertion that of course *kakalei* can be transferred. What would be the point of buying something if you didn't receive the *kakalei,* people said. They sometimes also suggested that this must be the statement of crooked old men who want to get money twice for the same piece of land. A.L. Epstein notes that sale by *kulia* never gives secure ownership because any one member of the vendor clan could a couple of years later stand up and claim not to have been consulted, causing the land to revert back (A.L. Epstein 1969:131–32). He implies that this is one of the mechanisms by which *kakalei* remains with the vendor clan. If so, this would be a mechanism for control of the land to pass back to the vendors, such as if the purchasers are remiss in maintaining an ongoing customary relationship with them following the *kulia* transaction. Today, this 'problem' has been partially resolved by the recent practice of witnessing purchases with statutory declarations, which all adult members of the vendor clan must sign before a purchase is finalised. This practice started in this part of East New Britain under the Australian Administration in the early 1970s, although T.S. Epstein's fieldnotes also contain governmental recordings of land purchases from the much less 'developed' Tolai village of Rapitok from the early 1960s.[6] Jessep (1980:123–24) documents the recording of land sales in East New Britain in the 1970s, and mentions that while the practice conferred no title it was 'apparently valued for the documentary evidence of the sale and the publicity of the payment made at the office'. Fitzpatrick (1983:19) drawing on Tolai evidence affirms that during the 1970s, 'Unofficial and semi-official land registers . . . had emerged' in PNG. He elaborates:

> . . . unofficial transfers of land as a commodity were taking place between members of different groups. Various operative strategies had developed to restrict the range of obligations effective in succession to land, to increase individual control over the process and to confine transmitted rights more to the nuclear family or a favoured son. Nor were these trends without suggestive precedent in the customary base . . . . With the extension of cash-cropping after the second world war . . . there emerged, a greater awareness of land as having a reified value and greater, and effective, pressure for more clearly defined individual rights in land.

I was often told by Tolai in the 2000s that if you have what is referred to as 'the paper', i.e. the statutory declaration, then you are safe. One old man explained to me that 'before we did not know how to buy and sell properly. Now that we have the paper, we have more *savvy* (know-how)'. This statement describes a clear feeling that the nature of *kulia* has changed over the years. In this new context 'papers' do have power as the practice of 'strengthening' (as one person described it to me) the buying of ground with statutory declarations is at least partly a process that Tolai themselves have developed in response to their own perceived need to secure land that they were buying for their children. The paper 'kills the talk' on a piece of ground, at least between the selling clan and the buyer (although of course there is always the possibility for a third party to claim that the vendors never had the right to sell the ground in the first place). I never came across a case where the selling clan was able to reclaim land from a buyer when the buyer had a statutory declaration. Of course a registration can be misleading to the outside observer, conflating a number of reciprocal customary obligations into one simple transaction (see Fingleton 1985:184–86). However, registration of the purchase transaction, at Matupit at least, does seem to set a kind of seal on the land transfer, making it harder for alleged oversights in the recognition of ongoing obligations to be used to overturn the transfer. Even if in many cases land transfers are unimaginable without a preceding history of relationships and an imagined future of ongoing relations, the act of registration does seem to give the transfer a degree of partial separation from these relations.

Registration is now semi-officially recognised by the Provincial Government, which has copies of all statutory declarations of land purchases at its Lands Division and has official guidelines for the practice. All reports of the origin of this practice claim that its impetus came from the village, not the government. In addition to the authorities cited above, Fingleton (1985:181–82) reports that at Rakunat the practice began as a continuation of an aborted attempt by the colonial government to register land in the 1960s, carried out by the villagers themselves in order to satisfy their own wish to secure land transfers, not as part of a government plan to reform customary land practices. As Fingleton (1985:178) puts it, 'The most important changes in ... land tenure ... are those which occurred internally, in transactions within the village community which continued the process of adjustment to changing land demands'. This is important to stress as it provides a different emphasis than the great attention that is often given to a history of unsuccessful state-driven changes in land tenure imposed upon an unwilling population (for example Fingleton 1985:iii with regard to the situation in the Gazelle). This ethnographic tendency fits into a what has become a wider theoretical concern in recent years, namely the ways in which the state needs to organise its subjects and their practices in fashions that enable it to 'see' and therefore govern them more efficiently (Scott 1998).

Such histories are rightly emphasised to counter the misguided arguments of those who suggest that Western nations should use their disproportionate economic power to force Melanesian nations into land tenure reform. But it is also important to acknowledge that in their engagement with the global economy, in certain contexts Melanesians are bound to explore the possibility of different ways of transacting land, and that sometimes they will seek the support of the state in making such new ways of transacting more secure. To acknowledge that it is just as possible for the state's subjects to be recognised by that state in a manner that fits their desires, as it is for the state to demand that its subjects be organised in a manner that makes it possible for the state to 'see' them, does not mean endorsing overarching schemes to revolutionise village life through legislative action. Quite the opposite, it shows the importance of a careful ethnographic attention to the different details of processes of contested commodification as they occur in different circumstances.

Land that is transacted by *kulia* that is strengthened through statutory declaration is still legally considered to be customary land, and although the purchaser, if a man, has the right to pass it on to his children, in the next generation it must follow matrilineal principles. Thus it will most likely go to one of his daughter's children. For example, if a man buys land from his own clan for his children, the land passes from his matriline to a section of his wife's matriline. For this reason Matupi will tend to refer to even 'purchased' land at Matupit as 'customary' land, as opposed to their land at Sikut that is referred to as 'non-customary'. However, they are also clearly aware that the 'custom' of *kulia* and its relationship to wider networks of customary obligation has changed in some respects in the past forty years. Land disputes at Matupit are not as widespread as they were in the years leading up to the eruption. But it was notable that of the cases I observed, not one was of an attempt by vendors to overturn a land sale that had been registered, and I was told by most Matupi that any such attempt would be fruitless. The Lands Division and the majority of Matupi clearly view *kulia* today as a transaction that implies the complete alienation of all rights in a piece of land from one group to another. A.L. Epstein's claim that 'the estate vested by a "purchase" is *always* regarded as inferior to a *kakalei*' (A.L. Epstein 1969:131, my emphasis) has, at the very least, been complicated by changes to Tolai *kulia* over the past forty years.

The Price of Land

With regard to 'market value', I conducted a village household survey and discovered that the average 'price' paid for a house had hardly risen at all in the past forty years. By contrast, the price of other essentials such as imported foodstuffs and the materials used to build permanent houses had risen dramatically. It is hard to ascertain what constitutes 'market value' in an environment such as Matupit.[7] Even so, prices as low as 50 to 100 Kina (the cost of two crates of beer) seem good value for the outright purchase of a plot of land on which one is going to build a house that will cost thousands of Kina. This stability and low value of land prices seems to bear out A.L. Epstein's original observations about the non-commodity nature of customary land transactions at Matupit, and to cast doubt on his prediction that trends were emerging in village life that were going to push land transactions in a more commodified direction. Matupi forwarded a number of explanations as to why they thought land prices had remained relatively stable. One was that land had for a long time been a part of the customary system. However, this answer was always accompanied by a caveat that this was changing and that prices for land were starting to rise. Indeed I was often told that the volcano had stopped an anticipated explosion in land prices, just as it had stopped the explosion of land disputes.

Another pattern was for people to affirm that many of the prices I had been given during my village survey were lies, and that the prices were much higher than I had been told. People would publicly 'buy' the land for a small amount of money, but behind the scenes hundreds or even thousands of Kina (or equivalents) would change hands. The larger amounts would be hidden out of shame.[8] Some at Matupit angrily denied that such a thing could happen, but the very suggestion demonstrates an awareness on the part of some Matupi that the low monetary value of a seemingly customary transaction can mask a more commercial exchange (just as on the other hand the legal registration of a seemingly commercial transaction can mask a web of customary obligations). Indeed a few people told me that _kastom_ was a means of 'hiding' the value of a land purchase. This again demonstrates that certain seemingly 'customary' transactions are capable of being viewed from a commercial perspective. In Melanesian ethnography there is a frequent theoretical pattern of stressing how relationships that have seemingly been Westernised or commodified are on closer examination still based on a customary ethic of reciprocity. This is undoubtedly often true, but perhaps in stressing such moments we sometimes lose sight of the logical corollary: situations in which what on the surface appears customary and reciprocal can simultaneously embody opposite ethical values as well. The ways in which Matupi discuss the 'commercialisation' of _kastom_ demonstrates that they have not lost sight of these possibilities.

Additionally there are tendencies emerging at Matupit today that suggest a more openly commercial attitude towards land sales. On a return visit to Matupit in January 2005, I interviewed one of the village councillors about land sales in his ward. He told me of one woman who had sold three separate plots of land for houses in the village on behalf of her clan section in the past year. Instead of the one or two hundred Kina that was the standard land sale price on my village survey, she had sold land for between two and three thousand Kina, a price much closer to the amount that similar plots would receive on the commercial market in Rabaul Town. The councillor was keen to stress that such price rises were the result of land registration that meant that purchase was secure. From the point of view of the state and Matupi themselves, although the land remained customary in contradistinction to the land at Sikut for example, the land in Matupit being transacted in this way does not match certain ideals of 'custom' at least as they are reported in many ethnographic and indigenous accounts.

'Only Custom'? Ritual and Land Tenure in the Twenty-First Century

The performance of customary ritual has always been of great importance to people's claims to reside on certain pieces of land. A man wishing to stay on his father's clan land after his death would pay close attention to helping his father's clan in custom, in particular distributing large amounts of customary shell-wealth on his death. Even someone residing on his own clan land would not expect residence by right, but would be expected to help in _kastom_. Someone remiss in their customary obligations would be considered to bring shame on the clan and would be likely to be given the worst pieces of ground to live and garden upon by the group's Big Man.[9]

Today the picture is slightly different. The decline of power of the big men in the clan means that complaints about young men simply building a house on clan land without consultation with elders are common. Some of the Matupit community at Sikut at the time of my fieldwork had just begun the performance of some customary practices at their new homes, such as the *namata*, a kind of initiation for the first-born son of a family. One of the minority of Matupi who hoped for a return to openly full-blooded 'customary' land tenure at Sikut was Isaac ToLanger.[10] ToLanger was a man from Matupit in his fifties who was now a senior public servant in Port Moresby, with responsibility for promoting and protecting culture. He was a man with a strong personal interest in Tolai customary practices. ToLanger was undoubtedly part of the new economic elite. He sent his children to international school in Port Moresby. He had rented a large block from the Provincial Government near to the Sikut resettlement camp which he had planted with cocoa, and he intended this land to be where he would spend his retirement. ToLanger told me that this emergence of *kastom* at Sikut was a sign of an inevitable gradual rise of customary land tenure, parallel to the earlier rise of customary tenure at Vudal.[11] He added, in English, that the Provincial Government's attempt to remove customary clan relations from land tenure at Sikut was a continuation of the Australian Administration's attempts to 'turn us into white men' when they tried to enforce patrilineal nuclear family inheritance at Vudal. For most Sikut residents, however, it is unclear to what extent the performance of *kastom* there heralds the re-emergence of customary land tenure. As one young man explained to me: 'when you do *kastom* at Matupit you are concerned with land. When you do *kastom* here it is *kastom* only (TP. *kastom tasol*)'. This man argued that many Matupit residents who had been heavily involved in *kastom* before they got blocks at Sikut were now involved in the bare minimum for social respectability. Now that they had their own land, they no longer felt the need to keep the clan happy by performing *kastom*.

Whatever the future at Sikut holds, these examples show the problems of defining land as 'customary' or 'non-customary' that are sometimes overlooked in policy debates. The land at Vudal is still formally 'non-customary' in the eyes of the state. Yet it is widely acknowledged to be land where '*kastom* has come back in' to such an extent that many people describe it as 'like customary land' or even as 'customary land'. The increasing performance of *kastom*, along with trends to 'acknowledge' the importance of customary relations to non-customary land at Sikut, may well have effects on land use and occupation. The question is how much effect this will have, and how much will inhabitants have to acknowledge that the land has become de facto 'customary'? Conversely, the land bought and sold by *kulia* at Matupit is still in the eyes of both the state and Matupit 'customary'. Yet Tolai described it in ways that make it appear less 'customary' (according to certain glosses of the word *kastom*) than would have been the case forty years ago. *Kastom* is as much a position taken on the morality of certain transactions, as it is an empirical description of a juridical process to be preserved or reformed in the interests of national development. In particular *kastom* acts as a means of taking a position on the appropriateness or inappropriateness of claims based on a history and expectation of reciprocal interdependence and exchange.

In the following chapter I examine in depth a land dispute at Matupit that illustrates, amongst other things, how *kastom* is a contested concept by which people attempt to resolve the extent to which their capacities as 'landholders' are held by virtue of individual right or are reliant upon ongoing ties of reciprocal interdependence.

Notes

1. See for example Mauss 1970 and Gregory 1982 for key discussions of the central importance of the non-alienability of objects in Melanesian societies in contrast to Western conceptions of alienable property.
2. Fingleton saw plasticity as itself a kind of fixed characteristic of a stable indigenous land tenure system under threat from policy advisors and developers blind to the advantages in such a system. My focus is different: namely how the very idea of customary versus non-customary land marks differing moral evaluations of differing kinds of social relations negotiated through land. In addition, both the resettlement at Sikut and the levelling of the ground at Matupit as a result of the volcano introduce new kinds of plasticity and fixity into the social relations negotiated through land among Matupi.
3. Simet refers to this transaction as *kunukul* rather than *kulia*.
4. Gregory seems subsequently to have retracted this position. See Gregory (1997:8).
5. I use the term 'morality' to refer to a process of ongoing and frequently contested evaluations of the appropriateness of acknowledging or denying conflicting obligations. As Laidlaw (2002:317) argues, 'moral thinking, then, is a matter of weighing obligations and deciding where one's duty lies, and moral judgment rests on whether one chooses, whatever one's desires or inclinations, to act in accordance with this duty'. Hence morality and moral reasoning forms a part of the central problem of ethics, namely how one ought to live, without fully exhausting it (op cit.:316–17).
6. T.S. Epstein fieldnote dated 14.05.1960, held in University of California San Diego library archives.
7. Although of course market value is often hard to ascertain in the U.K. as well, as ongoing legal controversies over fair pricing demonstrate.
8. If the practice of hiding additional payments was as widespread as some claimed, possibly it was also motivated by a fear of sparking jealousy or claims to compensation from other parties who might suddenly discover that they had an interest in the land.
9. 'Big man' refers here to a lineage leader, often known in Kuanua as *lualua*. This role is discussed in more detail in later chapters. According to T.S. Epstein (1968:6), 'A man who wished to cultivate a piece of land belonging to his kin-group could do so only with his *lualua*'s permission'.

10. ToLanger is a central character in the story recounted in Gewertz and Errington (1995:45–67).
11. This is in some ways similar to Tonkinson's (1968) early view of the social effects of the relocation of Ambrym villagers after the eruption of 1951.

What Makes a Landholder

A Case Study of a Matupit Land Dispute

In the previous chapter I described changes in *kulia* over the decades at Matupit, and how this transaction, commonly glossed in English as 'purchase', has become more akin to what we would understand as buying and selling. In this section I examine a case study of a land dispute whose origins lie in a contested *kulia* transaction. My intention is to demonstrate the rhetorical devices through which a form of individuality and individual rights are asserted and contested. This dispute does not centre on the nature of the transaction and the extent to which it implies absolute alienation of the vendor's entire claim to the land, removing the land from relationships of reciprocal obligation. Rather it is a dispute about who has the right to sell the land. Does that right rest merely in a small, named group of persons clearly associated with that piece of land, or do those with whom they are intertwined in wider relationships of reciprocal interdependence also have a claim? At its heart the issue is one of the integrity of the landholding social group. In the context of land tenure does the group exist as a discrete entity that is ontologically prior to relationships of reciprocal interdependence and is thus able to relate to the land as its collective individual owner? Or does it only exist as a contextual elicitation of those relationships of reciprocal interdependence, many of which are conducted through the land itself?

In order to analyse this question, I examine the language through which the dispute is conducted. Specifically I examine how naming works to describe and create social groups in this particular Melanesian context, and I analyse these processes as an example of a contest between contrasting language ideologies. The dispute is an example of how people imagine that particular uses of language affect social relations in different ways.[1]

The Nature of Social Groups amongst Twenty-First-Century Tolai

Roy Wagner's paper 'Are there Social Groups in the New Guinea Highlands' questioned frequent anthropological assumptions about the integrity of social groups in non-Western contexts. Often, when scholars find groups in places like Melanesia, it is the result of a tendency to hear indigenous names and terms as 'descriptions or definitions of concrete, bounded, and empirically existing groups' (Wagner 1974:106). In making this point he challenges the assumption that language simply refers to social entities that exist prior to their elicitation in language. Instead, in Melanesia, 'names may be said to "elicit" social collectivities in the act of distinguishing them' (ibid.:108). The divisions that are continuously made and remade through naming are contingent upon shifting networks of sociality. Consequently, when it comes to indigenous names and terms that serve to distinguish some people from others:

> [W]e would be well-advised to take the distinctions at face value, as distinctions only and not as groups. They only group people in the way that they separate or distinguish them on the basis of some criterion, and we cannot deduce from the conceptual distinctions an actual correspondence of the terms with discrete and consciously perceived groups of people. The terms are names rather than the things named . . . As names used to draw distinctions, these terms are very flexible. (ibid.:106–7)

The term 'Para', used among the people who Wagner describes as the 'Daribi', amongst whom he conducted his fieldwork, provides an example:

> Para can scarcely be said to represent a group, for it is impossible, given the range of usage, to determine which of the applications is the 'correct' one. Para is a name, not a group; it is a means of distinguishing, of including and excluding, and thus merely a device for setting up boundaries. Such a device can be used very flexibly, now drawing this distinction, now that, without ever being tied to a particular element or a bounded definitional 'domain'. (ibid.:107)

Wagner's analysis appears to support the view that reference is not the only or even prime function of language, even though reference is the function that is prioritised in most Western linguistic analysis, and in the explicit metalinguistic models employed by many language users in the West (Silverstein 1976:18–23, 42). Indeed Wagner's analysis of these Daribi group names seems to have much in common with Silverstein's description of 'shifters': terms that have a referential element, but for which '[t]he referential value . . . is constituted by the speech event itself' (Silverstein ibid.:29, see also p. 24). Shifters challenge a model of reference in which linguistic signs act as symbols arbitrarily representing entities according to a semantico-referential grammar. Instead their referential value is established within the context of a particular speech event. Silverstein (ibid.:23–24) gives the example of tense markers, where what is referred to, such as pastness, has to be indexed in relation to an aspect of the speech event itself, the time at which it takes place. Likewise what is referenced by Daribi naming terms such as 'Para' has to be understood in relation to other elements of the speech event in which it is used, such as knowledge of the social context of speaker and listener that would index which social differentiations were supposed to be evoked by the use of the name in that context. What Wagner's description of Daribi naming practices illustrates is that such overt referential context-dependency can extend to practices such as naming that we perhaps often imagine to be much more unproblematic examples of 'pure' lexical reference. The inability to imagine that indexicality-based reference could extend into such spheres could be seen as one way of describing precisely the problem that Wagner (1974:112) says faced Western outsiders who felt the 'strong obligation to discover groups'.

Silverstein (1976:52) is aware of this phenomenon, claiming that 'such lexical items as so-called kinship terms or personal names can hardly be characterised by a "semantic" analysis . . . it is the pragmatic functions that make them anthropologically important'. In other words it is the different ways in which such terms operate to create and describe social relations, rather than a referential description of that which we imagine they refer to independently of context, that is of anthropological importance. '[T]he interesting result is to see the ways in which societies use specifically linguistic means to constitute and maintain certain social categories' (ibid.:53).

Wagner's ethnography seems to describe Daribi language use as ascribing a pragmatic function to names that diverges from the more referential function that outsiders, such as colonial Patrol Officers, might have found more convenient. Wagner's position should not necessarily be taken as evidence for the existence of distinct 'Melanesian' and 'Western' language ideologies. Wagner makes no claims for a broader application of his position beyond the Daribi. And indeed, ethnographers of nearby Highland New Guinea societies have pointed to the ways in which social groups as entities do have an ongoing existence that continues before and beyond moments of their elicitation in naming (Lederman 1986:40–44, 52–55, Merlan and Rumsey 1991:40–41, 55–56). They have also questioned the extent to which Wagner's observations of the ways in which the group referred to by a particular name are context-based is necessarily enough to demonstrate that the groups have no enduring existence beyond their momentary evocation in speech (Lederman op cit.:55).

Wagner himself in other works describes Daribi sociality in a manner that suggests that social groups like Para have an enduring existence across generations, despite the fact that the name might refer to different levels of segmentation depending on the context of its use. In later work, although Wagner still points out the dangers of 'assumptions, ultimately Durkheimian, about the necessity for social groups' (Wagner 1988:39), his concern is to examine the points at which 'social units . . . are articulated through social relationships', such that 'a unit *in its constitution* is never really alienable from its relations with others' (op cit.:40, emphasis in the original). In this work, Wagner's concern is not so much to rhetorically question the existence of groups altogether as it is to question common assumptions about their necessity and nature, particularly implicit assumptions that the constitution of groups precedes their relations rather than being an effect of them. Wagner does see among Daribi points of relative fixity in the nature of groups that exist beyond moments in which they are named.

However, in making a didactic argument in that paper, Wagner is drawing our attention to an important point. Even if it is not the case that Daribi groups are not only ever momentary distinctions elicited through naming (or indeed if it is not always the case that Australian patrol officers imagined that names referred to social groups whose existence pre-exists the naming process), Wagner is making us aware of a difference between Daribi and Patrol Officers. The situation is not quite as simple as the stark opposition between total fixity and total fluidity that Wagner's 'Social Groups' paper might imply. But there is a clear difference between Daribi and outsiders who came to measure and regulate them regarding the degree of fixity of named social entities. Wagner's description of the ways in which names elicit groups in this paper and the way in which this led to a cultural confusion between Daribi and patrol officers, involves a difference between a name making a social group in the moment of its use or marking a pre-existing social group. In this chapter, I build on this insight to describe a situation in which different conceptions of the relationship between names and groups is also considered problematic: in this case a political contest over control of a piece of land at Matupit.

In doing so, I treat Wagner's analysis of Daribi naming as a point of theoretical departure that enables me to illuminate the shifting relationship between the description and evocation of social difference in language, in a manner similar to how Wagner himself takes assumptions about the existence of bounded social groups to be representative of an earlier British Social Anthropological tradition, whilst surely being aware that at times representatives of that tradition (e.g. Evans-Pritchard 1940:135, 147, 216) were as himself sensitive to the complex and contextually relative nature of group names. Wagner's work has been the main inspiration behind a fruitful trend in Melanesian ethnography over the past twenty years to take seriously the implications of the centrality of exchange for Melanesian conceptions of the person (a trend most famously exemplified by Strathern 1988). As important as this work has been, Scott (2007: 24–27, 30–31) is correct to caution against the way that the strength of its insights have on occasion blinded us to alternative idioms of sociality in Melanesia. My aim here is not to undo this work, but rather to draw attention to the ways in which we might look at the tension that Wagner usefully identifies between different presentations of the nature of social relations in contemporary Melanesia.

The Anatomy of a Land Dispute and the Contested Boundaries of Social Groups

This dispute in question is a long running one between Simon Turana and Andrew ToPal over a piece of land in the Rainatun area of Matupit. My observations of the case are mainly derived from land court hearings conducted in 2003 and conversations that I had with participants from both sides around this time. Turana and his supporters claimed the land as a gift from their father's clan. Andrew's father, ToBabat was the son of ToPal, a long deceased elder of the same clan (see Diagram 1). ToBabat allegedly 'sold' this land that had belonged to his father ToPal's clan to his son Andrew. Turana and members of his father's clan claim to have first been made aware of a problem, when in 1999, the bishop of Rabaul came to examine the site of the memorial marking the landing place of the first Catholic missionaries in the New Guinea Islands, and expressed concern that the view was blocked by the wall of Andrew ToPal's house. They approached ToBabat who asked why they were asking him, as the land had already been sold to his son.

There is often suspicion of a clan member who is making a permanent investment on his own clan land. People assume that he would want his children to inherit the investment rather than his clan nephews. It is therefore considered remiss of a clan not to enquire of one of its members what is going on when his child starts building a permanent structure on the clan's land. By this logic, it was doubly remiss of Turana and his father's clan not to have questioned a child of the clan about what was happening when *his* child, who did not even qualify as 'blood' (TP. *blut*) or a 'child of the clan' (K. *warwarngala na vunatarai*), started building on land that he was living on with the clan's permission. The fact that they allowed this to occur would raise suspicions that it was done with their approval, possibly as a result of *kulia*. Andrew claimed that the land that his house was situated on was his by right of purchase. Turana's supporters did not dispute that a payment had been made, but they rejected its legitimacy. Andrew claimed that part of the payment was taken by ToPokono, an old man controversial for the sale of much of what he claimed to be his clan land around Matupit. Turana and his supporters argued that ToPokono, along with his now deceased mother IaLouise, who was also implicated, had no right to agree to a sale or take payments, because they could not be classified as landholders. They claimed that ToPokono had previously agreed to compensate them with another piece of land, in exchange for the land that he and his mother had allegedly illegitimately taken payment for.

At the time of the compulsory pre-court mediation hearing in the summer of 2003, ToBabat had been dead for nearly two years, leaving Andrew to answer charges of wrongdoing. After short opening statements by the mediator, Brendan Laptikai tried to explain the situation. Brendan was a member of Turana's father's clan (i.e. the 'original' landholders) living at the nearby village of Malagunna, and acknowledged by many around Rabaul as an expert in clan and land histories. Brendan made his explanation by referring to *tubuans*, which are masked figures of a traditionally important Tolai male secret society. Different named *tubuans* are often associated with different clans (or clan sections or descent groups), and Brendan describes a commonly known history of *tubuans* to explain the relationship between clans and land in this instance, to the Provincial Government's Land Mediator. The discussion took place in Kuanua and is presented here in my English translation:[2]

> Brendan: My brother-in-law, ToBabat is the son of the clan. I'll have to say something here about our traditional custom. About ToPokono. It's a hundred years ago that they separated regarding the *tubuans*, IaTovo and IaMorogo ToPokono knows about this and he told us about this. For so many years they have been separated. He was looking after his own *tubuan* and selling other land at Matupit. And now we are talking about all the land under [the *tubuan*] IaMorogo. This is IaMorogo, but [the *tubuan*] IaTovo is different. And this is what brings the culture and the traditional ownership of the land.
>
> None of us know anything. We only know the land that my in-law sold and that's why we're here. None of us know anything about this. The family present here is uncles, nephews, nieces, and grandchildren. We always help each other with things like traditional custom and so on.

Later the mediator asked Andrew the details of the land purchase. ToBabat had apparently approached ToPokono's mother, IaLouise. When the mediator asked why ToBabat had approached Louise, and what they discussed, Andrew replied that his father had approached IaLouise, 'Because the land was theirs [i.e. IaLouise's clan]. They are the land owners'. Shortly after this, Brendan returned to his earlier theme, by saying:

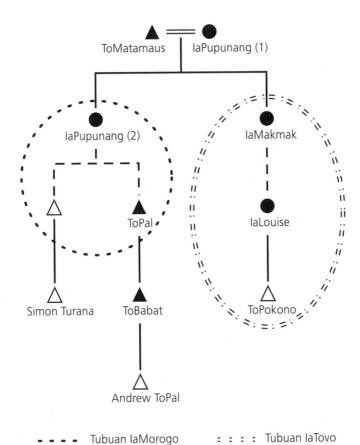

1. Genealogy of parties to the dispute

Brendan: So ToPokono, he's the one causing all of this, with IaLouise. The two *tubuans* separated a long time ago. The *tubuan* IaMorogo is where we are now. And ToPokono's *tubuan* IaTovo no longer exists. He's been selling all the land at Matupit.

At this point the meeting had been proceeding for nearly three quarters of an hour. So far, ToPokono had been sat listening in silence. Now he suddenly interjected angrily:

ToPokono: Now we're talking about the *tubuan*. I don't think we should, because this is a secret in Tolai society. These discussions in court should just be about the land, and things we can talk about in front of women. It's not right to talk about secrets and *tubuan* in the open in the court. Thank you chairman.

Brendan: All right, I'll talk about these things. All the land sales; ToPokono is not entitled to take part in them. Like the one that we are talking about now.

Andrew: Chairman, I'll answer that. My father knew all the land in our area. ToPokono stayed on the other side, and the land belongs to the clan. He's looking after the land. When they sold land, he usually got the *tabu* and gave it to the clan. My father knew about all the land starting from our home down to the beach and the bush. All the land belonged to *his* father, not him. My father could have solved all of these problems, but now who are we going to talk with. These people are the cause of all of this, because they should have come up with the dispute when my father was still alive, when there wouldn't have been any problems like this.

After further discussion revolving around why Turana and his line had not challenged ToBabat over the building of Andrew's house, the mediator returned the discussion to a previous theme, saying: 'There's a group here with the name IaLouise. Do you know about IaLouise?' This point was answered by Wilson, a supporter of Turana's case:

Wilson: It's been explained earlier, regarding the separation in our customs . . . I think it's good to know about this. That separation was there, there's no right for ToPokono to witness or support any payment for land, not at all . . . Now all the land is finished and there is no more land. We usually got him [ToPokono] regarding the other side, but for him to own the land; not at all.

Now ToPokono was roused to anger for a second time:

ToPokono: I tell you that there is no division in the clan. We come from one base. And not including me in the clan? At Rainatun? No, don't do it, I'm telling you. Now you're talking about division – why? And why are you cutting me out from the clan? When ToMinot was still living, why did he usually get me to witness the payments for the land at Rainatun and Rakar and why did he always give me all the payments? This is very clear. Hey – we never separate the clan or divide it . . . When I heard about the division within the clan, exclud-ing me, I would say no to that and don't continue with that practice. Without me, ToBabat wouldn't exist. If ToMar died, I'd get back all the land . . . They came and saw me at home (Sikut), and I said yes to them, with regard to me giving Andrew another portion of land. After that I heard about my exclusion; that I did not belong to the clan. So I changed my mind. I was not happy. I was sad because they excluded me and said that I'm not from Rainatun.

Brendan: Chairman. What he's complaining about now comes later. But we are still keeping him to his promise that he gave us when we saw him at his house in Sikut. And that's what we're basing this on.

Andrew: The statement that you are referring to is fine, but because of the division and exclusion from the clan, he changed his mind.

After this the hearing meandered towards an inconclusive finish. The mediator appealed to both sides to resolve the issue in the village rather than waste their time and money taking the case to court. He suggested that ToPokono could find some land with which to compensate Turana's party, thus ending the dispute. It was clear that this advice was unlikely to be followed. At the time I left the field in February 2004, the dispute was still unresolved and this appeared to still be the case at the time of my most recent trip in January 2010.

The Principles of the Dispute

The basis of the dispute is clear. Brendan's 'clan' who gave the land to their *warwarngala na vunatarai* deny any knowledge of the sale. They are descended from an ancestress called IaPupunang (2), who along with her sister IaMakmak were the two daughters of one of the village's founding ancestresses, IaPupunang (1). According to Andrew, the money for the sale was given to IaLouise and her son ToPokono who are descendants of IaMakmak. Consequently, the dispute centres on the right of Thelma and ToPokono to receive payment on behalf of the 'clan'. A constant theme repeated by Turana's party is the separate identities of the two clans. In particular they point to the publicly well-known existence of two separate *tubuans*, for the two separate lines.

This could be analysed simply as a dispute over the meaning of a word in a particular context (in this case: 'clan' or *vunatarai*). While the dispute does centre on this, it is about something more as well. It is about the role of language in making or describing permanent or group identities. The aggrieved party is clear that calling the names of the two *tubuans* should be seen as *describing* an immutable and ideally permanent division that has already occurred as a matter of historical fact. Brendan's statement makes this clear: 'It's 100 years ago when they separated . . . for so many years they have been separated'. The second witness makes it even clearer that the separation was a previously achieved fait accompli when he informs the hearing that 'the separation *was there*. What this means in terms of group identities is clear. 'This is IaMorogo but IaTovo is different.' Difference is not being contextually elicited here. Rather, the attempt is made to present language as merely describing or asserting a pre-existing group identity.

ToPokono, like everyone else, recognises the importance of the claims made on the basis of *tubuans*. His first interjection, even before his denial of the separation of the clan, is to dispute the legitimacy of Brendan's 'talk' about *tubuans*. He realises that accepting the legitimacy of this 'talk' virtually seals a description of clan divisions that leaves him on the outside. This intervention about the role of 'talk' is perhaps the clearest example of an attempt to assert a particular language ideology in the course of the hearing. ToPokono casts judgement on the appropriateness of different talk three times in the space of four sentences. ('Now we're talking about the *tubuan*. I don't think we should, because this is a secret in Tolai society. These discussions in court should just be about the land, and things we can talk about in front of women. It's not right to talk about secrets and *tubuan* in the open in the court.'). He claimed to be upset that such a discussion was taking place in front of women, who were barred from the *tubuan*'s secrets. Yet the universal response to this amongst all of the people that I spoke to was incredulity. Everyone knows that there are aspects of the *tubuan*'s work that are secret and the preserve of initiated men. But these aspects do not include the names of *tubuans*, and their links with certain lineages and pieces of ground. On the contrary, these aspects are traditionally made as public as possible, since they are a powerful sign of an association with particular pieces of land. ToPokono's anger was widely dismissed as a desperate attempt to deny the widely acknowledged separation of the two clan sections many generations ago. Unable to challenge the referential pragmatic function of IaMorogo as a name that describes a social group, he is forced into a different kind of language ideological strategy, in the form of a widely disparaged attempt to assert that such discussion is illegitimate owing to rules of customary secrecy.

Ritual Secrecy

Asserting the right of only certain people to discuss certain kinds of ritual knowledge can clearly be an important weapon in disputes (see Briggs 1998:242 for a case study from the Barao of Venezuela). Secrecy is naturally an important element of language ideology. The concealment of knowledge and its partial revelation have long been considered to be central aspects of Melanesian knowledge practices, especially in regard to ritual activities such as the *tubuan* (see Wagner 1986, Strathern 1979). Naturally a language ideology that stresses the importance of not talking about such matters is a central facet of such knowledge practices. Yet, to leave the matter there would be unsatisfactory. Ideologies of ritual secrecy are contested among the Tolai today. There is no unified Tolai view on what it is acceptable to talk about. For example, there have been several cases recently of members of evangelical Christian groups publicly outing *tubuan* secret knowledge, to discredit the *tubuan* society. Such moves are highly controversial, but have their supporters. Some powerful supporters of *tubuan* have responded by attempting to get allies in politics to pass laws protecting the secrecy of the *tubuan*. They desire the state to prop the *tubuan* up by imprisoning those who speak out against it or reveal its secrets.

Other people, both inside and outside the *tubuan*, often meet such attempts with suspicion. There is a feeling among many that contemporary leaders of the *tubuan* are not like the ritual big men of old who lived in the village. Instead, the new leaders are said to live in town and 'buy' their ritual power with money that they made as businessmen or public servants, and most importantly that they profit from ritual power personally. The complaint I often heard was that they 'commercialise' *kastom* and the *tubuan* (the word 'commercialise' is used in English conversations and frequently also as a loanword in Tok Pisin and Kuanua). People worried that a law protecting the secrecy of *tubuan* might be used by Big Shots to stifle what many saw as legitimate criticism of such activities.[3] Without going into detail here, it is clear that ritual secrecy is itself a highly contested aspect of language ideology, which in turn is a central part of the struggles over the perceived immorality of contemporary social changes, in particular widening social inequality. This case is slightly less complicated, as there is a general agreement that ToPokono's attempts to assert rights of secrecy are illegitimate. Apart from ToPokono himself no-one is willing to contest the issue. Brendan's response to ToPokono's outburst that he would talk about land should not be taken as an admission that ToPokono was right to reprimand him on this issue. Rather it was an assertion that if ToPokono wished to get to the real subject then Brendan was happy to do so. The point had already been made, and indeed it is returned to by Wilson later on in the hearing.

After being presented with the fairly damning evidence of the two *tubuans*, ToPokono uses a number of rhetorical devices to assert his common clan identity with Brendan's line, and thus his right and his mother's right to sell clan land. ToMar was a leader of Brendan's descent group who had died relatively recently. ToPokono was using ToMar's name to describe the group who were in dispute with him, in order to claim that if the line were to die out, then controlling interests in the land would revert to him, as the nearest related group within the wider clan. His statement that without him, ToBabat would not exist is in a similar vein. It is common for members of clans to make such comments about their clan's children. For ToPokono to make the claim that without him ToBabat would not exist is to assert a common clan identity with ToBabat's father, ToPal, and therefore by implication to assert a common interest in the land in question along with Brendan, who is indisputably a member of the same clan section as ToPal, identified with the tubuan IaMorogo.

'Confusions' of this kind abound in Melanesian ethnography, much to the frustration of outsiders, who as Wagner (1974:112) observes, 'faced with the task of building an interface between the native's "institutions" and their own', 'often felt a strong obligation to discover groups . . . Presented with a bewildering chaos of scattered homesteads and overlapping names, they reacted in the only way they knew how: they made groups'. However, as this dispute demonstrates, in many contexts Matupi are themselves keen to assert their membership of social groups, and in doing so use language in a way that suggests that it is a tool that describes such groups.

Turguvuai and the Separation of Clans

Such contests over the limits of the *vunatarai* in different contexts have long been at the heart of many Tolai land disputes (see A.L. Epstein 1969:149–64). The ambiguity of the term *vunatarai* that A.L. Epstein mentions as giving the Matupi a fertile language for controversy and dispute is best illustrated in this context by the custom of *turguvuai*, which literally translates as 'standing together'. A.L. Epstein (1969:126) describes *turguvuai* in the following terms:

> [L]iterally a standing together or alliance . . . The link is forged initially by contributing shell-money and other aid to some enterprise, perhaps a mortuary rite or dance festival that the 'big man' is organising. Gradually, a relationship of mutual assistance is built up until, having achieved a degree of permanence, the parties to it come to be regarded as belonging to one *vunatarai*. It is in this area perhaps that there is the greatest scope for ambiguity in the use of the term, producing the apparently odd result . . . that persons who in one context are recognised as belonging to a single *vunatarai* may not be so regarded in others.

I witnessed an example of this ambiguity during the last few months of my first fieldwork at Matupit at the start of 2004, when the village was gripped with a controversy over a burial that brought to the surface a long dormant land dispute. The person who had died was one of the most elderly members of the *vunatarai* that many had thought of as landholders of the land in question. He had been living with kin in another part of the village. The most influential member of the *vunatarai* was the senior civil servant, Isaac ToLanger, who lived in Port Moresby. He still, however, maintained a keen interest in village politics and customs, and he decided to bury the deceased on clan land.

These days it is unusual for anyone except well-respected elders to be buried on their clan land rather than at a church graveyard at Matupit. Everyone in the village understood the ownership claim that lay behind this move. Members of a rival clan made moves to stop the burial. On the day of the funeral itself, we left the church unsure as to whether or not members of this clan would be blocking our access to the hole that had been dug for the coffin.[4] The other clan claimed that they were the true landholders. They said that they had allowed the previous *lualua* ('big man') of this *vunatarai* to live on the land as recognition of the closeness of the ties between them, but that the land was intended to return upon his death. After that leader's death in the early 1990s, his son, a child of the clan, moved onto the land. The disputing clan claimed that they had been reluctantly prepared to accept this situation, but that the current attempt to bury a member of the clan on the land was too close to a permanent claim to be allowed to pass unchallenged. Eventually the burial was allowed to proceed, but not before the disputing clan had forced agreement to a meeting to 'straighten instruction' (K. *a warwe takodo*) to be held at a later date. What was notable at the funeral was that most people expressed surprise not only about the dispute but about the two clans being separate entities. Even ToNgala, who was acknowledged by allies and enemies alike to be one of the most knowledgeable people at Matupit about such issues, turned to me and murmured: 'They're the same clan. It's only now I hear they're separate'.[5] Even after the funeral ToNgala continued to refer to them as one clan, seeming to believe that mistakes or ulterior motives were behind the claims of separation. Most members of both clans were adamant in conversation with me that the two clans were genealogically separate, although one member of the first clan did raise the possibility with me that they might have been descended from a common ancestress, centuries ago, at the time that the Tolai first arrived in New Britain from New Ireland. Instead the two clans were related by *turguvuai* (K. 'standing together, alliance') to the point that most Matupi, even those who paid close attention to customary politics, appeared to assume that they were one clan. This is exactly how the situation was explained to me on the day of the funeral by the public servant who was taking a leading role on behalf of the first clan. 'It's a matter of standing together at <u>kastom</u>, but ToVata [his uncle, the Big Man who died in the early 1990s] told me, "look we are two separate groups"'.

A few days after the funeral I had the opportunity to discuss the history of this customary activity with ToLanger. In setting out the history as he describes it, I do not make any claims for its truth relative to other versions of events. Clearly the other side to this dispute would describe this history differently. ToLanger continued to describe the relationship in terms of *turguvuai*.

However, within this description he was keen to describe the relationship as one of unequal seniority with regard to this piece of land. He was also keen to point out how *kastom* was part of the ongoing battle over land:

> The first attempt to associate with the land by Remus clan was 1970s. One of their women died, and Remus sent someone to ask Vata if they could break *tabu* [i.e. distribute coiled shell money, a prototypic *kastom* activity] at that land. Vata said no. Vata said, 'do you know what's going on here?' to me. 'We stand together with these people but we are two different groups. What they're doing is okay, but later on it will not be good for you. These people haven't got land here, that's why they want to use the land for ceremonial purposes and this will become a land claim'. Then ten years later Samuel, Leonard and another came to ask the same, in around 1986 or 87. ToVata sent for me so that I could see what he did, and said, 'You must remember what I am doing now. You will face a lot of this in the future be careful or you will lose the land'. He was grooming me as a Big Man . . . Some members of Remus clan were allowed to live there. ToVata asked one of Remus's sisters to live there, but they wouldn't allow *kastom*.

Although the situation is one of two clans related by *turguvuai*, it is clearly important to control the nature of the customary activities that go on within that relationship. ToVata understands that if a dispute emerges between the two groups that brings their separate identities into the open, then the history of *tabu* being distributed on that land in memory of one of the other group's members will be a powerful weapon to be used in a land claim. An essential part of the Big Man's role is both to encourage this relationship of customary reciprocal interdependence, and to protect his own group's interests within it, if need be by drawing boundaries.

Ambiguities of *Turguvuai*

Hence we see that there is a long history at Matupit of this kind of 'ambiguity'. The main case that I outlined earlier in this chapter is slightly different than the funeral controversy, because in it no-one disputes their descent from a common ancestress. This is not as big of a difference as it may seem on the surface, however. The relationship of unity between the two sides that is accepted by both is based as much on a history of customary reciprocity as it is on bloodline. Although at one point in the hearing, Brendan mentioned ties of genealogy and customary assistance as a way of defining the identity of the group associated with IaMorogo as opposed to that of IaTovo, it is only the context of this dispute about land that gives it this particular gloss.

In another context, the very same statement could easily have been used to assert common identity with the IaTovo group. Indeed during the hearing and in conversations afterwards, members of the IaMorogo group were keen to acknowledge a history of reciprocal interdependence, largely conducted through *kastom*, with their relatives associated with the *tubuan* IaTovo. There is clearly at Matupit a history of attempts to assert a discrete group identity in certain contexts within relationships of larger reciprocal interdependence. It would be a mistake to presume these examples of assertion of discrete individual group identity were the harbingers of new kind of sociality. Equally, however, it would be a mistake to presume that structural precedents for the kinds of contextual corporate individualism that we see today are proof of an essentially unchanging sociality. The contexts in which such assertions are made are key.

Scholars in recent years have discussed the development of tendencies to assert clan identities in a manner that seems much more fixed and descriptive than the fluidity that has traditionally been associated with Melanesian sociality. Much of this work has concentrated on fairly rapid changes in how people talk about kinship and clans as a response to major developments such as mining projects. Jorgenson (1997) describes how the battle over anticipated mining royalties in the Telefolmin area has led to attempts by some to turn flexible social collectivities (the *tenum miit*) into something more akin to the kind of landholder group that the developers and the state can recognise as a unitary collective land 'owner'. Such attempts inevitably involve new uses of language, and a shift away from the kind of contextual elicitation of social difference described by Wagner. People 'who were familiar with government notions of landholding, began *talking* of traditional cognatic descent categories (*tenum miit*) as "clans", complete with patrilineal descent' (Jorgenson 1997:611, my emphasis). Such claims are contested, but they do show how dramatic social changes can inspire different language ideologies as people attempt to elicit or describe social difference in innovative ways.

Matupit has a much longer history of engagement with a global cash economy than other areas of PNG such as Telefolmin. Consequently, such tendencies are perhaps more deeply embedded and appear less as dramatic changes in Matupit than elsewhere. Although A.L. Epstein provides an impressive description of what a *vunatarai* is in various contexts, and in particular how the term's use is related to land issues, he does not discuss specific names, whether of *vunatarai* or of *tubuans*. However, there is evidence to suggest that, as landholding units, clan identities have perhaps become more unitary and fixed over the years.

A.L. Epstein's discussion of the term *vunatarai* makes it clear that it combines a degree of flexibility with a degree of genealogical fixity. On this basis A.L. Epstein states that although the:

Tolai model of descent might be simply represented by a three-tier model of categories, dispersed groups, and local corporations ... Such a model takes too little account of the flexibility of the system, and in particular the scope it provides for the voluntary contracting of new relationships or the transformation of remote ties into close ones. (A.L. Epstein 1969:125, see also Fingleton 1985:58–59)

Such a view makes Matupit kinship and clans of 1960 look somewhat like the model described by Wagner (1974:106), who is also keen to stress the dangers of describing 'a hierarchical arrangement of progressively more inclusive groups, based on genealogical reckoning and standardised into levels with corresponding labels, so that Para might be considered a phratry, Weirai a clan, Kurube a subclan'.

However, there is a limit to the flexibility of Matupit kinship. If a genealogical link can be convincingly proved, it overrides any link whose basis in common matrilineal inheritance is unclear. Thus the term *vunatarai* may at different times encompass different kinds of relationships, both genealogical and based on common work such as *turguvuai*. 'The *vunatarai* exists in neither of these two senses alone, but in both. Stated briefly, the term *vunatarai* has a built-in ambiguity' (A.L. Epstein 1969:164).

Within *vunatarai* as flexibly defined, there are possibilities for more irreducible, fixed units to be described on the basis of common genealogy. A.L. Epstein notes for example that, 'Where there is no influential leadership ... the *lualua* is likely to insist on the definition of the group in genealogical terms' (A.L. Epstein 1969:164). A.L. Epstein is clear that the *vunatarai* in its wider definitions is not 'a property-owning group, certainly not where land is concerned ... proprietary rights to property in land vest primarily in the local descent group' (A.L. Epstein 1969:124). Within the wider *vunatarai* smaller sub-divisions can exist on the basis of fairly fixed genealogy (see for example A.L. Epstein 1969:152–64).[6] A.L. Epstein (1969:191) also notes that the recent collection of genealogies by the Native Land Commissioner 'introduces an element of rigidity which was absent in the indigenous system'.

Such a position appears to suggest that the vision of discrete separate genealogically bounded groups with reference to land of the kind advanced by Turana and Brendan has been a feature of Tolai sociality for some time. Although specific instances of this differentiation are contested, the general principle seems, according to A.L. Epstein, to have been widely accepted (see also Salisbury 1970:71).

However, the examples outlined by Jorgenson and others also raise the possibility that such patterns of behaviour are at least partly responses to social and economic change. Some of the reports on the history of compensation claims prepared by Australian Patrol Officers in Rabaul in the early 1960s, now housed in the East New Britain Customary Land Offices in Kenabot, note that the tendency has been since the early twentieth century for control of land dealings to increasingly pass from the widest definition of the clan to ever smaller sub-lineages. Many reports attempt to deal with disputes that have their origins in the early colonial period. These often concern the 'problem' of overlapping rights, of the kind seemingly outlined by Jorgenson (1997:607–10), where a unitary clan owner for a parcel of land is hard to identify. For example, Officer Gaywood's gives a report on 'The Toma Case' of alleged unfair alienation of land by Europeans from Tolai villagers, at the start of the twentieth century:

> To begin with I assumed the correctness of the generally accepted pattern of life inheritance for the Tolai people, viz that each vuna tarai owns exclusively, or once did, one or more named and specific parcels of land . . . However, in dealing with specific parcels of land it is sometimes apparent that two or more vuna tarai have co-existing rights in the same parcel of land, and though these rights seem to be equal I cannot define their exact nature with certainty. (Gaywood 1959:3)

He also remarks that 'at the beginning of my investigation I found it difficult to disentangle any one part of the claims from the remainder' (Gaywood 1959:2).

And it is striking that those Matupi who have had cause to think deeply about the history of land dealings at their village see a tendency towards more unitary claims of ownership in land. PuiPui Tuna, the Head of the Provincial Government's Customary Land Division, told me that the problem today was that disputes were about 'ownership', which he contrasted to a situation that he believed existed generations ago characterised by overlapping interests in land. Jacob Simet, an anthropologist who is now Head of the PNG government's National Cultural Commission, agrees, arguing that 'ownership is a Western concept' that the Matupi had to engage with in the course of economic development.

This situation of overlapping rights seems similar to the situation described by Salisbury (1970:67–74) and A.L. Epstein (1969:110–37). Yet according to both accounts, by the 1960s many of these interests were becoming moribund; a trend that has continued in the years since. The *kakalei* of a *vunatarai* associated with a named piece of land has increasingly become the predominant controlling interest, moving the situation away from a conceptual pole of overlapping rights and towards a conceptual pole of unitary ownership (even if some of the overlapping rights that persist today do not sit easily with 'ownership' as it may be constituted in Western contexts). Such a move to increasingly prioritise genealogically determined matrilineal kin groups as owners parallels the trend at Telefolmin to transform flexible cognatic groups in which one can claim affiliation through male and female ancestry, into exclusively patrilineal clans as a way of 'insisting that only those descended in the male line should receive benefits' (Jorgenson 1997:618). The details of the two cases are of course different. What the ethnographer of Telefolmin is able to describe as a sudden change, is at Matupit more likely to be the result of a century of ongoing engagement with a global cash economy. Nonetheless, there is a common tendency across both cases, namely the privileging of 'new kinds of exclusionary claim based on a reification of privileged genealogical ties' (Jorgenson 1997:620). This inevitably involves particular ways of talking about social relations – and in some contexts attempts to assert that names *describe* genealogically fixed social groups.

Because most of the customary land on which gardening and cash cropping took place around Matupit was destroyed in 1994, there is no longer the same opportunity to see the extent to which interests other than those endowed by *kakalei* were tolerated. Yet it was stated to me that in the past there was much more reciprocal making of gardens in other clans' land. Interestingly this pattern of cross-*vunatarai* gardening was described in Tok Pisin as <u>halivim</u>, which is commonly translated into English as 'help(ing)', yet in Kuanua was described as *wariru*, more commonly translated as 'respect'. This situation is similar to that described by Sykes (personal communication) for gardening practices on the matrilineal Lelet plateau of nearby New Ireland, in which although land is associated with matrilineal clans, there is a great deal of cross-clan garden making, and gardens are often passed on through the male line. However, at Matupit this situation was described to me as having started to die out by the 1960s and to be largely moribund by the time of the eruption, with clans largely sticking to their 'own' land. The reason universally put forward for this trend was 'greed', caused by the money that could now be made from the ground as a result of cash cropping. Of course it is now impossible to test the veracity of this claim. However, the claim does seem to suggest a feeling among Matupi that the relationships between persons transacted through land were becoming more bounded and discrete.

The fragmentary evidence available, combined with the descriptions of changes taking place more rapidly in other parts of PNG, lead me to at least suspect that ToPokono's inclusive claims might have been taken more seriously at some point in the past. The referential language ideology deployed by Brendan and others with regard to IaMorogo, may at least in part be an element of a process of social change in which Tolai *vunatarai* have become in certain contexts a little more like the social groups whose universality was called into question by Wagner. Regardless of the extent to which the ways that Tolai talk about clan and land is the result of social change, what is clear is that the Tolai themselves ascribe the roots of much of their contemporary battles over language to their engagement with the 'modern' world. The point of view taken by most Matupi residents on ToPokono's use of language is particularly interesting. ToPokono's assertions that the clan could 'never be separate' were widely described to me as wrong, in conversations after this hearing. The majority of Matupi see this as an illegitimate attempt to join together what in this context should be seen as two separate social groups.

Social Change, Bounded Groups and Referential Language

Of course Matupi have not simply adopted a 'Western' perspective, regarding the relationship between language and social groups. But in contexts where a view of language as *describing* pre-existing social groups has become widely accepted, then language which attempts to draw attention to wider networks can be viewed as illegitimate, because it transgresses the boundaries of these discrete social groups. We often imagine that 'greed' is the assertion of 'exclusive' rights. But the widespread denigration of ToPokono's claims on the Rainatun land could be characterised as a matter of some in the community deciding that he was guilty of a kind of 'inclusive' greed, by illegitimately including himself in a legitimately exclusive bounded social group. ToPokono's often derided habit of allegedly claiming additional payments for land that he had already 'sold', on the basis of an ongoing customary relationship, could also be seen in the same manner (see Martin 2006a). The kinds of exclusive claims of ownership by genealogically bounded *vunatarai* on cash-crop land described earlier, which could be decried as exclusive 'greed' by many, could be defended by others as a pre-emptive defence against the inclusive 'greed' of relatives whose overlapping interests in a piece of land now threatened the interests of the 'landholding' clan in an era of permanent investments.

When it came to the assertion of a separate group identity regarding land, the vast majority of Matupi saw Brendan and Turana as describing a fait accompli. It is true that in certain contexts all the descendants of IaPupunang (Diagram 1) would be viewed as a single clan, in the performance of certain kinds of customary practices for example. Everyone involved in this dispute, including representatives of Turana's party, were at pains to point out that no-one was denying this. At certain times in the dispute, the common performance and preparation of _kastom_ is presented as evidence of the group identity of the particular section of the clan identified with IaMorogo, such as in Brendan's early statement that 'The family present here is uncles, nephews, nieces, and grandchildren. We always help each other with things like traditional custom and so on'. At other times, however, people went out of their way to dispute that they were attempting to 'exclude' ToPokono (as he put it) from the clan in the widest sense. When ToPokono states that 'there is no division in the clan. We come from one base', Brendan's response in the public arena of the dispute mediation hearing is instructive. First he says that: 'I've heard ToPokono's statement. It's a good statement . . . Really we respect him', before going on to insist that ToPokono still needs to give some land in compensation, as the histories of the two *tubuans* show that he has no right to accept money in exchange for interests in this piece of land. Later, towards the end of the hearing, when Brendan is attempting to find common ground that unites the disputing parties, he asserts that: 'I'm talking, because we are one family. We want to make things easier so that a good relationship must come between the two parties'. The history of genealogy and customary performances was well known enough to make any attempt to deny their common clan identity unthinkable. The argument was that in other contexts (such as land) they were known to be separate, and as this context was widely considered to be the most important, they would be described as separate clans more often than they were described as one. This was expressed by Wilson in a conversation I had with him months after the hearing in which he explained in Tok Pisin the relationship of the disputants with ToPokono as follows: 'We can't say that you're another clan; but you control this area, and we control this [other] area)'.[7]

It was often explained to me in discussion of this and other cases that two persons or groups may be 'one kind in custom, but it is different for controlling ground'. ToPokono himself inadvertently concedes some separation, when he states that 'If ToMar died, I'd get back all the land', strongly suggesting that as long as ToMar's line (i.e. Brendan etc.) survives, they have a right to be considered separately from him as far as exclusive interests in certain pieces of land are concerned.

Wagner (1974) argues that the relations of exclusion and inclusion referred to by any given name are inherently variable and dependent upon context. It is the calling of the name itself that makes affiliation and difference in any given context. In contrast, the view of most Matupi is that, *in the relevant contexts*, social group identity can be fixed, and is described by language such as the naming of the two related *tubuans*. It is not the case that the calling of the name is seen as *creating* a difference that is variable and contingent upon circumstances, at least not in the position being advanced by these Matupi. It was clear in discussions with people on both sides of this dispute that there could be no doubt, whatever the context, as to who was included under the name of IaMorogo.

The description of the social group bounded by the name IaMorogo could be said to be evoked contextually. It is ToPokono's claim to the land that evokes the response. However, descriptions of a socially bounded group if employed as a successful strategy bring to an end open acknowledgement of the importance of ongoing elicitation of differences in exchange and other social relations, at least in the particular context under discussion. ToPokono does not feel confident to openly dispute this use of language in which the function of the name is purely referential, a lack of confidence that perhaps reflects and partially explains the weakness of his case in the eyes of many. However, ToPokono's rejection of their claim does at least rely upon an implicit rejection of this claim for the referential stability of IaMorogo as a device to describe a social group that excludes him. This implicit rejection seems to suggest that the norms of language pragmatics that Silverstein describes are never absolute, and are themselves open to challenge and come into being, are maintained and decline as the result of negotiation and contest, like other aspects of language use. Silverstein (1976:45) suggests that what we commonly understand as 'grammar', namely the 'grammar' of semantico-referentialism, is merely a particular form of the general 'grammar' of pragmatic function. There are many situations where the referential value of a name like IaMorogo is more openly contested, where the pragmatic basis of a particular language use is disputed. As Volosinov (1973:68) puts it, for the speaker:

> the centre of gravity lies not in the identity of the form but in the new and concrete meaning it acquires in the particular context. What the speaker values is not the aspect of the form which is invariably identical in all instances of its usage . . . but that aspect of the linguistic form . . . because of which it becomes a sign adequate to the conditions of the given, concrete situation . . . the task of understanding does not basically amount to recognizing the form used, but rather to understanding it in a particular, concrete context, to understanding its meaning in a particular utterance . . . and not to recognizing its identity.

This description of how referential meaning in general is made is very close to Wagner's discussion of Daribi names. These names are an interesting example precisely because they are a case in which this context-dependent indexing of referential meaning is so overt that it becomes an unavoidable 'problem' for structural-referential linguistic analysis or colonial Patrol Officers. However, in many cases the indexing of referential meaning takes the form of a seemingly normative referential identity that makes mainstream propositional analysis less problematic. And it is these situations in which the elicitation of social differences appears to take the form of social groups. The distinctions evoked by naming in certain contexts are so widely and universally accepted that they come to be considered by those using them as descriptions or representations of an immutable pre-linguistic reality.

Perhaps Wagner himself is getting at a similar point when he argues that '"Groups" and "society" form a kind of modern shorthand for certain social phenomena' (Wagner 1974:119), just as Volosinov (1973:65–69) notes that language as a system of normatively identical forms is a kind of analytical shorthand for processes of ongoing inter-subjective social contest to create mutually intelligible signs. Although it is only relevant in certain contexts, unlike the names analysed by Wagner, IaMorogo is presented as non-flexible, and non-negotiable. The name of the *tubuan* IaMorogo can only relate to one social group and one identity, but is instead being one of the sign tokens that 'preserve their reference in all the speech events in which they occur' (Silverstein 1976:21). The boundaries that it describes are (for now at least) immutable and fixed, and ToPokono falls outside of them. ToPokono knows this and that is why he is forced to launch a doomed attempt to remove discussion of the *tubuans* from the dispute.

What the above description and discussion suggests is that naming, along with all other language, is best understood as a contested process in which meaning is made and distinctions are drawn in particular contexts of inter-subjective linguistic exchange. These contexts are themselves largely the result of a history of previous contests over meaning. At points, however, the process appears more fixed than others. Some names or words seem to have a wide range of potential nuances or meaning to them. Other words (or the same words at different times) appear to be more rigidly fixed, and this of course is itself merely one possible outcome of the ongoing process of negotiating and contesting meaning in different contexts. The current fixed association of the *tubuan* IaMorogo with a particular bounded clan section is one example of this, being the outcome of a previous contested history of exchange of gifts and words.

What is at stake is not a contrast between places where names describe fixed groups on the one hand or places in which they contextually evoke shifting groups on the other. As Lederman (1986:21) observes, 'adequate analytical models are likely to involve a complex articulation of structural principles'. In her discussion of Mendi kinship this means that notions of relatively fixed named corporate group identities and notions of more fluid interpersonal exchange relations, although contrasted with each other, are ultimately mutually constitutive (ibid.). And moments of what Rumsey (1981:184) refers to as 'contextual conditioning' in his discussion of kinship terminology among Ngarinyin are as much a part of the relationship between names and group identities in Western capitalist societies, as moments of fixed description are for the New Guinea Islands. The term 'cockney' for example can mean someone from specific areas of East London to other Londoners, any Londoner to someone from south-east England, and anyone from south of Birmingham with a vaguely working-class accent to a Mancunian.[8]

What is important is to focus on the different points at which and extents to which the process of making meaning and distinction from names is fixed or not. The Patrol Officers' problem with the Daribi was perhaps not so much that their names worked in a totally different way from Western names, but that they did not operate as fixed descriptors at the points at which the Officers would have found useful or familiar. Likewise ToPokono does not have a cultural inability to understand that at times the relationship between name and group can be relatively fixed (see also Merlan and Rumsey 1991:40), but instead in this instance he finds it inconvenient or objectionable to do so. Hence he attempts to dig up a process of exchange relations underpinning this moment of identity. No-one, including ToPokono, fails to understand that there is a group associated with the name of the *tubuan* IaMorogo. But what he disputes is how its description as having an existence outside of its history of customary exchange relations with his section, acts to 'disinclude' him. What is at stake here is not the existence of a group, but its nature. This dispute illustrates the point made by Merlan and Rumsey (1991:40–41) that: '"Groups" in general, and "corporate" ones in particular, should not be taken as preconstituted entities, but as contested ones, which are more or less problematically instantiated or reproduced in social action . . . much of what goes on at public exchange events can be understood as the reproduction or contestation of specific segmentary groupings'.

Analysis of the different contexts in which it is possible to assert or deny fixity within the process of negotiating the relationship between names and groups provides one of the key registers of processes of social change. It is possible to look at the tension between assertions of fixity and fluidity expressed in this case as nothing new, as merely the latest expression of what Wagner (1988:45), in a later reanalysis of Daribi naming and sociality describes as the 'fundamental contradiction within the ideology itself', when describing Daribi perspectives in which clans are clearly delineated. *Plus ça change, plus c'est la même chose.* Yet such an approach only tells half the story. For such tensions between fluidity and fixity, or relational interdependence and discrete individuality are inherent to the relationship between names and groups, not just as the expression of an underlying Melanesian ideology. It was in this vein that Mauss (1970:63–82) recognised that the tension between idioms of exchange based on reciprocity and non-reciprocity was central to understanding social life far beyond the domain of the *kula* or even the *potlatch*. As Volosinov's analysis of the ever shifting nature of linguistic meaning more generally suggests, such tensions are inherent in naming as a sociolinguistic process. Therefore to observe that such tensions occur in many different times and places is not to deny fundamental cultural difference or social change over time. Social groups 'are hard won social constructions, which, if they are to exist at all, must exist at least in part as more or less contested "representations"' (Merlan and Rumsey 1991:56). This is as true for 1970s Highlands New Guinea (or indeed 1770s Manchester) as it is for twenty-first century Matupit. But observing the shifting terrain on which it is possible to contest the boundary and nature of these 'representations' is to observe one of the ways that these names can mark a difference.

Notes

1. For discussions of the importance of language ideology, see, for example, Irvine (2006), and Woolard and Schieffelin (1994).

2. Transcriptions of recordings of this dispute hearing were produced with the assistance of Michael Waigoga, a resident of Matupit-Sikut who was unrelated to any of the disputants. Michael was responsible for the selection of English terms such as 'land-holder' as the best translations for Kuanua words or phrases relating to land and social organisation.

3. White and Lindstrom (1997:3) refer to the ongoing possibility of a tension between 'traditional' and 'legal-bureaucratic' authority in leadership institutions of Pacific societies. Any successful implementation of a law 'protecting the *tubuan*' could of course create another arena for the expression of potential legal conflict between these principles. This contradiction can no longer be unproblematically presented as one in which the customary law is a kind of indigenous buffer against the oppression of colonial law (e.g. Keesing 1992). Instead, in the context of widening postcolonial inequality the promotion of customary authority inside state legal structures can be seen, from some perspectives at least, as a spearhead for the intensification of elite power. PNG Prime Minister Michael Somare argued at the Pacific Science Congress in Honolulu in 1991 that 'traditional leadership and the democratic process are two completely different and opposite things' (quoted in White and Lindstrom 1997:3–4), before going on to call for 'greater recognition of chiefs and principles of indigenous leadership instead of the blind application of principles of Western democracy' (op cit.:4). Somare's position as a leading member of the national postcolonial political and economic elite, who also claims at least a part of his legitimacy on the basis of positions of 'traditional' leadership, should of course be taken into account when assessing his position. At the very least his position can not be taken as the unproblematic assertion of indigenous resistance to the hegemony of global discourses of 'democracy'. I am sure that many of my informants at Matupit would view his statements with as much suspicion as they view attempts to legally 'protect' the *tubuan*.

4. More of the background to this case can be found in Simet (1991:237–41).

5. ToNgala was the best known and most controversial 'Big Shot' at Matupit at the time of my fieldwork. His story will be told in more detail in subsequent chapters.

6. Smaller sub-divisions of a *vunatarai* are sometimes described as *vunatarai* or sometimes as *apik(tarai)*, when people wish to draw a distinction between the smaller section and the larger group. See A.L. Epstein (1969:124–25). The *apik* level of social categorisation will be discussed more in the next chapter.

7. TP. *Mipela no inap tok olsem yu narapela vunatarai; tasol yu bosim dispela hap, mipela bosim dispela hap*).

8. This is a point that Evans-Pritchard (1940:136) also makes in his discussion of the way in which the Nuer term *cieng*'s 'precise significance varies with the situation in which it is spoken' actually parallels the way in which its English equivalent 'home' is similarly speech-context dependent. I am grateful to Alan Rumsey for this observation.

5

Kastom, Family and Clan

Extending and Limiting Obligations

In the previous chapter, I analysed the changing ways in which Matupi have organised access to land, and the central importance of different kinds of kinship relations to that process. Kinship has long been central to the ways in which Tolai land tenure is negotiated. Or to put it another way, relations negotiated through land have long been central to how people recognise each other as kin. The institution of *turguvuai*, in which two separate *vunatarai* come to be recognised as one by virtue of a history of joint customary transactions, often performed on specific pieces of land, is one example. Kinship relations continue to be central to the negotiation of access to land, and relationships to the land remain central to how Matupi constitute and negotiate kinship relations. Economic development, political independence and the trauma of the eruption and resettlement to 'non-customary' land have not created a year zero in which these considerations have been wiped clean. But neither have the ways in which kinship and land are intertwined remained static over the years. Take Philip, who in previous chapters I have described as being keen to diminish the importance of his children spending time with their mother's brothers. This does not just exemplify an increasing desire to draw a line around the family household and protect it from the demands of wider kin-based obligations. When Philip announces that 'if I behaved like this on clan land, of course there would be talk', it also expresses a feeling that new ways of relating to land, in this case the government's moves to establish 'non-customary' land tenure at Sikut, make possible new ways of negotiating kinship relations. The family household is constituted as a social unit that stands relatively independent of other kinship ties partially as a result of state registration of land, much as the *vunatarai* can be constituted as a social unit by virtue of the relationships of reciprocally interdependent customary gift exchange conducted through land known as *turguvuai*.

In this chapter I begin to outline in more detail the importance of the ubiquitous concept of *kastom* as a term that, rather than carrying a fixed meaning, instead serves as a means by which the boundaries between different kinds of claims can be assessed. In particular contests over customary ritual can be best understood as a site in which hidden battles over issues such as the relation of family to clan or the morality of the new indigenous elite are brought into the public domain. Most fundamentally, these contests are often examples of the ongoing contest between reciprocal interdependence and non-reciprocal independence that marked contests over claims to land both at Matupit and at Sikut. Throughout this chapter I examine more fully the contradiction between family and more extended kinship networks, in particular the clan. The significance of this contradiction extends beyond merely that of 'land tenure'. The contradiction holds fundamental day-to-day significance, such that it is central to the constitution of many of the most important social trends in contemporary PNG, especially the variety of attempts to loosen the ties of reciprocal interdependence and to draw an increasing social division between Big Shots and grassroots villagers, something I discuss in the final chapter of this book. In this chapter my aim is to examine the term that perhaps more than any other exemplifies the ongoing social revolution in Tolai life across the past century, _kastom_. This concept also has a significance that goes well beyond the adjudication of land disputes or the contradiction between obligations to immediate family and to other kin. I argue that _kastom_ very often more generally marks an attempt to set the boundaries of reciprocal interdependence and obligation, and it often specifically does so in the space of contradiction between family and other levels of kin relatedness.

Kinship and Conflict

The situation that Matupi are faced with today is one in which different kinds of kinship relations co-exist, often in great tension or even open conflict with each other. Kinship is still one of the main ways in which social relations and obligations are negotiated and contested, but kinship relations of one kind are often opposed to kinship relations of another. Again this is nothing new, as is made clear by the conflicts between different clan sections over the nature of their relationship documented in earlier times by A.L. Epstein. These kinds of conflicts are still a feature of Matupit social life, as illustrated by the land dispute involving _tubuan_ names described in the previous chapter.

Kinship has always involved what Gregory (1997:50) describes as 'commonplace contradictions', but in new circumstances different contradictions come to the fore, or existing contradictions come to carry greater meaning.[1] In late eighteenth-century England, capitalism developed largely endogenously as a process of large-scale industrialisation, giving rise to many of the words that Hobsbawm (1962:13) identifies as markers of the scale of the revolution in social relations that unfolded in this period, such as 'factory', 'industrialist' or 'railway'. Tolai integration into a system of global commodity exchange has by contrast occurred largely on the basis of small-scale commodity exchange, in which cash cropping organised at a household or clan level has been of great importance. It is only in the years since independence that it has been possible for a very small number of Tolai to emerge as part of a postcolonial elite, whether as government bureaucrats or entrepreneurs. This development is reflected in the recent emergence of the term 'Big Shot'. But even now, there are no Tolai to compare with the tycoons of early eighteenth-century Lancashire or the mandarins of the Victorian imperial civil service.

The Tolai experience of integration into global capitalism is perhaps most acutely expressed in shifts in the contradiction between family and clan in relation to land. Cash cropping and the building of permanent houses has been part of a revolution in how Tolai relate to each other through land. This revolution, while very different in form from the industrial revolution that erupted in eighteenth-century Lancashire, is intrinsically a part of the specifically Tolai integration into a global capitalist commodity exchange economy.

I begin my analysis of the contradiction between family and other kinship obligations, and the importance of the concept of *kastom* to attempts to live with that paradox of daily life, with two quotes that contradict each other. Both speakers are grassroots men in their middle age, living at the resettlement camp of Matupit-Sikut. They both have a strong interest in *kastom*. They both seem to share an analysis of what underpins the concept of *kastom* too; both associate it with extended networks of mutual assistance that are stereotypically Melanesian, and are to be contrasted with the way of life of white people. The fundamental difference appears to be how they morally evaluate *kastom*.

The first speaker, my close friend ToAtun, was around forty years old at the time of my arrival at Sikut. ToAtun was a strong believer in *kastom*. He was very active in the *tubuan* society, and was often called upon for his expertise in conducting ritual preparations. This gave him a strong sense of self-worth and prestige among some people. But it was as likely to be the cause of hidden mockery amongst others, who wondered why he spent so much time on these activities rather than economically bettering himself. Many people viewed such customary activities as benefiting the new elite who were reliant on the goodwill and largely unpaid labour of men like ToAtun. But for ToAtun, *kastom* as a Melanesian practice based upon extended networks of mutual assistance and reciprocal interdependence is, on the whole, something to be defended. Here is what he said:

> The SDA (Seventh Day Adventists) don't like *kastom* . . . They want to follow Western ways . . . They think the *tubuan* is the Devil's work . . . The *tubuan* is part of the way by which we help each other. The Bible says we should help each other. The only reason they don't like

getting involved in the circulation of *tabu* is because they want to live a selfish life . . . You help whoever is in need. That's our way.

The second speaker, Luke Cada, was in his late fifties at the time of my first fieldwork and had a block at Sikut. Luke was well-educated and had previously worked as a clerical and statistical officer for the government. After the eruption, he had concentrated on his new block at Sikut and at the time of my fieldwork had already built a permanent house. Luke was also a senior member of the Seventh Day Adventist Church at Sikut. As such, he minimised his involvement in customary exchanges and rituals and would certainly have nothing to do with the *tubuan*. For Luke <u>kastom</u> is largely a problem to be resisted; rather than being of benefit it is an excuse for what at another point in this discussion he described as 'harassment'. Here is one passage from a longer discussion on the subject that he had with me, mainly in English:

> Martin, you have to condemn this idea that people have to support their father and mother's *tubuan* after they die, in your book. The *tubuan* has attendants like flight attendants. You have to pay these lazy buggers . . . We Adventists are getting rid of it. It's rich man's work, this stuff. We don't say some customs are no good, just burdensome . . . I have to busy myself with my immediate family not the extended family. Only occasionally the extended family. I waste my time and get nothing in return. Some of them are realising. Some of ToNgala's line are running away from ToNgala and <u>kastom</u> . . . All the time he's making them work hard to get *tabu* just for him. Who is he? Idi Amin? Your [white people's] style is better. When you want to go and see your friends you don't overload them all the time.

My fieldnotes are full of comments similar to both of these men's statements. One issue that arises starkly from these comments is the perceived contradiction between the 'immediate family' and the 'extended family'. Luke was using these terms to draw a commonly made distinction between obligations to one's family or household and one's clan-based obligations (whether to one's own clan or to other clans to whom one was reciprocally obligated). The desire to look after one's family first and foremost is often associated with the SDA. This desire is characterised by many SDA adherents as responsible, but is denigrated by many others as 'selfish'.

I have preferred to use the term 'family' to 'household' in this discussion primarily because it is a term that the Matupi themselves use in English and Tok Pisin, in distinction to 'extended family' or 'clan'. In a comparative discussion, Narotzky (1997:119) argues that the '"family" concept . . . is less useful as a descriptive term than that of "household", because the links that bind people into families – those of alliance and consanguinity – are highly

problematic cultural constructs that depend on the social and political relations in every society'. However, she goes on to point out that:

> the 'family' . . . has followed capitalist expansion around the world.
> As relations of production have developed differently according
> to historical and environmental, political and economic, local and
> regional constraints, the articulation of a Western 'family' ideology
> in different places will also vary according to local ideas about repro-
> duction-procreation, socialisation and maintenance – that probably
> will not be homogenous either. (op cit.:119–20)

Narotzky places great emphasis on conscious attempts by colonialists
(and presumably neo-colonialists) to enforce family ideology. However, as
we have seen with the case of land, it is important not to let this dynamic
blind us to the countervailing dynamic that on occasion people at a grassroots
level have an interest in using such concepts in their own face to face social
relations. In the current economic context many Matupi are keen to use the
concept of responsibility to their own family as a means of attempting to limit
the demands of clan-based obligations. Additionally, it is a deeply felt sense of
moral obligation to that 'family' unit that provides the motivation and desire
to resist those other obligations.

The Matupi family may vary from household to household (as the
Manchester family undoubtedly does), but the idea of a man's responsibility to his own children gathered around him in his house (even if one or two
children have left home or he and his wife look after a grandchild or two)
is thought of and referred to as his family. It is this idea that is consciously
contrasted and defended by many against the demands of the clan. Many
households do not simply have two parents and children. In some cases there
will be other relatives present, such as an elderly grandparent, married children's spouses and children, or sometimes matrilineal or patrilineal nephews
and nieces. Sometimes Matupi use the Tok Pisin or English word 'family' to
refer to the wider amalgamation of relatives living together, and here perhaps
the word is used in a manner closer to 'household', but it is normally clear
from the context which meaning is intended at any given time. Even at these
times the family unit of parents and immediate children is often presented as
the core of this household. For example, when context is not enough to make
clear the meaning, a person might refer in Tok Pisin to *famili tru tru* (real or
proper family) in distinction to wider groups of relatives that may be referred
to as *famili* in other contexts, such as clan relatives or the amalgamation of
relatives gathered in the family-based household.[2] Yet while Matupi sometimes use the category 'family' in different ways, this does not mean that the
nuclear family concept is unfamiliar to them. It may operate in the context
of other kinds of social relations in a uniquely Tolai manner, partly resulting

from the unique history of Tolai interaction with global capitalism. But the concept is central to how Matupi organise their households and to how they imagine future social relations.

Of course there have always been households at Matupit, and these households have been positioned within broader sets of social relations and reciprocal obligations. But it is the nature of those relations, how they are conceived of, and how they help to constitute the household unit that is the issue. These relations and the household unit that is constituted through them have changed over the years. For example the actual organisation of the houses themselves has shifted from a situation in which the social relatedness of each household was clearly visible to even outsiders by virtue of their organisation into clearly divided hamlets surrounded by fences. Living arrangements have also changed substantially over the years. For example, people told me that men's houses of the type that are still common in New Ireland used to be common at Matupit too, and that teenage boys would live most of the time in these dwellings, as is still the case elsewhere in PNG today.[3] Among the Tolai this is no longer the case. Male teenagers on the whole live with their parents. Philip's earlier-quoted comment about not wanting his children to go and stay with their maternal uncles is representative of a move away from what would have been an expectation in previous generations. Although the tendency for young men to be sent to stay with their clan uncles has not totally died out in the same way as the institution of the 'boy's house' (TP. *hausboi*), both of these changes involve increasingly prioritisation of the family as basic household unit. As Fingleton (1985:58) observes, 'One social unit which has enjoyed an increase in importance in the changing Tolai environment that shows no sign of abating is the nuclear or conjugal family'.

The rise to prominence of the Tolai family is signalled, as we might expect, by linguistic changes. Bradley (1982:191) claims that until the recent past, 'there appeared to be no Kuanua word to denote the unit of father, mother and child'. In the English-to-Kuanua dictionary produced by the Methodist Mission at Vunairima following the Second World War the word 'family' is translated as *bartamana*, and this translation was universally accepted by my interlocutors. However, in the Kuanua-to-English dictionary produced by the Methodist Mission at Rabaul in 1939 that was largely unchanged from the original version of 1888, the word *bartamana* does not appear. Instead, under the heading of the Kuanua word *bara*, we find the definition, 'Sign of the plural used only with words expressing relationship', followed by the example *bara tamana* 'father and son, or sons'. (Here, *tamana* is the third person singular possessive of *tama*, the Kuanua base word for 'father', thus literally meaning 'his or her father'.) *Bara tamana* thus appears not originally to have been a recognised word in its own right, but a way of expressing particular kinds of relations of a par with the other examples given in the dictionary such as *bara tana* or *nana* (mother and child or children), *bara turana* (brothers), *bara talaina* (friends), or *bara taulai* (husband and wife). Such phrases do not refer to fixed social groups. Who the 'friends' are that are referred to by *bara talaina* is of course indexed by the context of previous speech acts. Only one of these phrases by which people can describe a multiplicity of plural relations has become condensed into a single word that refers to a recognised social unit: *bara tamana* has become the word *bartamana*, universally recognised by Tolai as the equivalent of the English 'family'. That this relational phrase should become the basis for the description of a social unit seems to suggest the importance of the relationship between a man and his children as being the defining feature of that unit, as opposed to, for example, the matrilineal *vunatarai*.[4]

Simet (1991:169) refers to *bartamana* as one of three major kinds of Tolai kin relations, saying that it refers to 'those who belong to the father's clan'. Within this definition, however, he identifies 'six different kinds of relationship' (op cit.:170), of which the first is also called *bartamana*. This he defines as the relationship between 'a person and his or her father with his brothers and classificatory brothers'. It is true that as a result of this it is common to hear 'all the men in this category refer to the children as *natugu* ['my child' –KM] and the children refer to them as *tamagu* ['my father' –KM]' (op cit.:172). Hence the use of *bartamana* as a term that refers to a set of relations persists, and coexists with its use as the term for the family unit. Indeed it does so in a much wider and more flexible manner than the Methodist dictionary definition suggests, as that definition does not make explicit the number of persons that a Tolai may refer to as 'father'. To acknowledge all of this is not to deny the importance of the term's current use as the noun that refers to the family unit. When Simet (ibid.) goes on to state that 'The children's relationship with [their father's] brothers and classificatory brothers are essentially the same as that with their real father', this may be true in an ideal customary kinship sense, but it does not match the daily reality that I observed in most households at Matupit and Sikut. Although families vary massively in the amount of time that children spend with fathers' brothers and the amount of responsibility that these relatives take for the children, in most cases children mainly live in their parents' house and are primarily cared for by them. As Simet (op cit.:171) also observes: 'In the early years of the children's life, the father is the main provider of their sustenance such as food and shelter. And in conjunction with their mother, he is the most instrumental in the upbringing of the children'.

The emergence of the tension between family and clan can be seen as consequence and part of the process of ongoing Tolai reorganisation of social relations. Again it is important to stress that it is not a state of absolute war between these social affiliations that has followed an earlier state of absolute harmony. Older Tolai told me, for example, that when they were young they had been told that there was always tension surrounding men who wished to pass on magical or ritual knowledge to their children, magic that nephews believed was theirs by virtue of matrilineal *vunatarai* affiliation. Tensions over these issues persist today. However, such tension has become more pronounced. It emerges at new points (increasingly around the transmission of rights in land and tangible economic assets), as the increasing importance of the family household bears out. And it is a tension that Matupi themselves seek to historicise and to explain within a broader political economic context.

The situation faced by Tolai today is one in which they have competing moral obligations to their family household on the one hand and wider extended obligations on the other. This moral dilemma is one that is often felt particularly strongly by adult men. Such a man has to balance the needs of his children, who are of another clan, with those of his clan. But it is also a strongly felt dilemma for women, especially those in a wage earning household, who often feel the family budget to be under pressure from the demands of fellow clan members and other relatives (the much bemoaned and famous PNG '*wantok* system'). And in the Tolai context, the concept of *kastom* has become central to the ways in which persons justify their decisions to place one obligation ahead of another, or pass judgement on decisions of others. A claim may be described as legitimate or illegitimate with reference to its 'customary' status. Conversely one may choose to belittle the relevance of *kastom* in certain contexts, and hence reject a claim on that basis.

At another point in the conversation with ToAtun from Sikut (who denigrated the SDA for selfishness), he began to reflect upon how houses were built in the past. He had been led to believe that it used to be the job of the wife's clan section to build a bush material house for the newly married couple. (What I call a 'clan section' is a recognised unit smaller than a clan, often called *apiktarai* or *apik* in Kuanua. This smaller unit of social organisation is very prominent in Tolai thought about the kinds of social processes I discuss in this chapter, so I will be referring to people's *apik* groups a good deal across the discussion below.) This revelation intrigued me, and over the following months I began asking people of different ages what they knew of the situation in the past. There was not unanimity on the issue. Some claimed not to know. Others claimed that there had been no discernible pattern, and that whoever happened to be available would have helped on a basis of non-regulated loosely expected reciprocity (rather as much of the house-building and block development at Sikut had taken place). Still others claimed that it was the young man's responsibility to build the married couple's first house. Most, however, seemed to agree with ToAtun that the wife's *apik* would have to build the house, and that house-building by the young man was one of a number of tasks that he had to fulfil in the past to demonstrate that he was capable of supporting a wife and children, such as climbing a coconut tree to gather coconuts. It is impossible now to retrospectively ascertain the historical situation. Salisbury (1970:154) observes that in the late nineteenth century 'housebuilding and clearing bush for planting gardens were the main tasks requiring large labour forces'. However, by 1960 he was able to report that 'modern housebuilding is usually a job for a skilled carpenter rather than for a large crew of unskilled workers' (ibid.).

The Relations that Build a Household

What is undoubtedly the case is that the division of labour posited by ToAtun and most other Matupi that I spoke to immediately tied the very physical existence of the household into an ongoing relationship of reciprocal interdependence. As ToAtun described it, both *apiks* would try to ensure that a wife went back to the wife-giving *apik* in the next generation, thus ensuring that those who built a house in one generation had a house built for them in the next. This is an example of what A.L. Epstein (n.d.) in his fieldnotes reports Matupi in the early 1960s as referring to using the English phrase 'exchange marriage'.[5] More than simply observation of the taboo on marriage within each moiety, 'exchange marriage' involved two *apiks* from opposing moieties giving and receiving wives across the generations. It is under conditions such as this in which bridewealth can most clearly be presented as part of a cycle of reciprocal gift exchange. This contrasts with today's situation in which 'exchange marriage' is increasingly rare, and there is debate over bridewealth inflation and the alleged greed of some parents who treat their daughters as a 'market'.[6] Exchange marriage cemented ties between clans over the generations. The practice was particularly important in allowing children of a clan to reside on that clan's land after their father's death without the clan who were associated with the land feeling that their *kakalei* was under threat. This was possible because some of the male children of the clan would take wives from the original clan, such that occupancy would ideally revert to that clan in the next generation. It is no accident that the development of registered land sales at Matupit in which *kulia* is now described as involving a transfer of *kakalei* has coincided with widespread decline of this form of arranged marriage. If one can now transfer the *kakalei*, making it possible to buy land from one's own clan for one's children, then there is less incentive to arrange intergenerational reciprocal wife exchange in order to protect a *kakalei* that has been transferred anyway. Or, viewed from the other angle, young people's insistence on the freedom to marry as they wish means that the old way of a man ensuring that his children can continue to stay on his clan land after his death without a transfer of *kakalei* is no longer viable. It would be a mistake to spend too much time attempting to understand which development 'caused' the other. Rather they are two essential sides of the same coin: a partial removal of family-based households from the cycles of inter-clan, inter-generational reciprocity, within which those households' very existence was formerly more closely embedded.

This situation still pertains in parts of neighbouring New Ireland having many social similarities to the Tolai area of East New Britain. In most of southern New Ireland descent is similarly reckoned through the matriline, closely related languages are spoken, and there are many customary similarities including the practice of the *tubuan* society. The major difference that is admitted to by both Tolai and New Irelanders alike is that New Ireland is relatively 'undeveloped' compared to Tolai villages, especially coastal villages near Rabaul such as Matupit. Travelling in New Ireland I had the opportunity to spend some time with a Big Man from Tanga Island, who described reciprocal marriage as being a means to ensure that clans could allow their children to continue to live on the land without threatening their claim. He told me that in his village they had considered making it possible to buy land, but after a short period of time they went back on the decision as there was no way to ensure that purchases did not end up in dispute. A few people continued to try to buy land, but others stopped them. He gave an example of a land transfer from the 1970s where the person who acquired the land for his children today still had to 'pay and involve in *kastom*' in order to continue to secure the land, much as described by A.L. Epstein for Matupit for the early 1960s. He gave this as the reason why at Tanga they continued with exchange marriage of this kind. This man had spent several years in Rabaul in the 1970s, and immediately contrasted the Tanga practice with that of the Tolai around Rabaul whom he described as more 'individual'. 'In East New Britain everyone just follows money. Money is more powerful in East New Britain . . . In East New Britain, money is *kastom*.'

Although I did not have time to ask this man about how house building fitted into intergenerational wife exchange, it is clear that it is part of the picture in other parts of New Ireland. For example Sykes (personal communication) reports that on the Lelet plateau of New Ireland it is the groom's father's clan's responsibility to build a house for the newlyweds. Although this is a different state of affairs from that described by many at Matupit, it is still one that ties the household immediately into fairly fixed cycles of inter-generational reciprocal interdependence between a clan and its children (the same relation that as we have seen has increasingly become one of fraught tension among the Tolai). As we have seen, many Tolai describe the ideal relationship of reciprocal interdependence between a clan and its children as being increasingly difficult to maintain, partly as result of material changes such as cash cropping and permanent housing. Tolai regularly historicise the perceived increasing degree of household independence by linking this shift to the changing global political economy into which they have been integrated and the efflorescence of new material objects with which they now live. That much is made clear by the comment with which ToAtun ended his reflections on this subject: 'that's how it worked when things were easy, just bush materials'.

Philip, the Sikut resident mentioned in Chapter Four who talked about how his land and property was for his children and not his clan, provides an extreme example of how household independence is based upon a rejection of reciprocity. He does not just reject the demands of reciprocal interdependence within his own clan, upon which his ability to secure land and build a family would in the past have been dependent. (As the Big Man from Tanga told me, even if you settled on clan land if you weren't part of the clan's customary activity sooner or later problems would emerge and 'we would get you'.) Philip was also notable as one of those who had married within his moiety. Breaking the moiety taboo was in contact era Tolai society apparently often punishable by death. A.L. Epstein (n.d.) reports two cases of young people wishing to marry inside the moiety at the time of his own fieldwork. At this time, according to A.L. Epstein's fieldnotes, young people were successfully resisting attempts to enforce 'exchange marriage' between *apiks*, of the kind outlined above, although not without a fight.[7] Marriage within the moiety was considered to be a step too far, however, and both attempts were beaten down by community pressure. By 1986, A.L. Epstein (1999:225) was able to report two intra-moiety marriages at Matupit that, although disapproved of by most members of the community, seemed impossible to stop. Today marriage within the moiety, although still disapproved of by many and only practised by a minority, is now a recognised social phenomenon. It is not uncommon to find young people of the same moiety openly conducting a relationship or even cohabiting. Philip is unusual in that he is in his late forties and previously married. After divorcing his first wife he married a member of his own moiety in the face of opposition. However, as he himself pointed out to me, the high wage that he earned as a skilled worker at one of PNG's big mining projects meant that he was more able than most to ignore such opposition and pursue his own course. His wage was significantly higher than most of those still lucky enough to have work after the eruption, although nowhere near high enough – and his political influence nowhere near great enough – to qualify him as a 'Big Shot'. Many young men who end up living with women of their own moiety overcome this problem simply by avoiding paying bridewealth altogether. Although intra-moiety marriage causes many of the older generation great distress, they feel largely powerless to stop it. At the time of my fieldwork, it would be no exaggeration to say that intra-moiety marriage or partnership was becoming something of a norm for young grassroots men and women who wanted it at the time of my fieldwork.

Although the moiety is not a land holding unit, the *apiks* that have a claim (*kakalei*) to a particular piece of land engaged in exchange marriage would be members of opposite moieties, and, as A.L. Epstein (1969:192) points out, the moiety system provides the most powerful illustration of the general division into reciprocally interlocked parts by which Tolai have traditionally imagined their social relations to be organised. As such its breach is the most powerfully felt symptom and cause of the perceived general loosening of reciprocity and respect in Tolai society in general.

As statements by Philip quoted in an earlier chapter might suggest, he set a high premium on family independence. On one unprompted occasion he referred to <u>kastom</u> and the <u>wantok</u> system as: 'PNG's sickness. To become independent you must make sure everything belongs to your immediate family'. And even more importantly, it could be added, you must make sure that your immediate family belongs to your immediate family; that, as far as is possible, this family is removed from kin-based ties of reciprocal interdependence that make its very capacity to exist not its own.

When people talk about <u>kastom</u> not creeping back into land tenure at Sikut, if they are focused on a case where the named block holder is a man, primarily they are concerned with the man's *vunatarai*. It is his sisters' children that most conversations regarding the potential return of <u>kastom</u> revolve around. This is not the only 'customary' claim that is envisaged, however. On occasion people will discuss the possibility of a claim being made by other members of the children's own (that is the mother's) *vunatarai*. In the minority of cases where the named block holder is a woman, then this is the only matrilineal claim that would be possible. (At the time of my fieldwork over 75 per cent of blocks were listed by the Provincial Government as being allocated in a man's name.) To an extent this reflects the fact that as new land of a historically unprecedented variety, there is no set of 'rules' regarding which matrilineage the claim would be vested in if 'customary' principles were to be followed. Thus there is no clear 'customary' precedent for new land at Sikut. Perhaps the situation is one in which people will attempt to make claims on a number of bases, depending on what they think might work in different circumstances. In both cases, however, what is key is drawing boundaries around the degree of contact with clan relatives, be they the children's own clan or the father's clan. All sorts of relatives may come and stay for a day or two, and children may go to stay with relatives. There were some households surveyed at Sikut at which young clan nephews or nieces stayed at the block alongside of the block holder's own children, or instead of them. Such arrangements are viewed by many as a recipe for possible future disputes. But most households when surveyed are predominantly two parents and their children. And it is also worth noting that cases in which a relative of the block holder's brothers were staying with the family were nearly as common as those in which it was a clan relative. If they were to have a claim to the land in the future it would not be on the basis of any immediate matrilineal link, but as a result of a patrilineal one, combined with the wishes of the block holder or the history of work that they had put into the block's development.

Returning to the example of Philip, who mentioned the *wantok* system as PNG's sickness: he went on to explain that the reason he did not send his children to stay with their clan uncles was that he feared that if their uncles taught them and worked with them, then after his death his children's cousins would be able to make a claim on his children's work and inheritance. This is a clear example of an attempt to draw the boundaries around the family so that the children could not be held to be indebted and obligated to their cousins in years to come. I spent a considerable amount of time with this family. Although it will be impossible to tell how successful Philip's strategy has been for several decades, in my two years of residence the concern with limiting the children's links with the clan was not just talk, and this family was far from alone in its approach. By virtue of their state land at Sikut, and the male house-holder's significant cash income, this family had been able to limit their ties with either head of household's clan.[8] So for example the female householder was one of her *apik*'s experts in the knowledge (K. *varvateten*) of the history of transactions and genealogies that an *apik* needs to secure its *kakalei* on a piece of land. But the couple had decided that because they had the land at Sikut and were financially independent, she would cease to go back to Matupit to help out in disputes. If they were reliant on clan land they would have had no choice, but given their independence they would rather not risk the anger and potential sorcery of parties who disputed her evidence.

Interestingly Philip told me that the only activities that his children performed having anything to do with their clan and their uncles were *kastom*. In this conversation he seemed to be using the word in a manner similar to the man quoted in Chapter Four, who described how *kastom* at Matupit was to do with land, but *kastom* at Sikut was 'only *kastom*', and then going on to tell me that '*kastom* at Sikut doesn't have any meaning'. This man had no objection to his children taking part in *kastom* as a set of rituals, fearing that they might feel left out if not allowed to join in when appropriate, and also mindful that local 'custom' was now part of the compulsory PNG school curriculum. But he was keen to stress its separation from other parts of day-to-day life.

With regard to both potential claims made by the man's clan and potential claims made by other members of the children's clan, what seems to be key is limiting contact that could be seen to create an ongoing obligation. This would then potentially create the basis for a claim. Customary ritual maintains reciprocal obligations, and in the past land has been a key component of such obligations. However, as we have seen there are strong attempts to rhetorically separate *kastom* from access to land. How much land tenure over the next two generations will reflect these rhetorical attempts remains to be seen. But for the time being many people claimed to feel confident that allowing their children to engage in *kastom* with members of their own clan or their father's clan will not foster obligations that spiral out of the contained sphere of customary ritual.

Perhaps the most important thing to be wary of is allowing relatives to stay for too long and accepting their offers to 'help' with the development of the block. In my examination of a number of households at Sikut I found a variety of arrangements. People would perhaps pay a non-Tolai without work to clear a piece of their block, but then get a clan relative to prepare the wood to turn it into timber with a portable saw mill. Often people would try to find someone that they were related to in some way to do skilled work, such as constructing a permanent house. There was one man in particular with well-acknowledged carpentry skills who seemed to be responsible for about twenty houses that were constructed at Sikut during my fieldwork. Most Matupi can claim some kind of link to each other by virtue of relationships between *vunatarai*, even if the exact relations tying them together are not clear in more distant cases. What was interesting to me was that while hiring a relative always meant paying a cheaper price than one would have paid to a professional construction company from town, the amount that people paid tended to vary according to income. Those with higher incomes felt obliged to pay a premium and did not seem to resent doing so. Even though they benefited from lower than market prices, both they and those relatives that did this work often described the employment as a way of 'helping'. Although disputes over payment did occur, in general it was described as a mutually beneficial transaction. In this regard the prices paid for such labour are far from being a pure commodity transaction as understood in classical political economics in which the value of labour ultimately determines the price of the commodity.

However, in one respect payments that are made for assistance on the block are often presented in a very strong 'commodity' mould. Here I refer to help with clearing and planting land for cash crops rather than house building. People are very well aware that 'help' of this nature became one of the ways in which *kastom* reasserted itself at the resettlement schemes of the 1960s such as Vudal and Warangoi. People felt obliged to let nephews with no access to land 'help' on the blocks in exchange for food and for a little bit of land to garden on. Over the years this help and long-term residence became the basis of control over the land by the nephews. This was particularly exacerbated by the fact that some of the original block holders were well-connected Tolai, with relatively senior positions in the colonial Provincial Government whose own children were more likely to have gone on to higher education and full time employment, leaving the block subject to other relatives' claims by default. In one example of a block at Vudal that is under dispute, the original block license was given to a Matupit man in the 1950s. He was unable to look after the block for a long period of time and left it in the care of a member of his clan. Both of these men are now dead, but a clan niece of the second man now occupies the block and is listed with the Provincial Government as the block holder. The two sides differ over exactly how and when first this woman's uncle, and then she herself, came to be the registered owner.[9] But according to the original block holder's children, it is clear that if they had been on the block themselves at the time then the re-registration would not have happened. One of the children told me that he had been away studying for much of the period in question. Hence, he was not able to look after the block. He saw his case as exceptional or at least a result of the times in which that particular resettlement had occurred: he and his siblings had been the victims of unfortunate circumstances and skulduggery, rather than their misfortune being a sign that 'customary land was coming back'. He was convinced that his case was unlikely to set a precedent for the more recent resettlements such as Sikut. Although non-owning cousins might come and ask for help from the money made on a block, if it came to a legal dispute over ownership, he felt that title to the land would secure the owners' status. The only exception he mentioned, doubtless reflecting on his own experience, was 'if the title is with a man, and the kids don't stay there; if they're at school or work somewhere else and the relatives come and work then there'll be a dispute'.

At the end of the interview, he reflected wryly, 'before we didn't know how to hold onto ground'. To an extent this may be true. Perhaps the experience of resettlement schemes like Vudal will make this generation more wary of letting clan relatives outnumber children on their blocks. This is all the more salient for the many block holders at Sikut today, many of whom are grassroots villagers, for whose children access to land is likely to be their best route to economic security, especially with the decline of the PNG economy across the past fifteen years.

Paying off the Relatives

The wariness about allowing relatives to help remains. Although there are cases in which young close relations of the husband's or wife's *vunatarai* stay for long periods of time, these are the minority. What is interesting is how people attempt to characterise assistance that is made by such relatives. In every case that I was aware of, payment was made for the help, and that payment was always deliberately monetary. In the past, I was told, relatives would help each other out in return for a meal at midday, and the promise of assistance in the future. Such mutual assistance dovetailed with wider ties of reciprocal interdependence such as customary ritual and exchange marriage. Today there will nearly always be a cash element as well.

Often people who are paying relatives to do work on their block will ruefully contrast the greed of today with allegedly happier times. The longer I stayed at Sikut, however, the more I became aware that those making the payments were as likely to stress that these payments had been made at their own insistence. The situation is well summed up by a conversation that I had with Tony Danett, Param's predecessor as chair of the resettlement committee, whom I encountered one afternoon as he was entering his block near the care centre from the main road. Tony was an immensely forceful and articulate man who had been a senior Moresby public servant in the early 1970s in the last days of the colonial regime. He was well-educated and had the large English vocabulary that often marks former public servants of his generation. When I visited him, he invited me in, showing me the extent of the work that had been done on his block and his house so far. We sat down for a cup of tea, and I turned on my tape recorder and asked him what he thought the most important thing about continuing the development of the blocks at Sikut was. He replied in English, as follows:

> We need to keep the clan out of this land. The clan doesn't work in new economic situations. We are moving away from the clan to individual family responsibility. More like your custom. In the past we were tied by reciprocal obligations. Now when people work for me, I make a point of paying them individually. This negates their claim to the land. If you let relatives 'help' on the land, then the trouble starts. They can imagine that they're part of that old system and that includes rights to the land. I had to get relatives to help me on this land after the volcano, but *I made sure I paid them individually. That buys off any potential customary claim* .... Looking after our individual families is more important now than looking after the clan. This is because of economic changes. Now the land is like an investment. It's weak to let the clan back on the land, letting *kastom* in through the back door. You can protect your rights through the law if you want, but once you've let them on the land it's very difficult. [my emphasis]

Unlikely as it may seem, the phrase 'reciprocal obligations' was Tony's exact English phrase in this conversation. Perhaps the presence of so many anthropologists in the area, in particular A.L. Epstein at Matupit, has sparked an interest in anthropology among better educated Tolai (as witnessed by Jacob Simet's career), leading these concepts to become part of the intellectual currency of this strata of Tolai society. Tony was unusual in his familiarity with anthropological concepts. But the views that he expressed were far from unique. I knew of many others who insisted on paying for such labour for the same reason of preventing the possibility of the work being characterised as 'customary' and thus being the basis for a claim in years to come. Again we see that attempts to distinguish family from other kinds of kinship, such as clans, are indistinguishable from tussles over the nature of inherently ambiguous transactions. By characterising the payment unambiguously as a commodity exchange ('that buys off any customary claim'), block holders attempt to remove the transaction from the ongoing web of reciprocal exchanges that characterise *kastom*, simultaneously separating family from clan. Payments themselves are often inherently ambiguous. In a context in which many 'payments' have only made sense in the context of a wider network of reciprocal exchange it is understandable that payments can be characterised as part of such networks or as stand-alone commodity exchanges. But the fact that the reality of many transactions is ambiguous does not remove the need for conceptual clarity in analysing such transactions. When Tolai say that the payments 'buy off' customary claims based on reciprocal interdependence, they are making a clear conceptual distinction between the two kinds of exchange contrasted by Gregory (1982), gift exchange based on ongoing reciprocal interdependence, and commodity exchange based on non-reciprocal independence. The fact that others in years to come may dispute this characterisation as part of an attempt to claim rights to the land only emphasises the importance of such conceptual clarity at the very moment that it makes the transaction itself empirically ambiguous and difficult to define.

Any transaction is itself merely a moment in a chain of other transactions (see for example Sahlins 1972:187). But the extent to which that fact is emphasised or obscured defines how the transaction is characterised, and that characterisation in turn may retrospectively finally define its character. Many Tolai at Sikut attempt to characterise their payments to relatives as commodity transactions. If in years to come attempts to challenge this characterisation of the transactions fail, then the payments will not be integrated into ongoing cycles of reciprocal obligation. Hence the original characterisation will become self-fulfilling. For now, in the immediate aftermath of the volcano, there is no way of knowing which characterisations of these transactions will prevail and whether the work of the relatives will be bought off. We know from the case of Vudal that often such attempts failed. In the example recounted above, according to the original block holder's children, the clan member of the original block holder was invited on to look after the block and was paid for doing so. 'My father gave him the [cocoa] trees to harvest to compensate him for his work, but the ground stayed underneath my father.' Or as this man's wife, present during our interview, interjected at a later point, the other man was paid to look after the block 'like a labourer'. This phrasing implies clearly the idea that the monetary payment wipes out any other claim that could be made on the basis of the labour. In the case of this block the attempt to limit claims by characterising the relationship as one of wage labour failed, although the extent to which this sets a 'customary' precedent that the generation now settling at Sikut will inevitably follow, is open to question. A future generation of anthropologists may have the privilege of discovering the extent to which this is the case. For now we are faced with the different, but equally fascinating, task of ethnographically observing and analysing the moments in which the initial attempts to verbally characterise transactions are put in place. Such a moment, although it carries its own anthropological frustrations, offers a unique opportunity to observe how the distinction between gift exchange and commodity exchange plays out at a face to face level in the current Melanesian context. The two categories may sometimes be relevant less as alternative empirical descriptors of any transaction, than as alternative perspectives on what a transaction means depending upon how one sees its place within a wider context of transactions.

In forty years time, a follow-up study might find that attempts to divorce *kastom* as ritual from day-to-day reciprocal interdependence have been unsuccessful. There are a minority of Matupi who are convinced that such patterns should and will re-emerge at Sikut. For them the very emergence of customary ritual at Matupit is the first sign of this inevitable process. But even if this proves to be the case the rhetorical attempt to divorce *kastom* from day-to-day life is of immense significance. It shows at the very least that Papua New Guineans are conceptually separating the two, and in the process presenting the possibility of *kastom* as disembodied ritual.

Furthermore, Sikut block holders are not the only ones that seek to conceptually separate *kastom* from day-to-day life as a means of conceptually individuating themselves and their immediate families from kin-based networks of reciprocal interdependence. Such a strategy is central to the Big Shots' constitution of themselves as possessive individuals (after Macpherson 1962), as I describe in subsequent chapters. Many of those at the forefront of organising the introduction of customary ritual at Sikut are also the most adamant it will not affect their blocks or their children's futures. And even amongst the minority who are adamant that the introduction of customary ritual at Sikut presages the return of what is understood as matrilineal customary land tenure practices, I often heard comments at other times that seemed to express doubt as to the extent to which *kastom* was integrated with day-to-day life anymore. One person from among the minority who was convinced that customary land tenure would re-emerge at Sikut was Isaac ToLanger. He once told me that the big change was that in the past, feasts were almost an anticlimax and it was the work of preparing the feast that was important. 'Now we rely on the feast to be the actual glue . . . It is getting harder and harder to work *kastom*'. When I asked why, he told me that it was because *kastom* doesn't fit in with everyday life anymore due to each household now being individually more self-sufficient economically. From general observation and the detailed study that I pursued on a small number of household economies, it is clear that households vary widely in the degree to which they depend economically on ties of reciprocal interdependence or requests for assistance. Philip, who had a well-paid job working at a mine and who stressed his independence from *kastom*, was indeed the head of a household that was almost entirely economically self-sufficient, and he tended to buy what he needed out of his wages or cocoa money. ToAtun who denigrated the SDA for their selfishness, by contrast, was embedded in a myriad of webs of assistance involving circulation of labour, food and small amounts of money. Although it was not an absolute iron rule, there was a strong tendency for more economically successful persons to place greater stress on household independence, and to denigrate *kastom* or to stress its conceptual separation from everyday life. By contrast the less economically successful tended to place a greater emphasis on the importance of *kastom* in day-to-day life, and to express resentment of wealthier relatives who they claimed forgot their obligations. Among poorer Matupi there was, as one might expect, a greater reliance on day-to-day interdependence and reciprocal assistance. But even here, interestingly, there was much variation in the extent to which such networks or reciprocal assistance went along ties of kinship or had been negotiated on other bases such as friendship or household location. Each household was tied into a number of such relationships. Some of these followed ties of kinship of the kind that were expressed and cemented through customary ritual. Others seemed more 'voluntary'. Kinship provides a good basis upon which to build such relationships, but it is far from the only one, and not all kinship relations result in such day-to-day relationships of assistance. One cousin may live nearby and have an interest in pursuing such a relationship. Another may live several hours' journey away and have a greater interest in individual family independence. This shift in spatial organisation is another recent development. At the time of A.L. Epstein's original research, Matupi lived cheek by jowl with nearly all their significant kin. By the early 1990s, A.L. Epstein (1991) was writing about the social significance of Matupi being scattered all over the Gazelle, PNG, and even Australia. In the 1960s nearly all Matupi still lived in the village, but by 1986, A.L. Epstein could report that many were now living in other cities. He reports that according to Simet, there were 400 living in Port Moresby at the time, mainly as 'members of the new urban elite' (A.L. Epstein 1988:33). Many who worked in Rabaul Town now also lived there rather than in villages, which had the attraction of 'putting a distance between themselves and their kin, and escaping at least some of the burdensome claims that kinsfolk can assert' (ibid.).

Even the move to Sikut had significance in and of itself. One man with a well-paid clerical job with the Provincial Government living at Sikut told me that the *wantok* system had been 'much worse at Matupit, because everyone was living close together. Every fortnight on payday they were around. Here, even if they live at Sikut, it's harder for them to get to you. It's much better! I have to help them if I'm unlucky enough to bump into them in town though'. I observed that there tended to be a much greater frequency of demands and requests made during the course of the day at places where people lived close together, such as at Matupit or at the Sikut care centre, by comparison to the situation at the outlying Sikut blocks, and the man explained that proximity and convenience was itself the major cause of the difference in frequency of demands. Even amongst those poorer households that were more reliant upon ties of reciprocal assistance there was a wide differentiation in the extent to which such ties formed the basis of day-to-day household survival. Consequently they varied in the extent to which the kind of ritual described as *kastom* was felt to be separate from day-to-day life.

More generally, people's attempts to separate *kastom* out from other aspects of everyday life are another way in which they are using particular conceptualisations of *kastom* as an attempted means of limiting claims that can be made on the basis of a history of exchange and reciprocal interdependence. As we shall see in subsequent chapters, such a rhetorical strategy is central to the success of many of the emerging indigenous elite, the so-called 'Big Shots'. Very few Matupi, except members of the new evangelical churches and more devout members of the SDA, would be likely to claim to reject *kastom* in its totality. Yet the attempt to delimit *kastom*, or to claim that customary obligations and relations should be acknowledged in some contexts and not in others, is a key component of attempts to assert or reject claims to individual autonomy.

Notes

1. See T.S. Epstein (1968:126–29) for an example from the early 1960s of a man whose cash cropping led him to be 'caught in the dilemma created by the contradictory pulls emanating from his relationship with his kin-group on the one hand and with his son on the other'.
2. I discuss below the historically shifting meanings of a Kuanua word covering some of the same meanings as the English 'family' and Tok Pisin *famili*.
3. T.S. Epstein (1968:83–84) also reports this pattern for the Tolai village of Rapitok.
4. See also Bradley (1982:191–92) for more on *bartamana*'s origin in a term to describe 'people who stand in some relationship to each other'.
5. See also A.L. Epstein (1969:210–15) for another discussion of this.
6. This critical perspective was expressed in Tok Pisin conversations using the word *bisnis* (business), or alternatively using the English loanword 'market' itself.

7. See for example the entry headed 'Informant Tarai Herman and observation' dated 01.02.1960.
8. Indeed their major customary involvement seemed to be with the man's father's clan in New Ireland. There he had conducted a large feast involving 100 pigs in the late 1980s as a means of securing over ten hectares of land from his father's clan on which he was going to plant cocoa trees.
9. I do not give many details of the two sides' stories here for fear of prejudicing any possible outcome.

6

Kastom and Contested Reciprocity

Kastom has become central to debates about the how Tolai should behave in the twenty-first century. For example, as we have seen, this category is central to the negotiation of the appropriate relationship between the family-based household and the more extended kinship obligations of the *vunatarai*. This is the case both for the face to face interactions at the village level, and for the macro-level debates of policy formulation and implementation. The resettlement at Sikut, carried out under the auspices of the Gazelle Restoration Authority (GRA), is clearly operating under the premise of non-customary land holding. While the reality on the ground is more complex, the policy pursued by the GRA is premised upon an assumption that *kastom* would not be a positive influence in the arena of land tenure. This rests upon another assumption; that the extended claims of kinship-based obligation, often justified with reference to *kastom* are damaging to the potential for individual households to pursue economic development, and that it is with regard to access to land that this damaging effect is particularly noticeable. As such *kastom* is negatively evaluated in this context. However, *kastom* is not perceived as a universally negative category. By tracing some of the different ways in which the category is used we can begin to appreciate how for Tolai this term does not refer to a fixed set of practices, but is a tool in an ongoing struggle over the appropriateness of certain kinds of behaviour, and in particular, the appropriate limits of reciprocity.

Lindstrom (2008:162) discusses the ways in which *kastom* has become 'subject to much debate and revaluation . . . as globalisation has accentuated and further unsettled definitions of locality, indigeneity, and home'. Hence *kastom* today is best not understood either in terms of a quest for its origins, which some scholars understand as a kind of 'invented tradition' pursued by nation building elites in the run-up to and aftermath of independence (see Lindstrom op cit., for an overview of these debates), but rather as a shifting term of moral evaluation. Around this term, for example, elites make strategic appeals to aspects of a 'traditional' past in order to shape particular kinds of national futures. As Lindstrom (op cit.:168) notes, 'A symbiotics of *kastom*

remarked obvious differences between village uses and understandings of tradition and nationalist *kastom*, and also noted how *kastom*, at both the village and national levels, reflected those different contexts'. This means, as Akin (2004:299) astutely observes, that anthropological fixations on *kastom* as 'the objectification of culture' in 'the realm of overt cultural politics' misses the equally important continuous and ongoing 'subjectivization of *kastom* as culture'. Or as Tonkinson (2000:170) observes, *kastom* can be seen as 'a body of beliefs, orientations and practices that, while inviting perceptions of continuity, stability and shared identity, possess an inherent potential for manipulation and contestation'. Acrosss much of the southwestern Pacific region, *kastom* has become a battleground for contestation at all social levels, from elite contests over the nature of postcolonial nation building to village level land disputes. The category's salience in social contests is closely related to the ways the term that can potentially cover a wide range of social actions and be defined by opposition to a wide variety of other concepts (see Otto 1992, as well as Keane 2007:103 for a discussion of the wide range of meanings for the similar term *adat* in Sumba, Indonesia).

Kastom versus Business or 'Not-*Kastom*'

Although it is often contrasted with categories such as 'business', the modern world, or the ways of white people, *kastom* is just as often contrasted with its own direct negation, 'not-*kastom*'. The word *kastom* is used in many ways in contemporary Tolai society. One pattern is for the word to be unambiguously presented as something positive to be defended. This is the use that readers of Melanesian ethnographies will be most familiar with, and is perhaps closest to the one which most Tolai would give if asked to describe what *kastom* meant. It is this meaning that the ToAtun, quoted in the previous chapter, was invoking when he contrasted *kastom* with the alleged Westernised greed of the Seventh Day Adventists. Socially valued activities are frequently described as *kastom*. Often this refers to day-to-day patterns of respect, such as the ongoing reciprocal sharing of small items such as food, betel nut, and cigarettes, although this kind of activity would also often be described as *pasin* (TP. 'way, lifestyle'). Bigger ritual events that are often presented as being tied into this ethos of reciprocity are nearly always described as *kastom* in order to highlight their value, especially in contrast to the perceived corrosive effects of modernisation on respectful social relations. Among the Tolai, many of these ritual events involve the large-scale distribution of *tabu* to mark occasions such as marriages or deaths. The best known of these customary practices and the one that archetypally symbolises Tolai *kastom* to other Papua New Guineans is the raising of the *tubuan*: the masked figure that embodies ancestral spirits, and demonstrates the power and capacities of the clans and Big Men involved in its display.

The involvement of the indigenous elite, or 'Big Shots', in ritual is often dismissed as not being _kastom_. Their motives are allegedly commercial. They use their financial power to organise events that the previous generation of Big Men is said to have organised instead through careful attention to reciprocal obligations at the village level. Big Shots are accused of many sins, most notably 'commercialising' _kastom_ in general and the _tubuan_ in particular. Some of these stories seem a little far-fetched. One Big Shot is alleged to have sold photographs of the _tubuan_ to a 'German internet company' for 10 million Kina. On another occasion, I was told by one person that the same Big Shot had sold the right to paint a picture of one of his _tubuans_ to a Chinese owned supermarket in the nearby town of Kokopo. Again the story seemed unlikely, as dozens of Matupi visited the store every day and would instantly have noticed it. However, the story served to illustrate a general and ongoing fear that the Big Shots used _kastom_ for their own commercial advantage. It also served to illustrate their alleged hypocrisy. This particular Big Shot often accused the grassroots of having abandoned the meaning and correct practice of _kastom_ (see also Moran 2003:295). But look at the hypocrisy, my interlocutor demanded, adding that this is the same man who is firm about stopping men selling _kastom_ to other people. (In his capacity as a custodian of _kastom_, this particular Big Shot was well known for having stopped outsiders, in particular Australian businesses, from using _tubuan_ images for commercial purposes.) Due to their financial power, Big Shots often have leading roles in the organisation of customary ritual, but it is no wonder that they are often distrusted when they attempt to enforce what they see as the correct rules for the conduct of _kastom_. Their attempts to enforce rules forbidding the selling of _kastom_ are cast by many grassroots villagers as nothing more than self-serving efforts to preserve their monopoly on profiting from _kastom_'s 'commercialisation'. However unlikely some of these stories may be, and however much these stories are disparaged by Big Shots and their supporters as 'cargo cult' thinking, their resonance and persistence suggests that they deserve to be taken as seriously by anthropologists as 'cargo cult' stories of forty years ago, stories that were similarly denounced by the elites of that time (in the person of colonial rulers).

Other stories that seem to be more within the realm of possibility provide the context within which taller tales make sense. It was often said of a certain Matupit Big Shot that he gained large profits from 'customary' dances organised by his tourism company for the benefit of visiting Japanese tourists, but that he gave the boys from the village who took part nothing but a few uncooked bananas as payment. Such activities are denounced as not being _kastom_ as they are organised on spurious pretexts that are a cover for the real purposes of promoting tourism, making money, or as my previous interlocutor put it, 'selling *kastom*'. Real *kastom* of the kind supposedly organised by the big men of before was only carried out in response to the needs of village life, such as marking marriages or deaths or the relations between clans. On this basis, some people attacked not only tourist dances organised for commercial profit, but even government organised cultural events (also partly designed to promote tourism), such as the Mask Festival. One man from Matupit told me:

> You can't just raise a *tubuan*. *Tubuans* have work pulling clans together, showing who is related to who when someone dies. In the past the real big men would never have allowed a *tubuan* to be raised just for tourists. They would have said if a tourist wants to see the *tubuan*, they have to wait until the time for the *tubuan* to do its work. But now they just raise the *tubuan* to make money so they can pay off their debt to the lousy World Bank.

By contrast one Big Shot heavily involved in *kastom* and the planning of the Mask Festival told me at a later interview that all the talk about commercialising *kastom* and the *tubuan* could not be true because he followed all the rules for preparing these events. People who criticised him on this score obviously did not know *kastom*. For him commercialisation would have meant breaking the rules on raising *tubuans* or performing *kastom* – perhaps skipping the elaborate secret preparations that some customary events require and simply performing the eye-catching dances when the tourists arrive. For his critics, however, he and others had already broken an important 'rule' by raising *tubuans* and performing *kastom* for an illegitimate, allegedly commercial reason. The desire to use *kastom* to make money, and the lack of attention to reciprocal village relations in and of themselves made these events not *kastom* but 'commercial'.

Much of what happens in wedding or mortuary feasts is only understandable if one takes seriously the ways in which Tolai often describe them as events of making and marking significant social relations, in patterns that any student of Melanesian ethnography would find familiar. However, to leave the story there would be to mislead by significant omission. On one occasion I attended a mortuary feast known as a *minamai* for a well-respected Big Man in a nearby Tolai village. The journey to attend this feast was also made by many prominent persons from across the Tolai area and by 'expatriate' Tolai Big Shots, working senior public servants and the like, in the national capital of Port Moresby.[1] Afterwards I sat talking with Tony Danett. He described to me what had happened at the feast, in particular the rounds of distribution of customary shell-wealth or *tabu*. At the same time, he described the relationships – above all the relationships between the dead man's family and clan, on the one hand, and 'children' of the clan, on the other – that the distributions marked and cemented.[2] Following his description of the relations that were acknowledged in the exchanges of the feast, though, he turned his attention to one of the Tolai politicians who had returned from Port Moresby for the feast. When this man comes and throws around the *tabu* that he bought in Port Moresby, Tony told me, 'it's not *kastom*, it's a fucking pastiche'.

Rather than symbolising, confirming and remaking the careful attention to reciprocal obligations of village and clan life by which previous generations of big men were described as having accumulated their stocks of *tabu*, the Big Shot's distribution was merely a display of his financial wealth. His shells were likely bought in bulk from the Solomon Islands or Vanuatu, where some people made a business of selling them by the caseload to wealthy Tolai. Often in Port Moresby these Big Shots would pay less wealthy Tolai a wage to string the shells onto cane strips and thus turn them into *tabu*, in what was described to me as a '*tabu* factory'. As far as Tony was concerned, such a display could not be described as *kastom*, or at least should be contrasted with 'real' custom (see also Eves 2000, on denigration of 'store bought' customary shell-wealth in nearby New Ireland). Tony's disdain was not a rejection of *kastom* per se, in the manner for example of the most conscientious Seventh Day Adventists. Tony was a strong supporter of the potential power of customary ritual to stabilise social relations, and was responsible for the introduction of some customary rituals at Sikut. His son was the first to have a *namata* conducted in his honour at Sikut, and the ritual took place at his block. If anything, Tony's problem with Big Shots' involvement in customary ritual was that growing disdain for Big Shots and their wealth threatened the credibility of customs that he thought potentially still had social value.[3]

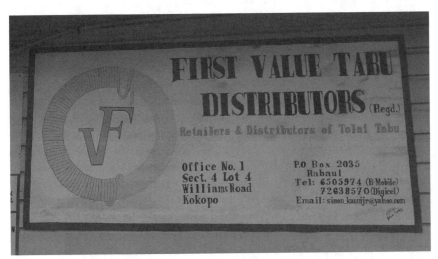

10. Sign advertising a business selling Tolai *tabu* in Kokopo Town

Likewise the Big Shot may have 'bought' the 'customary' knowledge that enables him to prepare these events with *tabu*. Previous generations of Big Men did this as well. But whereas the *tabu* that they acquired in the village reflected the respect they built up there, the Big Shot's *tabu* reflects nothing but his 'money-power' in the eyes of some critics. The Big Shots attempt to defend their right to be considered 'customary' against charges of commercialisation by reference to the observation of customary rules. This claimed adherence to rules for the distribution of wealth at customary events insulates their performance of <u>kastom</u> from any moral evaluation in terms of attention to what the grassroots consider to be suitable displays of day-to-day reciprocity. The attempt by Big Shots to claim customary legitimacy on the basis of adherence to codified rules (to which they have privileged access) is disputed by some as an attempt to escape moral accountability to the village. Matthew was a man in his early forties living with his parents at Matupit. He was well-educated, but was one of the many who found it hard to find employment in the aftermath of the eruption. Matthew now eked out a living from fishing and the <u>wantok</u> system. When I asked him to sum up the difference between the Big Men of today and before: 'You had to be chosen by the community. You had to have the respect of the community. With "money-power", you hold the power yourself' (TP. *yu yet yu holim pawa*). These disputes over the meaning and effect of *tabu* are important. Just as our understanding of key linguistic signifiers such as <u>kastom</u> requires a break with Saussurian assumptions of shared fixed codes of meaning, likewise our understanding of key material semiotic signifiers such as *tabu* requires a similar break and careful ethnographic inquiry into the shifting and contested meanings that people try to give to such signifiers in particular moments.

Critics question not just the origins of the Big Shots' *tabu*, but the way they distribute it as well. The returning politician from Port Moresby criticised by Tony was a child of the deceased's clan, and as such joined other children of the clan in distributing *tabu* to members of the dead man's clan at one point in the feast. ToAtun discussed the event with me a few days later and told me that he too was a member of the dead man's clan, but that this Big Shot and others avoided him and other grassroots villagers. Instead they picked out other Big Shots who were members of the deceased's clan to receive large public distributions of *tabu*. Of course, he complained, they would have known that he was a member of the clan; it's just that they were not worried about people like him. ToAtun made his complaint with an air more of wry resignation than anger, suggesting to me that such behaviour was so well-entrenched that it had long ago ceased to be truly shocking. This example illustrates well that it is the context within which customary practices are enacted that largely determines how they are morally evaluated, rather than such practices being a matter of uniform, cross-cutting adherence to 'custom' as a set of tradition derived rules. The ethnographic record makes clear that Big Men have long sought out fellow Big Men at such events and made a point of publicly presenting them with large amounts of *tabu*. Salisbury (1966:121) describes distribution at mortuary rituals in the following terms: 'Any important man present seizes the opportunity to *tabar* [K. 'give to' –KM] all and sundry, but especially other important men . . . Although these distributions are "made to everyone," larger shares are given to important people' (see also Salisbury 1970:295, 305; A.L. Epstein 1969:241, 1992:193). As one of the foremost grassroots experts on customary practice amongst the Matupi, ToAtun would have been aware of the long history of this kind of practice. But these actions are morally suspect by virtue of the new networks of political and economic inequality of which they are now a part.

Unlike the dances organised for tourists, mortuary distributions, such as those just described, appear on the surface to fit the criteria for 'real' *kastom*, as they are organised for legitimate customary reasons. But the involvement of Big Shots in them is still open to criticism from a grassroots perspective. Criticisms of the 'tourist' events and the Big Shot involvement in 'real' *kastom* have a common basis: the activities of Big Shots are not imbued with the reciprocal spirit that ideally marks *kastom*. The 'fake' *kastom* of events like the tourist dances was not part of the recognition of reciprocal obligations of the village, but instead was portrayed as a disembodied pastiche designed for commercial enrichment. The distribution of the fruits of these enterprises also leads to the Big Shot being devalued in customary terms. Rather than make payments in a manner that acknowledged ongoing reciprocal relations, by adequately recompensing those young men who danced for him, the organiser allegedly treated them, as one man angrily put it, as 'work boys': he paid them a simple (and allegedly low) wage from which he profited, as part of his general pattern of treating *kastom* as a 'business'. The phrase 'work boy' (TP. *wokboi*) has powerful connotations linked to memories of the colonial era and the alleged heartlessness of colonial overseers who forced Melanesians to labour like slaves on plantations for a pittance.

Yet this perspective is not universally held. Big Shots and their supporters among the village's grassroots present things differently. Tourist dances can be presented as providing a valuable opportunity to 'learn *kastom*'. One young man who had a marginal involvement in *kastom*, largely as a result of his distrust of the Big Shots, once described to me an argument that he had been involved in a few years previously. The Big Shot tour operator had returned to the village one day to recruit young men to dance for a Japanese tour party that was soon to arrive in Rabaul. This young man told other young men that they were fools to get involved because they would be 'exploited', as he put it using the English word. They angrily responded that it was their only chance to learn *kastom*, the Big Shot involved being an acknowledged expert in customary ritual and knowledge. Although the young man told me that subsequently many of them had come around to his way of thinking as the result of bitter experience, the strength of their initial response indicates that they felt at the time that they would gain more from the transaction than payment alone.

But from the perspective of those who have a negative moral evaluation of these events and the Big Shot's role in them, these 'customary' performances are the commonplace opposite of _kastom_: they are 'business'. Another man told me how arguments sometimes erupted when village men agreed to work for returning Big Shots preparing _kastom_: 'Why should you want to be his labourer?' others will challenge them. Again this vision of such practices is not held by all, but it is widespread, and many people's decision to withhold the description 'customary' from these kinds of events amounts to a powerful moral critique of what is perceived to be an unpleasant social change.

Likewise the Big Shots' involvement in 'real' _kastom_ can still be denounced as non-customary for the same kind of reasons. The *tabu* that they distributed is not the result of ongoing reciprocal obligations, but a commodity that they buy with what Matthew described to me as 'money-power'. Matthew told me that there wasn't this kind of 'money-power' before, and then went on to disparage Big Shots who came back to the village for _kastom_ and gave out five bags of rice. People may not publicly voice their discontent; grassroots find it hard to find the money to buy rice in postcolonial PNG, and not many people in that position are going to reject patronage. But they often describe the Big Shot's gift differently from a smaller one given by someone with less money. The Big Shot's gift shows nothing but their 'money-power', Matthew explained. Despite the fact that they show up to the village for _kastom_ to distribute rice, as far as he was concerned, 'they're not involved in village life'. Because they gain their power from a cash economy rather than the day-to-day reciprocal interdependence of village life, they can isolate themselves from day-to-day requests for assistance in a manner that was impossible for a previous generation of village-based Big Men. The way that they often distributed gifts at customary events likewise betrayed in the eyes of some grassroots villagers a lack of understanding or concern for the recognition of the ongoing ties of reciprocal obligation between persons and clans that are supposed to underpin the customary ethic. Instead they allegedly ignore those whose reciprocal indebtedness they should acknowledge, and only give gifts that cement their relationship to others of similar high esteem. In all of these examples a negative moral judgement has been made that the Big Shots do not embody customary values, even when they are performing _kastom_.

It is common to read in Melanesian ethnography of the ways in which _kastom_ absorbs Western commodities and turns them into gifts of the kind by which Melanesians make explicit their reciprocal interdependence (see for example Strathern 1988:81). Even a writer who places great emphasis on describing social change, such as Gregory, largely adopts this schema. In a discussion of ritual gift exchange depicted in the film *The Trobriand Islanders*, Gregory initially observed that:

> As one might expect, the chiefs have appropriated the symbols of commodity status and wealth . . . of importance today are the things that money can buy such as Benson and Hedges cigarettes, watches, cement for the graves of deceased chiefs, Toyota four-wheel drive vehicles, and so on. The borrowing and lending of money among chiefs has introduced a new element into their power game. (Gregory 1997:55)

However, the main point being made in this analysis concerns 'the crucial transformation of' commodities (via intermediary stages) into gifts (Gregory op cit.:56): 'This roundabout way of acquiring a gift keeps the alien world of commodities at bay, not by erecting a *cordon sanitaire* around the island, but by providing a means by which commodities can be domesticated and transformed into gifts' (ibid.).

While such an account may accurately describe many situations in contemporary Papua New Guinea, the examples I have cited above suggest this account does not fit *all* situations. In the Tolai instances, the commodity origin of the *tabu* or the rice being distributed by a Big Shot still shines through, leading to claims that its money-power origins make it non-customary. The customary *tabu* distributed along clan lines is not itself a commodity in these contexts.[4] But the commodity origin of the *tabu* is often not forgotten and hence the transactions are not worthy of the positive description of *kastom*.

The Pastiche Gift as Partial Social Fact

In later chapters of this book I discuss in more detail how Big Shots seek to restrict or 'delimit' *kastom*, and the ethic of reciprocal interdependence associated with it, to the sphere of customary ritual, as part of their self-constitution as Possessive Individuals with no inherent obligations. Yet it is precisely this effort that transforms their attempts at *kastom* into pastiche in the eyes of many. The gift that is given is partial by virtue of its delimitation, rather than being a '*total* social phenomenon', in which 'all kinds of institutions find simultaneous expression: religious, legal, moral, and economic' (Mauss 1970:1). Its effects of altering emerging social and economic relations of inequality are certainly minimal. Hence the money that bought it as a commodity is still visible to many Matupi, even as the object is exchanged as a gift. Rather than domesticating the commodity, in the eyes of many the gift's commodity origin and its delimitation turns it from a powerful total social phenomenon into a partial pastiche-gift. Indeed, when Tolai complain about Big Shots 'commercialising' or 'buying' *kastom*, in the context of conversations about bulk purchase of *tabu*, the gift exchange of *kastom* is presented as the means by which the Big Shots' 'money-power' manifests itself, rather than the arena in which it is domesticated.

So far I have concentrated on the moral judgements made about Big Shots' involvement in *kastom*, and the perspective on cultural change reflected in the judgement that their involvement is not customary. However, the activities of Big Shots are not the only focus of critical moral judgement on cultural change whereby villagers describe something as 'not *kastom*'. Other groups are also described as having 'commercialised' *kastom*. Matthew described in the following terms other PNG ethnic groups' practice of charging 'customary' bridewealth payments of up to 50,000 Kina: 'I can't see *kastom* in this . . . It's not *kastom*. You sell – you feel like you've gone to a kind of a market . . . another man's competing with you . . . it goes to the highest bidder . . . the highest bidder pays the "bride-price". Another group wants to buy this woman, they try to outbid the other group'.

Matthew went on to describe how when he was living in Port Moresby he had a friend from another PNG region who was the son of a politician. Because of his father's supposed wealth, this friend was expected to pay 35,000 Kina 'bride-price' when he married.[5] As with the example of the tourist dances, where a contrast was drawn between *kastom* and 'business', in this case there is a distinction made between *kastom* and 'a market'. In both cases *kastom* is clearly defined on the basis of the morality of exchange practices. Certain kinds of 'customary' practices (in the one case traditional dances, in the other the exchange of valuables at marriage) are denied the positive evaluation of *kastom* because they have allegedly become 'commercialised'. This example also illustrates the way in which *kastom* becomes a marker of group ethnic identity in postcolonial PNG, with Matthew contrasting this habit of people from another PNG region with Tolai bride payments which according to my him was 'still customary', as it was only shell-money, and maybe a little state currency. Papua New Guineans in general can present *kastom* as something that distinguishes them and marks their difference from 'Westerners', stating that 'our' custom that is based on sharing and respect is what distinguishes 'us' from 'you' with your lifestyles based on individualism, and so forth. In other contexts, *kastom* can be presented as the thing that distinguishes one ethnic group of Papua New Guineans from another.

This example also illustrates how what is referred to by the word *kastom* is context dependent. There is a seeming contradiction in the way that Matthew describes Tolai *kastom*. In one conversation it is positively morally evaluated, as still being *kastom* by virtue of the non-market ethic it embodies, by contrast to commodified bride-price customs in other parts of PNG. Yet in other conversations, he dismisses it for precisely the same reason, as having been corrupted by the 'money-power' of Big Shots. Matthew was very active in the Seventh Day Adventist Church at the time of my first fieldwork, and publicly eschewed involvement in *kastom*. As such his statements dismissing *kastom* might seem to make some sense, and his more positive evaluations of *kastom* could appear somewhat anomalous. Yet these different perspectives only constitute an insurmountable contradiction if we imagine that *kastom* is a word with a fundamental meaning; a linguistic sign that references a single concept. But instead of just being a word that refers to a certain set of practices or actions, *kastom* is often used as means of evaluating the morality of people's actions (whether the speaker's or others), and as such helps to form perspectives on social change. In particular it is used to form judgements regarding reciprocity and non-reciprocity. Is Tolai *kastom kastom*? That depends on what the speaker is attempting to morally evaluate with the word *kastom* at any given time. By describing something as 'customary', one is not necessarily assessing whether or not it fits within a list of certain practices that come under the heading of *kastom* in the Tok Pisin dictionary. Sometimes one is forming a moral judgement as to whether or not one judges it to still embody the requisite acknowledgement of customary reciprocity in an era of social change. In some contexts, such as denigrating the lack of moral obligation that is seemingly felt by a new generation of leaders, or the greed of Papuans alleged to proffer their daughters on the bride-price market in a commercial manner, then 'true' *kastom* and the ethic of reciprocal obligation that it ideally embodies is something positive to be defended. In this critique at least, it is necessary to uphold the positive ideal of *kastom*, in order for the Big Shots' fake *kastom* to be deprecated.

So far I have concentrated on the ways in which *kastom* is evaluated positively by examining contexts in which people declare an action or sentiment to be non-customary, as a way of expressing moral disapproval of it. I would like to briefly mention the ways in which *kastom* can also be given negative evaluations in people's views on social change. The most common of these is the argument that *kastom* is a large part of what holds PNG back. Expectations of sharing of material goods, and the performance of customary rituals, such as those outlined above are derided as costly and wasteful remnants of the past that leave people unable to develop business or look after their own family properly. On general election day in June 2002, I spent time outside of the Matupit polling station chatting with people waiting for their turn to vote. One voter put clearly to me why he felt that the problems facing PNG in general and Matupit in particular could not be solved by politicians: 'Lots of money goes on *kastom* . . . it's expensive'. Numerous businesses failed as a result, he told me, pointing to the big ceremony that had been held at

Matupit the previous year as an example. 'Men don't look after their own backyard, but they spend up to a thousand Kina on *kastom*, even if they've got leaking roofs'. Here as in many of the idealised descriptions of the 'true custom' of the Big Men of forty years ago, *kastom* is a thing of the past, but this time it is a hangover from an inferior past, counterposed to a superior modern way of living, much as living without cannibalism is counterposed to the previous state of 'darkness'.[6]

One example of this is a story told to me by a senior member of the Seventh Day Adventist Church at Matupit. He told me that as a young man, while the church tabooed nearly all customary ritual, he like many church members had a quite deep involvement with them in practice. As he became older, he claimed to have become increasingly aware of the wastefulness of *kastom* and its role in exacerbating the poverty of grassroots Papua New Guineans. In common with all Matupi senior enough to take a leading role in *kastom*, he kept a kind of ledger of accounts of customary 'debts' (TP. *dinau*) owed and due. If a person helps with a relative's initiation or mortuary rituals, that person is supposed to keep a record of this and wait for a suitable opportunity to repay the 'debt', which is most likely to be of food or *tabu*. Sometimes one may have to wait decades for a suitable opportunity to repay, but when such an opportunity occurs the parties involved will normally recognise it and 'repayment' will be expected. The SDA member I spoke with had made a decision that he wanted to remove himself from these wasteful cycles of obligation.[7] So one day, he collected all of his *tabu* and his ledger book and publicly went around the village 'repaying' each 'customary' debt that he was owed. He simultaneously told everyone who 'owed' him that their 'debt' was written off. Following this he gave all of his remaining *tabu* to a relative who was still involved in *kastom*, keeping back just a little for his son in case he needed *tabu* to buy a bride. He told me that this action 'bought him out' of *kastom*, and clearly was not a 'customary' act. And this view was shared by everyone else at Matupit who I discussed this story with. It was not a 'customary' act because the timing of the repayments was inappropriate. To pay off his debts at the 'wrong' time robbed them of the meaning they would have if he had patiently waited to pay them at a time that publicly acknowledged the importance of his relationship to that person. By instead publicly making a point of his right to discharge his obligations at a time of his own choosing, he was asserting the ability to treat his obligations as a pure commodity 'debt', and therefore cutting himself out of ongoing ceremonial cycles, even while he simultaneously acknowledged that he had previously been enmeshed in them.

Almost as striking as this man's act was the response to it expressed by non-Tolai from the neighbouring province of New Ireland, who were also members of matrilineal groups with many similarities of customary practice. When I relayed this story to them they were at first shocked: such a public removal from *kastom* would be impossible in their villages, they said. This was often followed by an assertion that of course one would expect that kind of thing among the Tolai, for whom money was now more important that *kastom* (see also Foster 1995:256 fn. 29). Whether or not a person sympathised with this total discharge of customary obligations or was horrified by it, everyone understood how it expressed this individual's underlying negative assessment of *kastom*. From the point of view of grassroots supporters of *kastom*, this action can be described as 'not custom' for similar reasons as Big Shots' involvement in *kastom*; namely that it does not adequately acknowledge and deepen ongoing reciprocal obligations. Many grassroots persons nonetheless positively evaluate this man's actions by comparison to the practices of Big Shots, in that at least the man's actions were 'honest' and not based on self-enrichment. He himself would wholeheartedly agree that his actions are 'not custom', but for him this is positive. Everyone would agree that, although his actions involved payment of *tabu* to discharge customary debts, the manner in which it was done made the act non-customary.

For some people *kastom* is so intrinsically 'corrupted' that at certain points they use the word in a negative sense precisely because *kastom* is now viewed as a central part of the inequalities that are viewed as being characteristic of social change. Sometimes *kastom* is described as being nothing more than a tool by which Big Shots use their financial power to assert control over the grassroots. Because *kastom* no longer lives up to the ideal, rather than contest whether certain actions fulfil the reciprocal morality of *kastom*, people turn the term itself into an insult. Often (though not always) this rejection of *kastom* is articulated by the same people who attack *kastom* for embodying outdated tradition (as outlined above), in particular members of the Seventh Day Adventists and other anti-*kastom* denominations. These kinds of views are expressed, for example, in discussions surrounding the national PNG Mask Festival that is held annually in the Rabaul area. The Mask Festival is organised by the National Cultural Commission, a branch of the PNG national government whose stated mission is to 'preserve, promote and protect PNG's custom and culture'. As such, the Mask Festival would appear to be one of the events that best illustrated the ways in which *kastom* is part of an elite-produced 'discourse of custom and tradition that seeks to ground national distinctiveness in definitions of indigenous ancestral ways' (Foster 1995:1). As we shall see, however, 'behind the scenes' it is more strikingly the focus of deprecation and a site of conflict between economic winners and losers in the postcolonial state. Some Seventh Day Adventists told me that it was wrong for church members even to attend the Mask Festival as spectators, as just viewing the dances and artefacts on display, especially those of the local *tubuan*, was to involve oneself in *kastom*. However, as we would expect, the Mask Festival could also be criticised for not embodying customary values.

There was constant complaint that the Mask Festival was used to make money and *tabu* for Big Shots who had governmental contacts, and that the ordinary grassroots Tolai who did the work in the bush of preparing customary displays did not adequately benefit. This complaint could take the form already discussed: a rejection of such activities' right to be described as *kastom*. Rather than embody the reciprocal ideology of *kastom*, the activities were for the personal enrichment of a new elite. The complaints could also, however, take a different form in which such manipulation by powerful elites was described as the basis of *kastom*. In such conversations, the ideal form of *kastom* as the manifestation of a socially egalitarian reciprocity was implicitly acknowledged. But rather than current practices being seen as particular examples of cases where *kastom* had been corrupted, critics stressed that *kastom* never attained this ideal – it was an inherently hypocritical word, always used in the interests of self-serving elites.

There is much ambiguity in these descriptions concerning how much the inherently hypocritical nature of *kastom* was tied to modern social changes. Sometimes Adventists were keen to stress that *kastom* had always been corrupt, and had always been about Big Men empowering themselves at the expense of other villagers. At other times, although they would often acknowledge the official church doctrine that most forms of *kastom* were inherently bad, they also made the familiar argument that *kastom* as performed by the previous generation of Big Men was different from the *kastom* of today's Big Shots.

During one Mask Festival, I mentioned to Eli, a senior Seventh Day Adventist at Matupit, that a female German tourist had gone right up to the dancing *tubuans* to take photographs, something that was allegedly strictly taboo. Eli was my host at Matupit for several months and I spent a lot of time with him and his family. In his early sixties at the time of my first fieldwork, Eli had previously worked as an administrator for mining companies and had enjoyed a very high standard of living that had largely been destroyed by the volcano. He was very active in rebuilding his family's life, however, having a resettlement block at Sikut and also renting a nine hectare block near the Sikut resettlement from the Provincial Government, a large section of which he had already planted with cocoa. Eli had been active in the *tubuan* society in his youth, but had ceased to be involved decades earlier, when he began to take the SDA's prohibitions on this more seriously. Yet his response to the story of the German tourist was a strong one. The *tubuan* organisers who were very strict to enforce customary rules in other contexts did nothing. Eli was clearly angry, and responded by saying, 'they can commercialise their *kastom* if they like, that's their business'. Although his statement carried the explicit meaning that he had given up his earlier heavy involvement in *kastom* and he didn't care what happened to it, the statement also expressed a great anger

11. Matupit residents on the beach at Matupit with souvenirs made of *tabu*

about the abuse of <u>*kastom*</u>, in particular the idea that customary rules could be broken for a few tourist dollars. While based on the same moral criticism of Big Shots as that of other people who denounce the commercialisation of <u>*kastom*</u>, Eli's rhetorical strategy is different. Rather than engage in a battle over ownership of the category, he cedes it to them, ('they can commercialise their custom') in the hope of underlining that as something solely owned by them, <u>*kastom*</u> does not embody the ethic of reciprocity. Rather than contest the Big Shots' right to claim the reciprocal ethic underpinning <u>*kastom*</u>, he instead aims to expose how <u>*kastom*</u> had been tainted by their ownership to the point of being inherently negative. This is backed up by the number of other occasions that Eli told me that <u>*kastom*</u> was a 'con', or a 'trick', by which Big Shots got the grassroots to work for them.

<u>*Kastom*</u> as Expression of Social Contradiction

These different tactics for dealing with <u>*kastom*</u> as a positively valued trait – either contesting the right of the elite to use it, or claiming that their ownership of it makes it inherently hypocritical – may seem on the surface contradictory. Yet we are familiar with a similar shifting of orientations towards key terms in political debates in Western societies. Radical critics of capitalist society may reject the concept of 'democracy' as being fundamentally bourgeois because it is based on a separation of the people from the state, but those same critics can also denounce the bourgeois state for being 'undemocratic' on occasion, i.e. for proving itself unable to even live up to its own limited ideals. Here, strategic use of the concept of 'democracy' depends upon the context of utterance, on whom one is addressing and the issues being discussed. It is this that gives 'democracy' its meaning as a: 'construct between socially organized persons in the process of their interaction . . . *conditioned above all by the social organization of the participants involved and also by the immediate conditions of their interaction*' (Volosinov 1973:21, emphasis in original). The same applies to the different meanings that *kastom* acquires in the interrelationship between speaker and listener at Matupit.

My aim in this chapter has been to present an ethnographic description of some of the ways in which the word *kastom* is used at Matupit today. We have seen that *kastom* is contrasted with both its axiomatic opposite ('not-*kastom*'), and with its commonplace opposites (such as a market, business or pastiche).[8] As a marker of adherence to reciprocity, as we have seen, *kastom* has no single meaning. And this should be no surprise. There is no consensus about the appropriate limits of reciprocity at Matupit today, so we should not expect consensus about the remit of words that refer to that ethic. Many disputes and arguments turn not on whether or not reciprocity is a positive value, but on the appropriate limits of reciprocity. At what point should one cease to acknowledge the interlocking obligations of oneself or one's group to others to whom one is socially related? The fraught relationship between a man's children and his nephews, or in other words between a clan and its children, is only one example. And it is a tension that Tolai continuously and convincingly aver has been intensified by integration into a global cash economy and changes such as the introduction of permanent housing or cash crops. Likewise the working through of the moral dilemma of how much Big Shots owe to the grassroots is also a process by which social change occurs and is assessed. In these cases and others, the word *kastom* becomes central to the positions that people hold and to the eventual resolution of disputes.

Sometimes *kastom* is presented in self-essentialising terms as the marker of a Tolai or Melanesian identity based on reciprocity that is opposed to the non-reciprocity of whites, all of this in a manner that will be immediately familiar to the student of Melanesian ethnography. For example, Kahn describes the way in which food, which is normally shared, can come to stand for the opposition between Melanesians and Westerners for the Wamiran of Milne Bay Province: '"We are taro people, but where you come from, people are money people"' (Kahn 1986:154). Both ToAtun and Luke Cada present this perspective, while differing strongly over which form of sociality is the most desirable. However, more often than not, appeals to *kastom* are best seen as a means by which people attempt to fix the appropriate limits of reciprocity, or attempt to fix the points and contexts at which ongoing relations need to be acknowledged or not, rather than *simply* being a positive reference to a reciprocal ethic as an absolute good.

Kastom reflects and constitutes differences of opinion over the appropriate limits of reciprocity between grassroots Tolai, as much as it does the emerging social cleavage between the grassroots and the Big Shots. So for example, a person might claim that *kastom* says that we have to help the children of the clan with this or that ritual performance, but we are not obliged to recognise demands for royalties from the government for use of clan land. Another person might argue that I have fulfilled my customary obligations by going through secret preparations for a dance in the bush (and by implication what I do with my money is not an issue), or conversely someone else might argue that that dance is not *kastom* because it was done with the intention of making money (that will not be shared with the rest of us). In another context someone might claim that I have largely ignored demands of my kin on my business to keep it afloat, but I am still respectful of *kastom* because I give more than most to sponsor ritually important feasts. A critic might then counterclaim that my involvement in *kastom* is fake because it is based on his 'money-power' and I ignore people's needs as kin in other contexts.

Even Luke Cada, the SDA member quoted near the start of the previous chapter, acknowledges that he is concerned 'occasionally [with] the extended family'. At one point he described to me how he had turned down a request of one nephew for him to help with *kastom*, telling me that: 'lots of people come and ask me for *tabu* and I say no. I'm self-reliant. A one-man army'. However, at a later point he told me that: 'Sooner or later I will bring food straight to ToBenjamin. It's a bridge over troubled waters. I will explain to him that this is for you and your family. They need to keep an eye on our relationship as they are our father's nephews. We are tied together'.

Likewise, ToAtun was at many times dismissive of those whom he felt pushed claims based on reciprocal interdependence too far in certain contexts. Luke tended to associate *kastom* with overly inclusive claims and thus liked to present those moments when he did acknowledge them as not being *kastom*. Instead, he carefully explained that the assistance was for the family, and he delayed it so that it was not clearly linked to customary demands. ToAtun pursues a different tactic, rejecting inclusive claims on the basis of reciprocal interdependence as being just as non-customary as exclusive claims based upon non-reciprocal independence.

Although *kastom* is rhetorically based upon an ethic of reciprocity, the category is actually working to express what a speaker thinks that he or she can assert as being the appropriate bounds of reciprocity in any given context. As such both *kastom* and its axiomatic opposite, non-*kastom*, vary in different social contexts. Both Luke and ToAtun use the word *kastom*, whether positively or negatively, as a yardstick by which the bounds of appropriate reciprocal obligations can be measured and hopefully maintained. Neither totally accepts or rejects demands based upon reciprocal interdependence in every context, but they do accept and reject them in very different ways from each other, and their different uses of the word *kastom* reflect and express those differences.

This moral dilemma of where to place the limits of reciprocity is far from being a uniquely Melanesian one. As Mauss (1970:63–82) recognised, it is perhaps the most pressing dilemma for 'modern' societies. And it is in this sense that *kastom* is best understood as a 'modern' Melanesian concept. For as Mauss also recognised, such a dilemma is far from being a uniquely 'modern' dilemma either. Mauss's discussion of Malinowski's description of the distinction between *kula* and *gimwali*, carries many echoes of the distinction that Matthew drew between *kastom* and 'a market'. According to Mauss's reading, *kula* 'is distinguished from the straightforward exchange of useful goods known as the *gimwali* . . . which . . . is distinguished by most tenacious bargaining on both sides, a procedure unworthy of the *kula*. It is said of the individual who does not behave in his *kula* with proper magnanimity that he is conducting it "as a *gimwali*"' (Mauss 1970:20).

This brief passage reveals an immense amount. It reveals that the contestability of the status of customary exchanges is not new. Just as my contemporary Tolai accuse those who claim to be conducting *kastom* of conducting a market or a business, so Malinowski's informants accused those who claimed to be conducting *kula* of actually conducting *gimwali*. Many transactions cannot be unambiguously categorised using opposed concepts such as *kastom* versus business, *kula* versus *gimwali*, or indeed gift versus commodity. Instead the different uses of such terms by those with different social interests to describe the *same* transaction reveal something of the nature of those divergent interests. It also reveals the necessity of such concepts to any analysis of the transactions that make up social life, be those analyses academic or indigenous. Even if these oppositions do not always neatly, empirically and unproblematically describe every kind of transaction, they are essential to the ways in which people involved take positions on them, and in the course of doing so lay the ground for future transactions. In both examples a commonplace opposition is set up, between two kinds of exchange practice, based upon (but not simply reducible to) an axiomatic contradiction between the reciprocal interdependence of gift exchange, and the non-reciprocal independence of market or 'straightforward . . . useful' exchange.

To acknowledge that drawing the appropriate boundaries around exclusive claims based on non-reciprocal independence, and inclusive claims based upon reciprocal interdependence has perhaps always been a moral dilemma across time and geographical location is not to deny social change. Rather, it is to draw attention to one of the main ways in which that change is constituted and expressed. As Keane (2007:6) observes, we live in an intellectual world that prides itself on having transcended both modernity and its now supposedly outdated dichotomies. But these kinds of oppositions have played and continue to play an important part in 'how Euro-Americans have under-stood themselves to be modern and construed modernity's others' (ibid.). The oppositions that concern Keane in the context of the mission encounter in Sumba, Indonesia, such as immanence and transcendence or determinism and freedom may be very different from the oppositions between *kastom* and its others by which Tolai construe some Tolai as modern and construe others as not. But such oppositions remain central to Tolai understandings, despite the often uncontrollable urge of some intellectuals to purify them from the era of postmodernity. The kinds of moral dilemmas around the appropri-ate boundaries of reciprocity expressed by the commonplace contradiction between *kula* and *gimwali* in a world of chiefs and canoe trading expedi-tions are different from those expressed by the commonplace contradiction between *kastom* and business in the world of *tabu* bought by Big Shots with money when they fly to Vanuatu. And that contradiction, in its turn, is very different from some of the other contradictions expressed by uses of the word *kastom* in other contexts, even if these too are often related to an axiomatic contradiction between reciprocity and non-reciprocity. Because *kastom*'s dif-ferent uses are part of the process by which the appropriate limits for reciproc-ity are morally debated and settled in different contexts, those different uses are an index of where those limits are being drawn. The term's life is both a marker and a maker of cultural change, or as Volosinov (1973:19) describes the evolving meaning of words, 'the most sensitive index of social changes'. In *kastom*'s character as a means by which Melanesians draw and redraw the boundaries of reciprocity in response to an ever-changing world, the category can be understood as being a cultural phenomenon that 'continues in rela-tion to and frequently in opposition to the claims of [the] world system' (Jolly 1994:10). The different changing accents carried by words such as *kastom* are one of the best markers we have of the ways in which Matupi themselves form moral perspectives on these changes and in doing so themselves become part of the processes by which such changes are made.

Notes

1. This category of ritual and other categories of mortuary feasts are described in detail by Simet (1991:252–311).
2. Simet (1991:279–80) gives this account of the ritual's social embeddedness: 'After the second phase in which non-relatives and relatives distribute some of their own *tabu*, it is time for the *warwangala* (children of the clan or the deceased: all people who were fathered by the clan), to stand up and distribute small pieces of *tabu* to the remaining members of the deceased's clan. This phase of the ceremony is known as *warap* (token reimbursement). A number of old people whom I approached about the significance of this distribution said that it was a way by which the "children" (which also includes adults), reimburse the members of the deceased's clan who had gave them life and

reared them. It is said that although these "children" do not belong to the clans of their fathers, it is these clans which gave them sustenance in the way of food and care. It appears to me that the significance of this action goes further than just token compensation for the provision of sustenance, because it is repeated by the "children" at the death of every member of their father's clan. It seems that by distributing *tabu*, the "children" are resettling the relationship between them and their "fathers", which has been temporarily broken by the death. It is a way of saying that in spite of the death of a "father" (in the case of a male), who is the link between "children" and his clan, the relationship between children and "father" clan still continues for good social relations. For many people, the maintaining of good social relations through this means is important because they are residing or gardening on land which belongs to their fathers' clans.' Hence, following Rio (1997:453), we could say that the *minamai* is an example of how in 'life-cycle ceremonies . . . people are pressed to recognise . . . the Outside', here the 'Outside' of the matriclan.

3. As we have seen, he was also keen to delimit the social contexts in which customary relations had an effect. He wanted to promote customary exchanges whilst at the same time keeping customary land tenure out of the new land at Sikut where these exchanges would be taking place. In this respect his position was similar to that of those Big Shots who also wished to promote *kastom* but restrict it to ritual exchanges that did not threaten their ownership or tenure of their businesses. The extent to which it is possible for *kastom* to remain 'just custom' is an ongoing battle at the very heart of contemporary Tolai sociality.

4. It is notable, though, that *tabu* can be transacted in a commodity fashion on the margins of these events, such as when women sell crisps, ice-creams, betel nut and cigarettes for *tabu* at the end of the events, to the people to whom *tabu* have been distributed (see for example Bradley 1982:110).

5. 'Bride-price' is the English term used by this and most other of my Tolai interlocutors to talk about marriage payments. The role of *tabu* in Tolai marriage is examined in A.L. Epstein 1969:216–18, Salisbury 1970:115, 291, 316, 328, Bradley 1982:166–77, Simet 1991:379–421, A.L. Epstein 1992:154–59.

6. Tolai often have a very ambiguous attitude towards their 'pre-contact' past, simultaneously worrying about the positive aspects of it that have been lost in the rush towards modernisation (such as the disintegration of the taboo on marriage between moieties, lamented by many) whilst also describing it as a 'time of darkness' (K. *a bobotoi*), when cannibalism and unrestrained warfare blighted lives before Christianisation and pacification (see Martin 2010). When people talk about keeping *kastom* they certainly are not referring to the revival of such practices, but selectively looking at aspects of past practices and evaluating them in the light of current moral dilemmas and then using elements of past practice in order to justify particular positions that they can take regarding those current disputes. This ambiguity towards the past illustrates Keesing's (1992:123) point regarding *kastom* among Kwaio people of the Solomon Islands that the category has a 'political force that go[es] far beyond any ideas Kwaio people may have had about their way of life prior to European invasion'.

7. See Rio (2007:452) for an example from Ambrym of a man embedded in these cycles momentarily expressing weariness with the seemingly endless pointless effort that they demand.

8. See also Guha (1983).

7

Big Shots, Corned Beef and Big Heads

The example of the Big Shots provides perhaps the best illustration of how the contradiction between family and clan crystallises the wider contradictions of a global capitalist economy in East New Britain. This contradiction between family and clan is one of the key sites at which the emerging elite pursues strategies of individuation and hence are seen by others as abrogating their obligations to the grassroots. I examine this issue in more detail in Chapter Nine. The overall pattern, though, is one of 'extended' kin of Big Shots tending to feel that they have a greater claim on the Big Shots' wealth and persons than the Big Shots are willing to recognise. Stories describe a history of ongoing exchange-based reciprocal interdependence into which the Big Shot was born, and on which his personal success is based. These stories are told as the foundation for claims on his wealth and person. Conversely, the Big Shot has to reject or restrict these stories and claims, as part of his effort to individuate himself. In this context, accusations of corruption and theft on the part of Big Shots abound. I soon came to recognise these accusations as often being more about the moral legitimacy of how Big Shots transacted with their relatives, than as being descriptions of actual legal crimes. The common complaint made between grassroots villagers that a man forgets his extended obligations to his own clan or his father's clan by 'selfishly' protecting the interests of his own family is repeated five times as often and with ten times as much force and venom behind the backs of Big Shots.

If there is one figure at Matupit that embodies the distrust that many feel for Big Shots, it is ToNgala. ToNgala, like most Big Shots, no longer lives in Matupit. But as the owner of an East New Britain-based business, he has to remain in the area, and has lived in Rabaul Town for many years. This means that he has been able to remain involved in village politics and customary ritual to a greater extent than other Big Shots. At the time of my arrival, he was the undisputed customary expert and ritual leader at Matupit. This proximity led to other problems, however. Over the years he had become subject to much more criticism than other wealthier Big Shots who lived further away, in places such as Port Moresby. Some Port Moresby-based Big Shots, who were not subject to the same degree of opprobrium as ToNgala, expressed sympathy with him privately to me, because his position made him a more accessible target. I had many opportunities for conversation with ToNgala, and I sometimes found it hard to match the open and careful person that I was interviewing with the image of disreputable corruption that I had been led to expect. But the point is that the accusations made against ToNgala should not be seen as the result of his moral character, but as the inevitable result of his position in an ever changing network of social relations. In order to preserve his family's social position, he had to draw limits around the demands of extended kinship obligation. This is easier to achieve if one lives in Port Moresby and only returns to the village once a year. If one is living in town a short bus ride away, and returning to the village frequently for *kastom* in which one deals face to face with many of those persons with whom one has such extended relations, then the very act of drawing such limits is more apparent, and hence more open to criticism.

The Weakening of the Clans

One afternoon towards the end of my first year of fieldwork in East New Britain, I was walking to someone's house in Sikut, when I bumped into a man that I knew quite well who had just been allocated a block near the care centre. We began talking, and he brought up a subject that he and many other Matupi often raised with me, what he described as the 'weakening' of the clans. As he clearly had something to say, we sat down to share a cigarette, and I began to make notes on our conversation. According to his description, the clan was still important, but there were now points at which its ties were 'looser'. This was an analysis that I had heard before from others, and it is one that I myself have adopted as a part of my own analysis without major revision. The problem, he felt, was that too many people were favouring their own families over clans, leading to splits and conflict. I already knew this individual to have good reason to see the world in this way. He was a new block holder who was only just establishing himself economically, and although he had carpentry skills for which he was occasionally able to get small amounts of money, his economic position was precarious. He had a large number of brothers and sisters, some of whom were more economically successful, having white collar jobs in government or private business. He often complained that they 'forgot' about him, rarely visiting or providing his family with financial assistance. As his siblings were all members of his own clan, such complaints were often voiced in terms that pitted the selfishness of concentrating purely on one's own family against responsibility to remember the clan that gave birth to you and brought you up. So when I asked him for an example of the weakening of clans, I was expecting to hear more details of his own situation. Obviously, I thought, this is the specific problem that is aggravating him.

Instead, my request for an example led the man to bring up the name of ToNgala. Yet this too was not a complete surprise to me. I had already lost count of the number of times that ToNgala's name was raised in the context of complaints about the behaviour of Big Shots. The man told me that he had bumped into one of ToNgala's clan nephews on the previous Friday, and that this nephew was saying that he and his siblings were planning to break away from ToNgala's *apik* (clan subdivision), as they were sick of having to do *kastom* with him while he favoured his own children over them. I attempted to clarify what 'breaking' from the *apik* meant, and was told that it did not mean forming a new *apik*, but rather that they would 'stand at the back', withdrawing from all but the bare minimum of clan obligations and look after their own business first. I was unsure as to how exactly ToNgala was treating them badly, but the problem centred on customary ritual knowledge that ToNgala was allegedly using for his children rather than the clan that, strictly speaking, it should belong to. My interlocutor was unwilling to go into the details of the case, and knowing the sensitivity and secrecy that often surrounds such issues, I was unwilling to press him on the issue. Unfortunately this also makes it hard to check the veracity of his claims. It would have been impossible to directly question any of ToNgala's clanmates on this issue. I knew from private conversation that some of them were extremely supportive of ToNgala. Others I was less close to, and it would have been impossible for me to approach any of them directly to ask about such sensitive issues. I spoke to ToNgala himself on a number of occasions, but here too it would have been extremely difficult to raise such issues with him directly. On one occasion, he did inform me, unprompted, that he had very good relations with all of his clan, including all of his clan nephews. I have no doubt in my mind that he dropped this into the conversation out of awareness that I had been living in the community for nearly two years, and would know the rumours surrounding his relations with his clan. Ultimately it is hard to get at the 'truth' of issues like this, as they largely surface through gossip and innuendo.

Such a situation has made me uneasy about writing on cases like this. The need to be sensitive in reporting gossip and slander in an era in which my writings will almost certainly make their way back to my fieldsite means that my reports inevitably have an ethnographic 'thinness', compared to the wonderfully detailed reports of an earlier age (such as A.L. Epstein's descriptions of how land disputes at Matupit illuminated how different categories of kin came into conflict with each other in the early 1960s). Furthermore, no matter how careful I am in setting forth elements of this kind of case, I am ultimately still reporting gossip, with all of the problems that this entails. Although everyone at Matupit and Sikut knows the rumours surrounding ToNgala's family and clan relations (and indeed every other person's family and clan relations), I know that the transformation from open secret or rumour to reported ethnographic data could be significant, perhaps giving the rumour an additional legitimacy by placing it in the public domain. However, to choose not to report this material would be to give up on the attempt to honestly record the changing nature of Tolai social relations in the early twenty-first century.

Land disputes often provided a public arena in which underlying kinship tensions were played out. For example, I knew that the tensions between ToNgala and some members of his father's clan had in the past been expressed through a dispute over his building a permanent house at Matupit on what they considered to be their clan land. This dispute may well erupt into the public again at some point in the future, but in the current climate it remains below the surface of public debate. In the relative absence of large numbers of public land disputes, gossip, innuendo, and talk about kinship has become a more important expression of such tensions. In my opinion it is sufficient to emphasise that to report on adverse moral judgements made on individuals is not to endorse them. Moreover the moral judgements made on individual persons are best seen not as judgements made upon them as individual persons, but as critiques of new forms of social division: in other words as critiques of their position within new and disliked constellations of social relations. The sympathy expressed by Tolai Big Shots living in Port Moresby for ToNgala illustrates this perfectly. They know that his relative unpopularity is at least in part a result of how his decision to stay close to his home community has made him more of a target. Many of these elites told me that ToNgala had stayed around Rabaul partly out of a sense of concern for his home village and a desire to look after it and help preserve its _kastom_. It was this concern that had paradoxically made him in many quarters public enemy number one. In this book, I have tended to prioritise the grassroots perspective on social differentiation. In practice, that has tended to mean a negative evaluation of Big Shots in general and ToNgala in particular. However, it is important to keep in view also some people's *positive* evaluations of Big Shot figures, and also to emphasise that the ethnographic value of people's evaluative statements about the motivations of others lies mainly in what those statements reveal about the social perspective of the person making the judgement, rather than in what they reveal about the person judged. It is not my intention to attempt to decide which judgements of a man like ToNgala are 'correct', but to point out ways those judgements are themselves powerful indicators of an entrenched socio-economic divide in contemporary PNG.

If land disputes no longer provide such a public arena for expression of tension between different kinds of kin, another arena that still does provide such an arena is that of of kin-based ritual performances often referred to by the Tok Pisin word _kastom_. When I returned to Matupit around Christmas

2004 for one month, after having left the previous February, the intervening event that many people were keenest to tell me about was the raising of a new *tubuan*. It was younger members of ToNgala's *apik* who had raised the *tubuan*. What stood out about the event, as one knowledgeable Matupi put it to me, was that ToNgala 'was on the outside looking in'. The man told me that what had happened was the continuation of what we had talked about two years before. At first the younger men's break with ToNgala was hidden, but now with this action it had burst out into the open. Everyone I spoke to on the issue agreed that this act marked a new stage in the expression of discontent with ToNgala amongst his own clan: 'Now they have raised a new *tubuan*, when they previously stood under ToNgala's *tubuan*'.

I did not get the chance to question ToNgala directly about these issues. My visit was short, and as a busy businessman it was not possible for him to meet with me on this occasion. I have no doubt that he would have glossed these events differently if the opportunity had presented itself. Everyone admitted that he had helped with the event's preparations, and indeed his *tubuan* was one of the ones that attended. He would have presented these facts to me as exemplifying his good relations with his junior clan members and his desire to help them establish themselves in customary activities. For his grassroots critics, however, this participation was something he had carried out in order to avoid embarrassment. His nephews had provided so much assistance for him in *kastom* events in the past that it would have been impossible for him to refuse to help them now, even though he knew that the whole village would see the performance for the rejection that it was. As one grassroots Matupit man told me, 'you already know, Martin, they give help but help doesn't come back'.

To me, this sentence encapsulates the difference in class perspectives between grassroots Tolai and Big Shots. I cannot think of a Big Shot Tolai, even those who were not particularly well-disposed to ToNgala, who could wholeheartedly have endorsed this statement. And I cannot think of many grassroots Matupi, except for ToNgala's most fervent supporters (some of them members of his own clan), who would have totally dismissed it. ToNgala's sympathisers could have pointed to several instances of how he helped his relatives. As the Matupi wealthiest in *tabu*, he had provided shell money to his relatives on many occasions when their involvement in *kastom* would otherwise have been impossible. However, as we shall see, the new political economy of *tabu* production and distribution makes the moral status of Big Shots' *tabu* a subject of great controversy. The real issue is one of whether or not grassroots Tolai get adequate recompense for their assistance in the preparation of *kastom*.

It is impossible to go into many details concerning preparation of customary ritual without making public knowledge what many Tolai still consider should be taboo. It would also not be fair to comment on the details of any particular case. Suffice it to say that 'payment' for customary preparation has in general become a vexed issue among Tolai. I often heard from grassroots Tolai a feeling expressed that Big Shots who were preparing *kastom* did not 'straighten' the grassroots participants properly for their work. From the perspective of Big Shots, especially those who considered themselves experts in *kastom*, such complaints were by and large viewed as opportunistic. Once again there was particular sympathy for ToNgala who was considered by many other elites to be among the most criticised, despite actually being amongst the most conscientious with regard to these issues.

People widely agree that there is a greater tendency today towards demanding direct payment for *kastom* work. This fits the wider tendency I observed towards demanding direct payment for all varieties of work. For example, in my research into how people had built houses at Sikut, there were examples of people giving and receiving assistance on the basis of informally contracted or kin-based reciprocal relations, but in most instances I was told that to get someone to help with chopping wood, or transporting materials or clearing bush that they would demand a cash payment. Everyone that I spoke to contrasted this with the situation forty years previously. With regard to *kastom*, again the interesting contrast was with New Ireland, where *kastom* was said to be similar to Tolai *kastom*, but still more 'traditional'. I was often told that in New Ireland people less frequently demanded payment for help with *kastom*. Big Shots in particular stressed this point to me as an illustration of how grassroots Tolai had 'forgotten' how *kastom* really worked, and saw it as an excuse to make money, or to 'consume' and be 'spoon fed'. From a grassroots perspective the situation of course looks a little different. As every Tolai would acknowledge, they are, more than almost any other ethnic group in PNG, a group that 'lives by money'. To give up large amounts of time to pursue customary activities on behalf of one's clan is to pass up opportunities to improve one's family's financial position. Here it is the grassroots' desire to protect their families' interests that comes into conflict with the customary demands of clan. Even Big Shots themselves are capable of acknowledging this. So ToNgala, in the course of the same conversation in which he claimed that there was no tension within his clan could tell me that there had been a decline in the amount of work done 'free' for the clan. In the past people had done work for the Big Men, but now 'people are worried about survival, and they need to think what comes back for me and my individual family'. He then volunteered the example of one of his nephews at Sikut, who was known to be one of the next generation of customary experts among the Matupi: 'If I asked him about helping with *kastom*, he would say, "what about my cocoa", because that's where he gets his living. Thirty years ago we were doing nothing in the village. You were sitting on the beach. You might as well go and do *kastom*. It's more difficult today'.

Again we see how Matupi tend to explain changes in how they organise their own social relations in the light of wider political economic changes. In this quote, the condemnation of the grassroots is replaced with a position that shows a degree of sympathy with their position. The same geographical and social proximity to the grassroots that leads to ToNgala being one of the most distrusted of the Big Shots also paradoxically makes him one of those who is most sympathetic to the grassroots' position. Perhaps the most significant part of this statement is the contrast with the past that ToNgala draws, in saying that formerly people worked for the Big Men, whereas now they demand direct payment. As I shall argue in Chapter Nine, the 'traditional' Tolai Big Man's power was a result of his conscientious observance of and willingness to enforce customary obligations of reciprocal interdependence. If one wished to marry, obtain good land, or gain assistance in customary activities then one had to have the support of Big Men who would be impressed by one's willingness to play one's part, perhaps by not shaming the clan by non-attendance of rituals honouring the clan's reciprocal obligations to another clan. This is what I believe is meant by working for the Big Man rather than demanding immediate payment. Conversely the Big Man only became a Big Man if he was willing and able to organise such assistance for one who had proven himself worthy of it. It is in this vein that T.S. Epstein (1968:84) describes a situation in which Big Men (described as 'elders') and young men were part of a 'system' of ongoing 'reciprocal obligations' within the *vunatarai*: 'the elder did provide for the needs of young men of his matrilineage while in return they worked for him and helped him cultivate his gardens'.

Already by the early 1960s, however, T.S. Epstein reports that 'some of the young men were getting dissatisfied with the system' (ibid.), and relates a 'typical dispute', in which a young man complained that after planting cocoa with the Big Man's permission, he had begun pocketing the profits. The Big Man's response was that he had supported the young man for several years in various ways. T.S. Epstein's (op cit.:84–85) ideas about the importance of this dispute are worth quoting at length. The dispute:

> show[s] a breaking down of the traditional reciprocal obligations between elders and young men. This breakdown can be expected eventually to undermine the strategic economic position occupied by the matrilineage sector elder . . . Secondly it indicates the germ of the development of a system of individual land-ownership, though this is not yet explicit . . . the vesting of usufruct rights in the young man pointed to the beginning of vesting full rights of ownership in an individual.

T.S. Epstein correctly predicts that the loosening of reciprocal interdependence within the clan would lead to the weakening of Big Men of the traditional type (a process I trace out in subsequent chapters). Although 'a system of individual ownership' has not in fact replaced the system of gaining of access to land through careful observation of ongoing reciprocal obligations, the Tolai situation today *is* one in which the concept of individual ownership is increasingly asserted as the rhetorical justification for restricting others' access to one's own land. T.S. Epstein is correct to describe the increasing assertion of individual ownership as being fundamentally intertwined with the partial breaking down of ongoing reciprocal obligations. One could almost describe them as two sides of the same coin.

Today, however, traditional Big Man-ship no longer exists at villages like Matupit, and people no longer secure their individual or family existence through relations of reciprocal obligations with these figures. Indeed given the decline in Big Man-ship they are compelled to look elsewhere. In the past there was doubtless tension between individual family households and clans, but the family's very existence was nonetheless largely dependent upon both men and women fulfilling customary obligations to their clans and other clans. Today, although families are still tied into such reciprocal obligations in ways that might bewilder many Westerners, such ties have been loosened by phenomena such as the partial commodification of *kulia*, state conferral of land at Sikut, the opportunity to buy blocks of land in other parts of the province, and changes in bridewealth (detailed in Chapter Eight). These processes have simultaneously made ties of reciprocal obligation easier to partially avoid, and also a less reliable source of support. Many households I observed at Sikut and elsewhere did not receive much day-to-day support from their clan relatives. They were not reliant on these relatives for the land, for assistance in clearing and planting it, or for building their house. The family's very capacity to exist is not totally divorced from such networks of extended kin-based customary obligation, but is less intertwined with these networks than in the past.

The Tension between Clan and Family

This analysis is broadly shared by the grassroots. For example, Philip, who had got involved in *kastom* in New Ireland to secure a claim to some of his father's clan land, once reflected on the biggest difference between New Ireland and Tolai *kastom* to me: 'At New Ireland they listen to what the Big Men say. If you help another clan, you know that help will come back'. Again there is the contrast with a situation in which reciprocity can be relied upon, and one in which, according to many Tolai, it cannot. This explained for this man the tendency for Tolai to demand payment for *kastom*, which was one of the factors that led him to sometimes contemptuously dismiss Tolai *kastom* as not really being *kastom*. For him the situation was summed up by the use of tins of corned beef in Tolai *kastom* distributions, which he contrasted to the pigs distributed in New Ireland. He pointed out to me that one could not simply go and buy a pig and then make *kastom* with it in New Ireland. Rather, one could only pay for a pig with shell wealth from someone one already had a relationship with, be it a kinship relation or an ongoing customary exchange relation. 'Ox and Palm [corned beef] doesn't have the meaning of *kastom* in it. *Kastom* is to show the work you have done together. That's why you can't just buy a pig. Ox and Palm is nothing.'[1]

The 'meaning' of *kastom* is to display the work of reciprocal interdependence, but Tolai *kastom* has in this man's eyes become devalued by becoming more like one-off payments. Patterns like the purchase of tins of corned beef to distribute at *kastom* are reminiscent of the widespread theme in Melanesian ethnography that *kastom* movements involve appropriating Western commodities to Melanesian ends. It stands to reason, though, that Melanesians would sometimes consider the opposite process to taking place: namely the commodification or commercialisation of *kastom*. The actual moment of customary exchange may not have changed in any major respect. But this does not mean that it is not evaluated differently. It is evaluated within a wider context of exchange and social relations, and it is this wider context that leads it to be judged as an exchange doing work of displaying reciprocal interdependence or judged to be a one off payment, 'not *kastom*'.

The best examples concern the large numbers of young men with seemingly nothing to do circulating around Matupit and Sikut. The destruction of land and business caused by the volcano has exacerbated the economic problems that started to beset PNG in the late 1980s. In the past fifteen years foreign aid has been massively cut and civil disturbances such as the civil war that closed PNG's major source of foreign currency, the Bougainville Copper Mine, have crippled the PNG economy. In the years leading up to and immediately following national independence in 1975, large-scale development programmes funded by foreign governments and international agencies helped large numbers of young men in 'developed' areas such as the Gazelle find employment. Today in an era of neo-liberal globalisation, the economic orthodoxy has changed. The large numbers of young men aimlessly wandering the villages of East New Britain are one of the costs of this particular economic medicine. Although many Tolai are aware of the economic changes that have led to this state of affairs and therefore have some sympathy with the plight of these young men, on a day-to-day level the youths are frankly experienced as a problem and an embarrassingly visual display of the Tolai people's inability to preserve their previously privileged position. Many times I have heard older Tolai refer to the actions of younger 'big head' Tolai with the contemptuous remark, 'they're not Tolai, they're like Highlanders'. Given the traditional Tolai contempt for the 'backwards' Highlanders, this is a powerful statement of disdain for the speakers' own children and nephews. In the past there was universal agreement among Tolai and expatriates alike that all violent crimes and robberies committed in Rabaul Town were the result of gangs of youths from other provinces, living in squatter camps with no access to employment or land. Now there is reluctant acknowledgement that young Tolai men from the villages surrounding Rabaul and Kokopo are themselves increasingly involved in such activities.

These young men's style of involvement in <u>*kastom*</u> is one focus of the larger disdain that is expressed about them, and exemplifies the way customary exchanges and payments that are formally unchanged from decades ago are now differently evaluated, owing to the changed wider political and economic context within which they are made. Take for example the *minamai*, a mortuary feast in which *tabu* is distributed amongst the mourners by relatives of the deceased. Formally the *tabu* is distributed exactly as it has been for decades, but the presence of young men is now often a focus of controversy. Attending such events has long been recognised as one of the main ways in which poorer Tolai can acquire *tabu*, but the young men are accused of attending the *minamai* of those with whom they have no real relation in order to acquire *tabu*, and more importantly of getting *tabu* just so they can spend it on items of immediate consumption such as tobacco, betel nut, or rice. This is contrasted with what they 'should' be acquiring *tabu* for, namely building up a stock of *tabu* to fulfil customary obligations, such as their own obligations to honour dead relatives or to help contribute towards their own bridewealth payments. The way in which they both acquire and spend *tabu* is morally suspect. They allegedly acquire it simply to use it as a commodity rather than

12. Young men gambling with cards at Matupit

as a way of entering into customary obligations of reciprocal interdependence, the work of _kastom_.

Similar expressions of suspicion and hostility towards young men in ritual performances now arise regularly in the context of the *namata*, a ceremony that is conducted when a family's firstborn son is revealed after a period of seclusion in the 'bush' away from the village.[2] The major purpose of the *namata* is to help collect *tabu* that will be used for the young man's bridewealth payment. Relatives and clan members of both parents are involved, and the ritual is one of the events that best demonstrates the interlocking ties of reciprocal interdependence by which _kastom_ is supposed to work. A.L. Epstein (1969:218–21) provides a description of the *namata*, in the course of which he observes:

> [E]ach contribution imposes on the recipient an obligation to reciprocate on some subsequent occasion. From this point of view, the *namata* provides an arena within which standing obligations are fulfilled and new debt relationships incurred. The full significance of the *namata* . . . only emerges therefore when it is set in the context of an ongoing series of exchanges and distributions of various kinds. (op cit.:220)

In common with much customary ritual, a wide variety of other payments take place at the same time. One of these is the *iap* (K. 'fire') which is made to other young men who go into the bush to help the young man while he is in seclusion.[3] The *iap* payment is made when all of the young men who have been in the bush come out with customary face and body decorations. I attended many *namata* during my fieldwork, and observed a numerous interesting events (including on one occasion a man passing out and requiring resuscitation after over-enthusiastic consumption of home-distilled 'jungle juice', and on another a near fatal altercation amongst some of the young men over alleged drug dealing). What sticks in my mind most, however, is the occasion when after the *iap* payments had been made the councillor who was acting as master of ceremonies turned on the young men who were assembled for this purpose and roundly berated them for their laziness and lack of morals. Although I knew this to be a widespread complaint, occasions such as the *namata* were one of the few occasions on which these young men could actually legitimately be the centre of attention and occupy a position of esteem for an hour or two. Yet now even this was being taken away from them. It was for me a moment of some drama to see the sudden reversal of fortunes as these young men, sitting in a circle at the middle of the crowd with every eye present upon them and previously basking in the glow of attention, were publicly shamed and humiliated. Almost everyone present applauded the councillor's words, and several senior men got up after him to reinforce his message. For me it was the most remarkable spectacle. It was as if the village had collectively decided to use *kastom* as a means to publicly and deliberately shame an entire generation at the very moment when they were least expecting it.

What was most fascinating, however, was the substance of the councillor's attack. Many young men were going along to the initiate's aid with nothing except a couple of pieces of cooked taro as 'assistance' and then expecting to get *tabu* in return. More to the point, many of them were not related in any meaningful way to the young man in seclusion, clearly making this an attempt to simply gain a bit of *tabu*. The councillor said he knew of some families who had sent four or five sons to gain *tabu* in this manner. It wasn't fair that the family trying to collect *tabu* for their son should lose half of it on the *iap*. In future, he said, they would limit it to one boy per family, as 'lazy people were using it as an excuse not to work'. After this event the same complaints came up as with regard to the *minamai*. Such activities were seen as the abuse of *kastom*. People without a real customary link were using the event as a way of getting *tabu* to spend on themselves.

As we will continue to see, semi-destitute young men are far from being the only ones who are accused of abusing *kastom*. The new elite, the Big Shots, are subjected to similar criticisms of abusing the ethic of reciprocal interdependence that is ideally supposed to underpin the work of *kastom*. Again, though, the exchange of assistance for *tabu* is formally the same as ever, and occurs at the same point in ritual proceedings as before. But the wider context in which it occurs has led to it being differently evaluated. It is no longer seen as a part of an ongoing ritual cycle of reciprocal interdependence, but as a means by which the 'lazy' generation of young men try to exploit the system for short-term personal gain. Although at other moments many Matupi would accept that the young men themselves are victims of economic changes beyond anyone's control, most of the time they are cast as the problems themselves. They are a whole generation that the new economy seems to have cast as being surplus to requirements.

What all of these examples illustrate in different ways is the tension that most Matupi acknowledge between the needs of clan and family. Whether this tension arises in the form of poorer families allegedly sending their children to clan-based customary events with handfuls of cooked taro in an attempt to squeeze *tabu* out of the sponsors, or of Big Shots who acknowledge their kin-based reciprocal responsibilities at customary events but then allegedly favour their families in real life, the tension is one of the key ways in which Matupi discuss the various crises of conflicting moral obligations with which they are faced. It should be clear that the choice between clan and family is not a matter of absolute good versus bad for any one person, although certain persons will tend to be more or less sympathetic to clan-based responsibilities than others. For example, someone may well support the continuation of customary practices such as the *namata* that tie clans together, whilst denying that such relations have any effect on their state land at Sikut. The key debate is always over the contexts in which it is legitimate to prioritise family interests over wider clan-based interests. And this in turn should be seen as an example of the wider dilemma and contest over when and where to acknowledge claims that can be made on a person on the basis of a history of reciprocal interdependence, or in other words the struggle to set the limits of reciprocity. As I have illustrated, the concept of *kastom* often is key to discussions and arguments surrounding such issues. In the next chapter I examine in more detail the ways in which uses of this concept shape and reflect people's conflicting ideas about reciprocity's limits.

Notes

1. Ox and Palm is PNG's best known brand of tinned corned beef. See also Rio (2007:451) for a discussion of the customary importance of pig killing, which 'has not been replaced by monetary contributions in the ceremonial economy' in Ambrym (Vanuatu), largely because 'the way pigs are thought of in the society, connects them closely to the person who breeds them' (op cit.:452). See also Strathern (1988:264).

2. Given that at most Tolai villages nearly all available land has been cleared and cultivated or built upon, finding a suitable piece of 'bush' can quite often be a challenge. The 'bush' is today often within earshot of traffic on a nearby road.

3. Subsequent to fieldwork, I have noticed that A.L. Epstein does not refer to the *iap* in his description of the *namata* ritual. It is possible that its name has changed over the years, along with other changes in language and ritual practice. For example the 'house' that accompanies the men out of the bush in Epstein's description is known as the *pal na mamarikai* (K. 'house of emergence, house of revelation'). Today it is universally known at Matupit as the *pal na pidik* (K. 'house of [the] secret'). Most significantly, A.L. Epstein describes the ceremony as being performed in honour of a recently married young man. Today it is commonly performed for a young bachelor who often will not even have a prospective bride lined up.

8

A Fish Trap for _Kastom_

Across the previous several chapters I looked at the concept of _kastom_ and how its meaning has constantly been creatively re-invented in new social contexts, as a marker of the ever shifting boundaries of appropriate reciprocal interdependence in postcolonial PNG. Across those chapters, I examined concrete examples to illustrate the different ways in which this one word can mark out a moral position on the appropriate limits of reciprocity in a variety of different contexts. In this chapter I take a different approach, looking in detail at a single issue, namely changes in fishing technologies over the past fifty years at Matupit, and the social significance attached to these changes by the village's residents. These changes again reflect and are part of a process of the ongoing renegotiation of the appropriate limits of reciprocal obligations.

A useful starting point for the examination of these issues can be provided by a quotation from A.L. Epstein's Matupit fieldnotes from the early 1960s:

> Went along to Raulai this afternoon. Turpui was helping his son ToKaul to make a second or spare _a varkia_ as the one now at sea is old. TurPui himself belongs to the matonoi of ToUraulai, but as he remarked, we old men wander everywhere so as to see that the youngsters are doing it properly.[1] As they worked ToKaul, a young man of about 30, said: from this much tambu will emerge. Young lads who spend their time just wandering idly about and leading a useless existence don't know how to make a basket. But from this comes the tambu with which one marries. I pointed out that a man did not buy his own wife. TurPui said it was only if they saw a young man busy on a fish trap that they would help him by buying a wife for him. Many men had never found wives because they were too idle to make baskets. (A.L. Epstein n.d.)[2]

This quotation raises the issue of the relationship between the acquistion of _tabu_ both as the outcome of respectful relations of reciprocal interdependence (learning how to make baskets with senior kinsmen) and as the technology for their recreation (the basis for bridewealth payments). ToKaul and Turpui's description provide an ideal type outline of the role of fish traps in the recreation of respectful social relations: an outline that, as we shall see, was complicated by the perception of countervailing tendencies at the time of Epstein's fieldwork and that is now viewed by some with nostalgia as being iconic of a better bygone age.

Fishing for Respect: The Relationship between Technology and Good Behaviour

I have noted how Matupit is widely regarded as a unique community by comparison to most other village communities of PNG. One respect in which Matupit is not unique is in its residents' conviction that there is less respect today among the young. Such complaints are common in most PNG communities, but I was struck by the frequency of their repetition at Matupit. I was also struck by the frequency with which the end of the construction of traditional fish traps at Matupit was linked to this loss of 'respect' (K. *variru*). Such stories made clear that fish traps (K. *babau*) were seen not just as a technology for catching fish, but also a tool for the making of certain kinds of desirable social relations, in particular marriage and other relations built upon reciprocity and respect.

Fish traps have long been important to the economies of Matupit and other coastal Tolai communities. The technical details of their manufacture and use are described by Parkinson (2000) and A.L. Epstein (1969). Salisbury (1970:151–54) in his discussion of fishing at the nearby Tolai village of Vunamami draws a distinction between labour that is provided between equals on a basis of reciprocity, and labour that is paid for. According to him, manufacture of fish traps is an 'instance of non-reciprocal labour'. Each skilled adult man nominally makes his own trap, but he often:

> makes only the most difficult part of his trap – the springy central core through which fish enter, but through which they cannot escape. He then gets a less skilled person, often one of the youths . . . to do the tedious job of tying hundreds of cane strips to the spacing rings to make the basket. Food is provided while a youth is so working, and usually a final present equivalent to about half a fathom of tabu for a day's work. Reciprocity is again possible, for the skilled man may eventually make a core for the youth, but it does not necessarily occur. (Salisbury 1970:153)

Other stages of fish trap labour unfold on a more overtly reciprocal basis, with the anchoring of fish traps in the ocean providing 'the occasion of reciprocity par excellence' (Salisbury 1970:152–53). The large group of men who anchor the basket are made up of those whom the owner has helped in the past, or who hope for his assistance in the future. They receive only a meal for their efforts (although the owners of the canoes used must receive a little *tabu*). The collection of fish from the traps is a process in which '[r]eciprocity is involved to some extent' (Salisbury 1970:152). Among the regular fishermen there is reciprocity, in that people use each other's canoes and check each other's traps. However, there are also 'casual visitors at the beach, or young men not yet owning a canoe and still learning how to weave fish traps, who are only too willing to work for a morning with the near certainty of a meal, and the expectation of half a fathom of tabu as well. Reciprocity is unlikely for such young men, who form a labour pool' (Salisbury 1970:153).

Salisbury's distinction between labour embedded in networks of reciprocity, and non-reciprocal labour more akin to wage-labour is an analytically useful one, helping us to avoid Western essentialisms that presume the universal predominance of commodity exchange. However, distinguishing different moments in the manufacture and use of fish traps by whether they are occasions of reciprocity or not does not tell the whole story. The larger network of social relations, within which these moments occur, also needs to be taken into consideration. For example, we do not know if the youths who tied the cane strips to make the basket tended to be kin of the skilled trap maker, or reciprocally obligated to him in other ways. When it came to learning how to make traps, it is true that the old men tended 'to wander everywhere', to check that the youngsters were making the traps properly. But the people that I spoke to also tended to describe one old man to whom they were related, as having taken particular interest in their progress. They reported learning much from this old man, not least learning respect.

Marx (1976:182) stresses that non-reciprocal exchange (i.e. commodity exchange or what he refers to as exchange based on 'reciprocal isolation') is not unique to capitalist society. What distinguishes capitalist society is a tendency for production to be organised according to the needs of generalised commodity exchange. This wider social context in which we acknowledge the immense power of non-reciprocal economic relations over our lives is important in defining the meaning and importance of the moments of reciprocal or non-reciprocal exchange that we live by from day-to-day. For Marx, the tendency for commodity transactions to reify social relations by virtue of their non-reciprocal nature (commodity fetishism), which is only embryonic in societies in which commodity exchange is of marginal importance, reaches its apex in capitalist society (see Marx 1976:172, 176). By virtue of this wider social context Marx considers commodity exchange in a capitalist society to acquire an immense social power to influence the ways in which people imagine their relationships and entailments to others.

The perceived importance of the wider social networks within which fish trap manufacture and use were embedded is well-attested in A.L. Epstein's (1992:87–93) discussion of fishing technologies at Matupit. During his first fieldwork in the early 1960s, elder men stressed the importance of fish traps as a means of acquiring *tabu*, which as opposed to Australian money was 'not to be frittered away on everyday purchases' (A.L. Epstein 1992:89). Instead, individual trap owners held the *tabu* collected through sales of fish, but only so that this shell currency could be pooled in an account held at the beach segment from which the trap had been launched. At the end of the fish trap season, the amount of *tabu* collected would be publicly counted at an occasion known as *vevedek* (see A.L. Epstein, ibid., and 1963:190).[3] For the elders this was imagined to be a means by which they could display their ritual prowess. A.L. Epstein describes how one elder, Turpui, announced at a *tabu*-counting event how the people of the nearby village of Talwat had organised an impressive display of *tabu* that they had earned from trap fishing, and how this should be a role model for Matupit: "'Then our young men will see and begin to understand the ways of our forefathers. This is the road we are talking about through which a lot of tambu will arise. There is no work like the babau [fish trap]"' (A.L. Epstein 1992:89). In working hard to acquire the *tabu* that could be displayed in this manner, young men proved themselves worthy of the assistance that they required from elders in making a bridewealth payment. This explains the assertion of Turpui's son ToKaul that from the fish traps would come the *tabu* with which one married, even if one did not directly pay for one's wife with the *tabu* that one earned fishing. Rather than pay for one's wife oneself, a variety of related kinsfolk (in particular, members of one's matrilineal clan) would contribute (T.S. Epstein 1968:93).

Rather than an act in which one 'bought' a bride, marriage became an event in which reciprocal interdependence with others was demonstrated and mobilised. Hence the importance of being seen to learn how to make a trap: the learner demonstrated that he was willing to fulfil his end of the bargain and work hard to produce *tabu*, not necessarily for immediate individual gain but to assist with moments of ritual display. In return, the elders would help the young man with his needs, such as acquiring a wife. Instances such as the display of *tabu* described by Turpui, and bridewealth exchanges became sites at which the powers of this ongoing reciprocity were publicly displayed. The display is a moment of great power, as Turpui expressed in his already-quoted statement about young men learning 'the ways of our forefathers' through these events.

However, even by the time of A.L. Epstein's first fieldwork in the early 1960s, this picture had been complicated by fear that social changes were dislocating the wider networks of reciprocity within which fish trap manufacture and use occurred. A.L. Epstein reports that 'Turpui knew in his heart that he was talking into the wind' (A.L. Epstein 1992:89). In private Turpui told A.L. Epstein that 'Our fathers used to beat us so that we paid heed and learned the customs . . . Pa ave nunure boko – "We no longer know about these things"' (ibid.). Turpui's pessimism proved to be correct. When A.L. Epstein returned to Matupit in 1986, he found that 'the babau [fish trap] had become a thing of the past' (A.L. Epstein 1992:90). Yet nearly twenty years on, there is a sense in which this object is still a technological item of importance at Matupit. It remains one of the most popular illustrations of and explanations for a perceived lessening of respect. Why did the fish trap die out, and why is its demise still considered to be so important?

Contemporary Discussions of the Fish Trap

One afternoon I was discussing with my host family the behaviour of a young woman who frequented nightclubs in town. Although I was told that the clan had a stake in her behaviour, their will was not as strongly enforced as in the past. Now young people were more 'individualistic' and 'Westernised', and they 'followed the lifestyle of white people'. In the past they would not have got away with it, but today the attitude was, 'this is my life, not the clan's'. Both of my hosts laughed at the thought of someone putting forward that argument when they were young. When I asked why things were different now, there was initially no clear answer. Education, greater freedom of movement, and the impact of television were all put forward as partial suggestions. But what really got to the essence of what had changed was the end of fish traps. Eli, one of my hosts, described how when he was young, he sat down every morning with his grandfather as he made fish traps. It was there that he learnt about the past, and about the correct way to show respect. Young people today don't have that. 'There aren't,' he told me, 'any old people anymore!'

Clearly there were still old people at Matupit. But why were today's old people thought incapable of passing on habits of respect, and what did the end of the traditional fish traps have to do with it? Eli was returned to the example of the fish traps more than once. As a Seventh Day Adventist, he often told me of his opposition to *kastom*, which usually meant ritual obligations that he considered to be wasteful and backward. Yet sometimes he discussed *kastom* in a more positive light. One afternoon, I mentioned to him something that I had heard about men's houses in the nearby province of New Ireland: when the old people there say that the young people don't want to learn, what they really mean is that the young people are not showing the correct respectful demeanour. Eli agreed enthusiastically, saying that this was the 'real' meaning of *kastom*, rather than *kastom* meaning adherence to a set of rules for the preparation of a ritual performance. And where you learnt this 'real' *kastom*

13. Old Tolai-style fish trap on display at a tourist lodge in Kokopo Town

was not at the *tariau*, a secret place in the bush for activities of the male *tubuan* cult, but on the beach, making fish traps with the old men. This was where you learnt to put others before yourself, learnt not to eat before others were ready, and learnt that one only got food after displaying good behaviour to the satisfaction of the old men. It was where one learnt to open one's ears and close one's mouth.[4] Men such as Eli were comparatively uninterested in describing the technical details of fish trap manufacture, but greatly stressed the general point that in being seen learning to manufacture the traps, one learnt – and earned – something of more fundamental importance: respect.[5] The hours spent on the beach making the traps with the old men have thus become an archetypal social scene by which elder Matupi such as Eli describe how they demonstrated respect to their elders when they were young.

Such an insistence that respect was learnt on the beach, not in a hidden men's cult meeting place, might be expected from a member of a denomination that denigrated customary rituals. But the fish trap scene was also raised by others who were enthusiastic supporters of such rituals, especially in the course of conversations about why these practices sometimes failed to produce the respectful behaviour in the young that they were supposed to. Hence the comment of one advocate of customary ritual, Isaac ToLanger, that I already quoted in Chapter Five, to the effect that feasts were almost like an anti-climax. It was the work of producing the feast that was actually important: 'Now we rely on the feast to be the actual glue ... It's getting harder and harder to work *kastom*'. Clearly moments of public ritual performance were of importance, as registered in the example of Turpui's admiration for the display of *tabu* at Talwat. But these events of display only made sense as moments in ongoing networks of reciprocity. ToLanger's comments referred to a widely expressed fear at Matupit that *kastom* had become 'commercialised', meaning that public displays of *kastom* had become divorced from the reciprocity that gave them meaning and that the capacity and power that they now displayed was of a different order. For ToLanger what had changed was that individual households had become more economically self-sufficient.

One particularly strong example of this feeling is the distrust of the role of the new indigenous elite, or Big Shots. As we have seen, their participation in customary ritual is often derided because they do not live in the village like the idealised Big Men of previous generations, and because the shell-money they use in ritual is bought with cash rather than being earned through careful attention to the ongoing shifting reciprocal obligations of everyday village life. And the fish trap again serves as a powerful metaphor for this development, as the following statement from one grassroots block holder at Sikut illustrates:

> The Big Men before were Big Men in the gardens or in making fish
> traps, it's not like ToNgala with his big belly pulling the men to get

tabu for himself. Before Big Men became Big Men with their own strength, it's not like JK or ToNgala, you can't see their big garden.[6] How many gardens have they got, how many pigs have they raised? Before men became Big Men in the *tubuan* through their work, and people recognised the Big Men. How did ToNgala come up, he hasn't got a garden, he hasn't got a fish trap for <u>kastom</u>.

Why Did the Fish Trap Disappear at Matupit?

A number of explanations are advanced for the decline of fish trap technology at Matupit. The most drastic is that after the war an increased volume of large ships using Rabaul Harbour destroyed traditional wooden fish traps. (These traps, once set up, permanently remained in the water.) One evening I had a conversation about compensation claims with two Matupit men in their mid-forties. Both men were grassroots villagers. I was thus not surprised to discover that they were more sympathetic to compensation claims than economically successful 'Big Shots' who, like expatriate businessmen, tended to disparage compensation claims as being the last resort of the lazy and unsuccessful, and a deterrent to investment and development. The two men complained that expatriates, the Government and Big Shots often dismissed claims without taking into account the damage that occurred on their land. They explained how the building of roads and the expansion of Rabaul Town before the eruption had made it harder for them to get to their gardens, a problem that seemed to be invisible or irrelevant to the more economically powerful. Then one of the men became animated and said that it was like the fish traps. He knew that I had heard a lot about the fish traps. But did I know that the reason for their extinction was the number of big foreign boats that ploughed in and out of the harbour, moving close to the Matupit coastline despite repeated requests from the Matupi not to do so?[7] Had I not noticed that once I got away from Rabaul I could still see the poles marking fish traps sticking out of the water at other villages? But they didn't care about our fish traps or us, the man remarked. We were just an irritation to be brushed aside while they made money.

This description acted as a kind of metaphor for one view of economic and political changes, casting them as invasive forces that callously ripped up previous ways of life. Such a view was not the only way of describing economic development, but it was one that I had come to increasingly associate with Tolai of this socio-economic status. And it also tied into a view sometimes expressed by Matupi that the rapid development and social change that their village had experienced had been a double-edged sword. As Isaac ToLanger put it to me, 'In a way, you could say, the Tolai have been victims of our own advanced development'. He was talking about the perceived partial unravelling of traditional patterns of respect and authority in general, and the death of the traditional 'Big Man' in particular, and then went on to claim that such trends had a longer history and were more pronounced at Tolai villages near Rabaul like Matupit. The case of the fishing boats destroying the fish traps at Matupit almost acts as a Tolai parable of such changes. The Matupi had had advantages but there was a price to be paid as well, in terms of a perceived disintegration of traditional cultures, whether the technology of the fish trap, or the traditional culture of respect that was made in the course of their manufacture.

This way of discussing economic change also had implications for how one viewed the plight of men who had not achieved great economic success, or laid down secure roots for themselves and their families. Just as the option to build the fish traps had been ripped away from them by large foreign fishing boats, meaning that they could not be held morally accountable on the grounds of 'laziness' for their failure to learn their construction with the old men, so is it not also reasonable to infer from this description an implicit claim that they are not to be held to blame for their failures both to succeed financially, and to follow old customary practices of respect to the satisfaction of other? According to this particular narrative the conditions that would have made it possible for them to do all of these things had been ripped asunder by overwhelming outside force. This is the sense in which Matupit had become the victim of its advanced development; forced by its proximity to town into radical cultural discontinuities whether they were desired or not.

Another reason given for the end of fish trap manufacture was lack of materials. We have seen that the population of Matupit had grown faster than that of other villages, and much of their customary land was developed, either by outside business interests with the expansion of Rabaul Town, or by the Matupi themselves planting their own coconut plantations for cash cropping. In conjunction with these changes, local Tolai claimed that the materials necessary for the construction of traditional fish traps were no longer available. In this narrative, rather than being a direct result of externally imposed economic exploitation, here the material inability to continue making fish traps (and by implication the inability to continue with the old way of doing things) is seen as an unintended, but equally inevitable side effect of Matupis' own involvement in development, a process that was always bound to have benefits and drawbacks. A similar tale is told by some about the replacement of bush material housing with permanent housing at Matupit. This change is presented as being as much a response to the increasing difficulty in obtaining bush materials at Matupit, as it is the result of positive desire to modernise among Matupi.

But the most common explanation is that young men began to abandon the making of fish traps out of 'laziness' or 'big headedness'. What sense are we to make of this seemingly circular argument that because the young men were big heads they stopped making fish traps, which in turn made them big headed? On one level it can be explained by the fact that the introduction of new technologies was co-temporal with other changes that were perceived as loosening the ties of customary village authority, surrounding wage labour, money, education, increased mobility, and distrust of the perceived increasing corruption of village Big Men (see A.L. Epstein 1969). This is an argument that seems to place much more moral responsibility for the decline in fish trap making and the culture of respect associated with it on recent generations of young men at Matupit themselves. New technologies such as store bought fishing nets (K. *umbene*) theoretically cut someone out of the need to spend hours with the old men on the beach, in the time it took to hand over a few bank notes at a store in town.[8] As one man told me: 'Fish traps; who wants to do that? All the work is in the bush. You just use a net'. The same man went on to tell me that people don't have the time to work *kastom*, being primarily concerned with 'quick money'.[9] In other words, this new technology provided an added opportunity to cut oneself out of certain extended face-to-face social relationships at a time when wider socio-economic changes were already thought to be promoting such tendencies. Money is not merely gained quickly by virtue of the nets, but money and modern technologies such as the nets are considered to be 'quick' technologies that enable shortcutting of dependencies on other people.

But what was the nature of the networks that people are sometimes imagined to have freed themselves from with this simple commodity transaction? The extract from A.L. Epstein's fieldnotes that opens this chapter gives a clue. When the men talk about the link between being seen to make a fish trap and receiving assistance with bridewealth, they are describing an ethnographically familiar Melanesian norm of reciprocity, according to which one has to act in a certain manner and acknowledge one's obligations to others, just as one is dependent upon them acting in the same manner of acknowledging their obligations to oneself.[10] Consider how they respond to A.L. Epstein's observation that a man does not buy his own wife. That is true, they tell him in these conversations, but it is only by showing himself willing to work and acquire the *tabu* that is needed to buy a wife that he proves himself worthy of others' assistance. A young man demonstrated the willingness to be respectful of his ongoing obligations to others that would be the precondition of them assisting him by showing the discipline to sit down with the old men and learning how to make fish traps. According to Epstein's informants, a young man demonstrated worthiness of receipt of the *tabu* required to buy a wife, by showing willingness to learn the techniques that will enable him to fulfil his reciprocal obligations to others over the years to come.

The situation today, however, is in many ways very different. Nowadays men with the means do sometimes in fact organise their own bridewealth payments. This is a development that has been observed in other parts of PNG, with attendant effects on the respect shown to elders and customary norms (see Carrier and Carrier 1989:91). Even when grooms themselves do not pay their own bridewealth, the parents alone may make the whole payment in families with the money to buy enough *tabu*, or an individual Big Shot sponsor may do so. In either case, the payment is no longer a composite of a large number of offerings drawn together by a Big Man from a variety of persons (above all, matrilineal clan relatives), with whom the groom is entwined in ongoing networks of reciprocal obligation. Although it would be wrong to say that this organisation of bridewealth payments no longer takes place, during my fieldwork I was often told that in the past *kastom* was for maternal uncles and the clan to pay bridewealth, but now the new *kastom* is that it was the parents' responsibility.

Additionally many young men live with partners for years without organising bride payments, even building houses with them and raising children. Although these actions provoke some to anger, it is not always considered possible to enforce bridewealth payments from them. One afternoon at Sikut I walked up to the block of a friend who was preparing a small wheel of *tabu* for display at a forthcoming ceremonial event. He was being helped by a friend. As we sat and chatted, this man picked up the *tabu* and suddenly exclaimed how sick he was of people calling him *tambu* when they had not paid any *tabu*. *Tambu* is the Tok Pisin word for an 'in-law', and is itself derived from the Kuanua word *tabu*. He was referring to young men who had relationships with relatives of his without marrying. It was bad enough that they were able to get away with this, but for them then to call him *tambu* as if they had been properly married was adding insult to injury as far as he was concerned. As he put it, 'it's the *tabu* that makes the bridge'. He told me that often parents left it too late to ensure bridewealth was paid, perhaps because the young man had helped them in some other way such as assistance in building a house. By the time that a couple split up after a long period of cohabitation, it was too late to insist on anything.[11] Young people were not so concerned about *tabu*. When I asked why they thought that such customary obligations were no longer being so strongly enforced, I was told that it was because the councillors were no longer doing their job. Two out of the five Matupit councillors were outsiders (K. *waira*) married to Matupit women, and the others were said to be too young to know what they should be doing, namely going around talking strongly to those remiss in their obligations. 'The *waira* don't know our *kastom*', one of these men told me. 'All they know how to do is to go round trying to get taxes off people.' One of the most interesting aspects of this discussion is the light it sheds on contemporary attitudes to village level leadership.

Following the cross-societal death of the traditional Tolai figure of the Big Man as village leader, the vain hope is expressed that the councillors should step into the breach and take over that role. But in their heart of hearts every Matupi knows that this is a vain hope. Whereas the Big Man had a real power to organise social relationships by virtue of the reciprocal obligations that tied young men to him, the councillor has no such equivalent authority. And even if it were possible for councillors to take on such a role, it is not a vision that meets with universal approval. A few days later I mentioned this conversation to a friend of the two men. This man was slightly younger and much less interested in customary ritual, so to an extent his response was no surprise. He told me that 'it's not the job of the councillors to look after *kastom*, it's their job to look after the people *tasol* (only)'. This statement would have been readily agreed to by most young people at Matupit and Sikut. It is the complement to the previously mentioned statement that *kastom* at Sikut is *kastom tasol*. In both statements people and the relationships that they conduct around land or marriages are imagined as being potentially separable from *kastom*. *Kastom* is partially delimited to the realm of optional ceremonial that it is possible to live outside of to an extent. It may have been the case in A.L. Epstein's day that 'many men had never found wives because they were too idle to make baskets', but if that is no longer the case today, it is not merely because fish trap basket technology is obsolete, but because many no longer always respect the particular networks of reciprocity that were encapsulated in relationships to that technology.[12]

This respect the loss of which is so frequently lamented is, in essence, the measure of attention to a multiplicity of ongoing reciprocal obligations. This is a trope that will be familiar to any student of Melanesian ethnography (see for example Gregory 1982:52–53). Respect as a marker of attention to reciprocal obligations amongst the Tolai is well-illustrated with regard to discussions of marriage, and in particular the collapse of marriage prohibitions. All Tolai belong to one of two moieties, and marriage inside the moieties is supposed to be strictly prohibited. Yet over the past thirty years these prohibitions have been increasingly ignored, with allegedly catastrophic social affects. As one Tolai political leader put it to me, the collapse of what he referred to as 'the incest law' caused 'death because you spoil the life of the Tolai society and the relationships within the clan. If we had that [i.e. if the "incest law" was well-observed] in today's society we wouldn't have law and order problems . . . You bring back respect to society'.

The respect that is lost is the loss of attention to one's obligation to reciprocate the exchange of spouses between moieties, an exchange that made one's own existence possible. In marrying inside one's own moiety, a person does not so much break a law as show disrespect to one's own father's moiety, by not acknowledging the obligation to reciprocate the spousal gift that moiety made to one's own mother and clan. Marriages ideally express and constitute

14. Supermarket at the border of Rabaul Town

this ongoing reciprocal exchange and interdependence between clans. Such respect is also made explicit in the exchanges that occur around marriage, in particular the exchanges of *tabu*. This was particularly the case in those situations in which particular *vunatarai* became involved in a process of exchange marriage, a process that was tied into residence and use of parcels of land. As we have seen, it was in acquiring *tabu*, particularly in the course of learning how to build fish traps, that young men in the past ideally demonstrated the demeanour that showed their willingness to respect reciprocal obligations that made them worthy of a bride.

At Matupit today, not only do many young people find ways around reliance on networks of respect in finding a mate, but it is also commonly complained that when they do need assistance, they demand it as a right, rather than recognising it as needing to be earned through demonstration of respect for the principle of reciprocity. Reciprocity is not a 'one way street'. Yet the phrase 'one way street' is frequently used to describe the attitude of young men at Matupit concerning the famous Melanesian '*wantok* system'. Lacking the economic opportunities that were available before the collapse of the PNG currency and the volcanic eruption in the early 1990s, many of them seem to wander aimlessly 'house to house' or as 'local tourists' as the sayings go, demanding food and money from anyone they can claim a relationship to. What angers many is not their requests for help as such, but that they hold an expectation of help without reciprocal shows of assistance or respect. Stories of this attitude abound, ranging from mundane day-to-day complaints, to tales of young men showing up at customary events demanding to be fed even though they have no right to attend and have not assisted in the preparations.

One example was typical of these complaints. A young man allegedly showed up at his mother's house one evening after having been aimlessly circulating around the village for several days. Angry that there was no food ready for him, he picked up his bush knife and cut a cup of tea out of his mother's hand. In the past, I was assured he would have been severely dealt with, but now people were too scared of young men to take action.[13] With the decline of traditional Big Men, there was felt to be no power to contain these youths. What angered people in the telling of this story, almost as much as the dangerous assault on the young man's own mother, was the perceived arrogance of his demand for unearned and unreciprocated assistance. Yet the anger was mixed with resignation, and the story was told to me not merely as a horror story of a particularly bad family situation, but as an illustration of a general trend. Indeed the story was told in the context of a wider discussion of the tendency of young man to grab things from others on the basis of an alleged *wantok* connection, yet to offer very little in terms of assistance or respect in return. The contrast with Eli's description of the respect that he and others of his generation learnt on the beach making fish traps could not be clearer. (This contrast very much parallels the contrast at the opposite end of the social spectrum between stories of the Big Men of old who acquired customary prestige and *tabu* through careful attention to the reciprocal give and take of everyday life, and modern Big Shots who allegedly try to short-circuit such reciprocity by buying *tabu* in bulk with money.) Instead of displays of respect and an understanding of reciprocal obligations, it was often the threat of anger and even violence that inspired compliance with these demands.

My argument is not that things in the past were as perfect as they are sometimes retrospectively presented to have been. The point is rather how people see the customary values ensuring correct demeanour as having disappeared or been corrupted. Rather than being frameworks in which the young learnt about reciprocal respect, *kastom* and the *wantok* system had become a means by which they forced others to feed and assist them.

Nets, Bigheads and the Fetish of the Commodity

Complaints about the big-headedness of youth are not a new phenomenon. The extract with which I started this chapter acknowledges the existence of 'young lads who spend their time just wandering idly about and leading a useless existence don't know how to make a basket'. But the powerlessness to affect their behaviour is felt as a worrying change.

In an interview with two senior Gazelle Regional Authority administrators I asked them about the poor state of repair of much of the infrastructure that had been established in places such as Sikut, at considerable investment cost. I asked who was responsible for maintenance. The GRA, I was told, was not responsible. Their job was simply to build. It was the job of the Provincial Government to maintain these projects afterwards. One of the interviewees was a white expatriate married to a Tolai woman, who lived in a local village and was well known and respected for being close to local people. This man further asked rhetorically, why should the Provincial Government look after the assets? Why not the community? Both men admitted surprise at the level of vandalism of public assets and the inability or the unwillingness of the 'community' to stop the young men's vandalism. They had both expected 'customary' authority in the village communities to provide 'sanctions' against anti-social behaviour. The expatriate official told me that 'communities need to learn to look after these assets. No-one is going to repair continuously vandalised assets'. His colleague, a Tolai man from one of the local villages, added (continuing our mainly English-language conversation) that years ago, respect was there for public projects. Now it had gone:

> When the big men were there, there would have been respect, and you would have been sanctioned. What we have now is totally different from twenty or thirty years ago. It's Westernised life. People are struggling for themselves especially their families. It's not the kind of relations we had before working together . . . Today we don't give things freely, we sell . . . today it's an individualistic approach. As for me, my brothers, my sisters they don't support me I have to struggle for my wife and my kids.

The irony is that in many contexts it is bodies such as the Provincial Government and the GRA that have encouraged a rejection of *kastom*, such as by prioritising individual family households over clan-based claims in matters of land tenure at the resettlements. Yet these bodies simultaneously expected customary authority based on an ethic of 'relations' that are not 'individualistic' to look after the assets that they had provided. This is not to say that the situation is one in which the government has started to get rid of *kastom* and customary authority in the aftermath of the volcano. Such a view would far overstate the government's power, and ignore the extent to which many grass-roots Tolai are suspicious of customary obligations independently of government policy. It would also ignore the ways in which political economic changes have already for several decades been undermining customary leadership by loosening ties of reciprocal interdependence. Even by the mid-1980s, several years before the eruption, A.L. Epstein (1988:26) was struck by the contrast between Matupit of the early 1960s, and the same place he was now revisiting:

> one's overall impression was of shabbiness and decay that spoke to a pervasive malaise. Most of the houses, which had been relatively

new and looked well-cared for in 1960, still stood . . . but many of them were no longer properly maintained: walls were often broken and windows smashed – commonly, I was told, the result of a bout of drunkenness. Around the houses, too, there were frequently littered the bodies of abandoned cars, discarded metal and other detritus. A number of factors undoubtedly contributed to this situation: changing economic circumstances appear to have brought increased differentiation in terms of wealth among the islanders, all, and the poorer in particular, being affected by steep rises in the cost of materials . . . Other considerations too seem to have played a part. Thus some Matupi, themselves keenly aware of the changes in the appearance of the village, spontaneously voiced their concern to me; in their view the signs of increasing neglect were pointers to a decline in communal authority and social control.

A.L. Epstein (op cit.:36) goes on to mention other changes that he noticed that resulted from 'the decline of political authority on the island', including 'the rising incidence of theft, particularly of coconuts from the gardens by young people'. If there has been a loosening in customary authority, the GRA and the government cannot claim sole responsibility. But it is worth drawing attention to the inherent contradictions of the governmental elites' position in this regard. They simultaneously berate the grassroots for not having preserved customary relations in one context, while attempting to engineer weakening of those relations in another.[14] In their dealings with grassroots villagers, they struggle to demarcate the contexts in which _kastom_ is appropriate or not, and in which ties of reciprocal interdependence should be recognised or not: just as grassroots villagers do in their dealings with each other.

The situation is not simply one of the corrosive power of commodities freeing those with money from reciprocal obligations. For example large fishing nets are often purchased today with loans from kin or in-laws, tying the owner into obligations to those who helped.[15] Debts may have to be repaid or school fees contributed to. Relatives of the lender may be employed operating the net, or assistance may be provided at the performance of some of their customary obligations. Perhaps _wantok_-ism may affect the price at the shop or who gets nets from government assistance schemes. Often those whom the owner recruited to help with operating large nets were close young kin, in particular members of their own clan, with whom they would have the closest customary relationships and mutual reciprocal obligations.

One fish net owner that I spoke to at Matupit told me that all of the young men that he paid to help with the fishing were members of his _vunatarai_, his brothers or cousins: 'I chose them because if I say something they will listen. If I got another group of people, maybe they'd get other work. Other people would give excuses.' His fear was that if more rewarding work options came up at the last minute, other people would desert him when there were plenty of fish to be caught. He felt more confident that his own junior clansmen would not desert him in this manner, because for them working on his net was not a stand-alone labour transaction, but a moment in a history of mutual entailment. This man had bought his net second-hand for around 2,600 Kina with money that he had borrowed from an in-law, a debt that is itself the result of a previous history of exchange. Net fishing is possible for several months of the year at Matupit, and on a good day he reckoned that the net could make five or six hundred Kina, although much of this money would have to go to his relatives working on the net. This man had also opened a trade store in mid-2004, around the same time that he launched his fish net, and he told me 'A net is better than a store. The fish net is a very good business. A store you have to run with money, but not a net. The thing with the store is credit. I worry about credit'.

Any business is susceptible to demands from those who feel they can make claims on the owner on the basis of a history of mutual entailment. But a fishing net, once bought, does not need replenishing. Even if *wantoks* claim his entire catch for a week, he can still fish again the following week. If they claim his trade store profits for a week, then the business is finished, because he cannot afford to replenish his stock. What this small businessman is saying, in effect, is that businesses that only require a single fixed capital outlay at the start, are more resistant to the *wantok* system than those that require ongoing capital reinvestment. Demands made on the basis of ongoing reciprocal obligation will continue to be made, and certain kinds of business are better able to survive those demands.[16] A.L. Epstein (1992:91) describes how the large numbers of men required to operate a net, as opposed to a trap, can encourage the public affirmation of reciprocal interdependence. The culmination of the launch (K. *popoai*) of a new net is the distribution of food and *tabu* to those present, 'not so much for past assistance in the preparation of the net but to secure their future help in "working" the umbene and helping to bring in the catch' (A.L. Epstein, ibid. and 1963:190).[17] Nets made in Japan did not have the power to magically transform those Matupi who bought them into the fantasy bourgeois individuals of certain Western economic theories. But equally we should beware of simply asserting that purchase of 'Western' commodities leads to recreation of Melanesian networks of clan and kin. Doing so would not take into account how kinship relations mobilised in the purchase and operation of store bought fishing nets are described as not having the same power to create respect as the long days sat learning how to make fish traps with the old men on the beach. The 'big head' youth also utilise the terminology of kin relations and *wantok*-ism to frame their aggressive demands, yet in the eyes of many Matupi these demands are so objectionable precisely because they do not embody an ethic of reciprocity. Maybe reciprocity is always held up as an ideal, that people worry they do not live up to sufficiently. Yet it is also clear that Matupi themselves worry that recent social changes have created a situation in which demands for assistance ideally based on reciprocity are increasingly being abused. And Matupi clearly recognise at least the potential for money to act as a social technology that is corrosive of certain kinds of social relations and constitutive of others in their discussions of the demise of the fish trap.

Foregrounding and Backgrounding Reciprocity: An Ongoing Tension

Much of Matupit social life still centres on cultures of reciprocity. I do not mean to imply that such patterns have totally broken down at Matupit any more than I would for the case of Manchester. But it is important to trace in the never ending flow of sociality those points at which reciprocity is fore-grounded or backgrounded, where its role is accepted or contested. Moments in which reciprocity is foregrounded or dismissed themselves occur within wider contexts in which reciprocity and non-reciprocity are of differing importance, and held to have a greater or lesser cultural significance. While Salisbury may be correct to describe certain moments of fish trap manufacture at Vunamami as being largely non-reciprocal when taken in isolation, A.L. Epstein's description, and the memories of my older interlocutors, make clear that the cultural significance of the fish trap lies in the wider network of recip-rocal relations within which the trap is embedded. Changing social relations, including technological relations, are processes of change in the degrees and contexts in which reciprocity and non-reciprocity are each stressed. We have already seen that both net fishing and trap fishing have potential to support both reciprocal and non-reciprocal relations. However, it is a shift in the broader social context – the perceived relative importance of reciprocity and non-reciprocity – that is of importance here, rather than simply whether the moment of non-reciprocal fish trap manufacture described by Salisbury has become more or less reciprocal. Marx's analysis of the changing importance of commodities in a society where production is now organised primarily for the purposes of generalised commodity exchange is one description of this kind of phenomenon. Matupis' analysis of the cultural significance of the decline of fish trap technology is another. Only a quarter of the fish caught in traps in the early 1960s at Matupit were sold for the *tabu* that was displayed at the end-of-season public count (A.L. Epstein 1963:192). Yet it is this *tabu*, visibly embodying reciprocal interdependence and obligation, that is high-lighted in period accounts, and in recollection of fish traps by older people today. This is because it is this *tabu* that displayed and helped to constitute the wider context that gives significance to the fish traps when Matupi of the 1960s and today have talked about their importance.

Reciprocity has clearly not disappeared. But its scope and social significance are in question. It is feared not to be the force that it was before at Matupit, and the decline of fish trap manufacture has become emblematic of that fear. Whether decline of the fish trap at Matupit is described as cause, effect or both of these changes, it is clear that for Matupi this technology was deeply tied into networks of reciprocal interdependence and respect. Its replacement with new technologies, in the Matupit imagination, is tied in with wider ongoing social changes. Such discontinuities have implications that go beyond those directly involved in fishing. Women have never been involved in the production or use of fishing technologies at Matupit (whether fish traps or store bought nets), yet for the earlier-quoted Seventh Day Adventist man Eli it was a small step from a discussion of the behaviour of a 'Westernised' young woman to a discussion of the demise of fish traps and respect in general.

There is a seeming contradiction here in the way that the money and nets that seem to shorten social relations simultaneously tie Matupi into networks of commodity exchange that extend across the world. But the issue is what kinds of relations are foregrounded in different contexts. With money and nets as social technologies, what is more immediately relevant to Matupi is not the labour of factory workers or dockers in Southeast Asia who make and transport the nets, but the perceived effects of these social technologies' displacement of earlier technologies. The ways people at Matupit describe the impact of new fishing technologies thus serves as an ethnographic demonstration of both sides of Marx's analysis of the fetishism of the commodity (Marx 1976:163–78). The tendency of large-scale commodity exchange to remove from the forefront of consciousness certain kinds of social relations is apparent here, but this pattern is complemented by its logical corollary: a tendency for these commodities to be ascribed certain kinds of moral agency with regard to other, more local social relations.

Notes

1. The *motonoi* (Epstein spells it 'matanoi') is a piece of beach reserved for fishing activities, only open to adult men. It is also the name of the group that exists as the 'structural expression' of '[t]he necessity for co-operation' in tasks such as launching the fish trap (A.L. Epstein 1963:189). Members are expected to help each other and often check each others' traps (A.L. Epstein 1963:190).
2. This incident is recorded in A.L. Epstein's fieldnotes in an entry titled 'Fishing-tambu' dated 01.02.1960, and is also reported in A.L. Epstein (1992:88–89).

3. At Matupit during the 1960s, the proceeds of both trap and net-fishing were displayed in the collective *motonoi* account (A.L. Epstein 1963:189–90). At Vunamami, by contrast, the proceeds of the trap went directly to the individual owner (unless someone else checked the trap on his behalf, in which case the catch was split), whereas net fishing proceeds were collectively organised by the clan, rather than the *motonoi* (Salisbury 1970:239). By the time of my fieldwork at Matupit, profits from the net went to its owner, be this an individual or a group. One owner that I interviewed told me that a net owner would have to pay the landholder of the *motonoi* where a net was stationed, but at the time it was unclear who had jurisdiction over the *motonoi* he was using.

4. Similar complaints that young people today do not display this correct demeanour are increasingly commonplace throughout PNG. For example Tuzin (personal correspondence) reports for Ilahita Arapesh, Sepik Province, that people complain that the young 'close their ears'.

5. In this, Eli's interests contrasted a bit with older men of the early 1960s, who Epstein says 'seemed to take particular pleasure in explaining the finer technical points [of trap making] and in instructing me in the terms for the various operations I was observing' (A.L. Epstein 1992:87).

6. 'JK' was a common nickname for John Kaputin across the Gazelle Region.

7. This claim seems to be corroborated by an entry in A.L. Epstein's fieldnotes, titled 'Council Meetings-1/60', dated 29.01.1960, which refer to a meeting of councillors for the Rabaul area in 1960. In this meeting, ToGoragora, a Matupit councillor, asks what has happened to the letter that they sent the Rabaul Harbour Master on 15 January asking about safeguarding the Matupit fish traps.

8. The same word, *umbene*, is used to describe both contemporary store bought nets and their hand-made predecessors.

9. A.L. Epstein (1992:92) describes how the different techniques for collecting fish could also lead to the nets being associated with laziness. The trap was not too time consuming (a small group just paddled out in a canoe to check it), whereas the net required large amounts of time spent waiting for a large school of fish to arrive, before a sudden frenetic and co-ordinated attempt by at least twenty men to catch them. It is the enforced hours of idleness associated with net fishing that led to disapproval. A.L. Epstein describes being told in the mid-1980s by one old man who part owned a fish trap, but preferred to work in his garden that the net was for those: 'who did not know the meaning of real work. "See, they will sit there," he would add, "from morning to night just waiting"' (A.L. Epstein, ibid.). A.L. Epstein further states that he himself could understand why the net might be more attractive in the changed economic climate of the mid-1980s, 'to many of the younger people who could no longer find jobs around Rabaul' (A.L. Epstein, ibid.). For them, a fishing technology that could be fitted in around the demands of paid employment was no longer a priority. One could also add that a similar effect might have been caused by the chronic shortage of land for gardening or cash cropping at Matupit, a major problem for young men in particular at this time.

10. Being seen to behave in a manner that publicly acknowledges one's reciprocal obligations to others is also important to Tolai in many other contexts. Consider for example the interesting judgements that some people articulate about the practice now common amongst Seventh Day Adventists of providing hidden assistance to

relatives preparing for customary ritual, in order to fulfil their obligations without provoking disapproval from the church. This practice was disparaged by some of my informants who took a keen interest in custom. To them, the fact that you could not see the person giving the assistance invalidated it. It was felt by these informants that to 'send one's hand', rather than to 'send one's face', was not showing respect.

11. I did come across one case in which a young woman and her family successfully took a young man to court for a *tabu* bridewealth payment after the relationship had fallen apart owing to his philandering, but he was appealing the decision, and several months later no payment had yet been made.

12. Hence the perceived breakdown of 'customary' authority at Matupit can be seen to a large extent as another way of describing a perceived breakdown or disappearance of appropriate reciprocity, where it is once imagined to have usefully existed. This breakdown of authority is in essence the perceived breakdown of reciprocal recognition and respect between generations. A good example of intergenerational authority and leadership being rooted in this reciprocal recognition is provided in Petersen's discussion of 'demand sharing' (1993). He draws on Myers's (1986) description of authority among Pintupi people to observe that 'Collectively and individually, members of the senior generation are obliged to look after and nurture the succeeding generation, preparing them for holding the law. Hierarchy and authority thus come to be presented in the guise of concern and nurturing, and in consequence, generosity becomes the complement of authority. In return for respect and deference, the subordinate generation can legitimately make demands for goods on their relatives in the senior generation. Of course, such demands are not made at random, but where a history of services leads to an expectation that they should or will be met' (Petersen 1993:869–70). It is this exchange of deference for nurture, of respect for goods that is precisely what many at Matupit fear has broken down. Many elders complain that the respect is not forthcoming, such that the 'subordinate generation' now only make illegitimate demands. This feeling of lack of respect is mirrored by many persons in the younger generation claiming that their elders do not school them in *kastom* properly because the elders are lazy and cannot be bothered. On my last visit to Matupit in 2010, I spent time with some young men at the village of Malaguna Number One, which is now adjoining to the edge of Rabaul Town and is if anything even more 'urbanised' than Matupit. They were extremely scornful of elders who told them to go to the bush to learn *kastom* and respect, pointing out that their village had no bush anymore because previous generations of elders had sold it all off to foreigners or the government.

13. A.L. Epstein (1999:61–62) mentions the case of one man in the early 1960s who assaulted his own mother and subsequently knocked out his uncle's teeth. He was pulled before a village moot and ordered to pay compensation. A.L. Epstein's description gives the impression of a man who was widely considered to be uniquely and pathologically unbalanced, not the exemplar of a worrying new social trend.

14. See also Gewertz and Errington (1999) for parallel examples from another PNG area of the emerging middle class simultaneously berating the grassroots for being too individualistic and not individualistic enough.

15. According to A.L. Epstein (1992:91) most fishing nets at Matupit in the mid-1980s were owned by groups. While I did not have time to conduct a full survey of every net at Matupit during my fieldwork, I found that group ownership was still common, but that there were also many nets that were individually owned.

16. Salisbury (1970:239) describes net fishing as 'more clearly a business in the European sense' than trap fishing, as: 'more than mere investment is needed if a good yield is to be returned. Not only must a substantial labour force be organised but the net must be dried and repaired after each use.' This is true, but compared to the need to buy goods from a Chinese or Australian wholesaler in Rabaul, these labour requirements are a comparatively easy hurdle to negotiate. If the _wantoks_ bleed a fish trap owner dry, he can still convince young men to work for him on the basis of future expected returns. A trade store owner who goes to a wholesaler in town and explains that his relatives have eaten all of his profits, so that he needs to get stock on credit to make up the difference, is not likely to receive quite so enthusiastic a response.

17. A.L. Epstein (1963:190) even claims that the large numbers of men required to operate and maintain a net means that net fishing 'therefore, has a corporate aspect lacking in the case of trap fishing'. However, we have seen that the cooperation of large groups of men is also required at certain moments in the career of a fish trap, such as its launch and at the time of fish collection. More significantly, events such as the *vevedek* (the end-of-season count) demonstrate a corporate aspect of fish trap use that is not simply determined by the kind of material technology being used, but is also partially the consequence of its position within wider networks of exchange. Fish nets at Matupit today, in which the net owner simply keeps the financial profit after paying those who have worked on the net, give the appearance in this respect at least of being less 'corporate' than the traps of the 1960s as described by A.L. Epstein and my older informants.

9

Big Men, Big Shots and Bourgeois Individuals

Conflicts over Moral Obligation and the Limits of Reciprocity

One evening towards the end of my fieldwork, I was accosted by a drunk. I was in a bar in Kokopo, the Provincial Capital and my friends and I were chatting in Kuanua, when a well-dressed middle-aged man grabbed me by the shoulder and insisted that I speak in English, as the poor standard of my Kuanua made me 'sound like a dog'. For the past few weeks, national news had been dominated by the Australian government's attempts to get the PNG government to agree to the placement of Australian officials in overseeing positions in PNG governmental departments to counteract perceived corruption and inefficiency, and as a precondition of continued economic aid. As the evening progressed it emerged that my new friend, a non-Tolai from the neighbouring province of New Ireland, was a senior public servant, determined to let off steam at the alleged arrogance of white expatriates. Our debate was concluded when he grabbed me by the face, necessitating a measured but equivalent physical response on my own part. Shortly after this he left the building, escorted by the club's security.

The next morning, I dropped into the bar for a coffee, and recognised one of the security men from the night before. He told me that when they escorted my sparring partner to his car, he was so drunk that he had spent a minute trying to open the car door, before the security informed him that his car was parked on the other side of the street and that this car belonged to another man. I laughed and replied in Tok Pisin, '*kain stail bilong ol bikman*' (that's typical behaviour for big men). He shook his head and told me that 'in Tok Pisin we don't call this kind of man "Big Man", in Tok Pisin we call this kind of man "Big Shot"' (*long Tok Pisin mipela no save kolim dispela kain man, 'bikman'; long Tok Pisin mipela kolim dispela kain man 'Big Shot'*).

The Emergence of the 'Big Shots'

I have told this story because it is a particularly clear observation on the reasons for the emergence of the term 'Big Shot'. By correcting me on my use of language, the security guard was drawing attention to the perception that 'this kind of man' represented a type of person so different from the figure ideally described by the Tok Pisin term *bikman*, that a new word was required to describe him. The emergence of the term marks a local acknowledgement of the fact that new types of social practice are becoming possible (and older types of practice no longer sustainable), and it marks a negative moral evaluation of these possibilities. As such, it is a specific Melanesian instance of a global phenomenon of renegotiations of moral obligations in the context of postcolonial disillusionment and neo-liberal economic restructuring, renegotiations that are commented upon through emergence of new terms that take their power from creative subversion of older well-established local expressions.

Often the alternative to the assumption of a tidal wave of globalisation leading to blanket commodification and Westernisation is the mirror assumption of deep-rooted cultural continuity that underlies surface changes. In this picture there tends to be an 'indigenization' (Sahlins 2005:28) of Western commodities by local cultures that then turn them to their own ends.[1] Such models often tend to amount to a mirror-image of the notion of universalisation that they seek to critique, sharing an assumption of a discrete, separate and essentially ahistorical indigenous culture that is either destroyed by or survives the threat of Westernisation. Given this impossible choice, anthropological theory, as Robbins (2007:301) notes, has tended to overstress 'cultural continuities' in the South Pacific and beyond.

The analysis in this chapter builds upon previous analyses that stress the historically shifting coevality of different types of transactions (Gregory 1982, 1997), and most importantly the contested differing evaluations of the same transactions and relations (Mauss 1970:20, Martin 2008c). In East New Britain, as elsewhere, this means understanding the ways in which different people make different moral assessments of particular transactions. In particular it entails paying close attention to how those people's divergent evaluations are partially contingent upon their position within global political economic flows of commerce and power and the social perspectives might make sense from particular social positions. Such assessments do not provide evidence for either a deep-seated cultural continuity or an unproblematic process of commodification or individuation, but rather display the continuing importance of ethnography in demonstrating the nuances of judgement by which people make sense of their particular position in a global political economy.

The term 'Big Shot' is a commonly used slang term in English throughout the world, leading one to suspect that it was probably introduced to East New Britain from the outside, whether by an expatriate resident or through the global media. The origin of the term's introduction into everyday Tolai Tok Pisin is not important, however, to the analysis I develop here. What is important is that it has been adopted in recent years by Tolai at a time when its use in deliberate rhetorical contrast to the well-established Tok Pisin term *bikman* makes sense to increasing numbers of people. Its very emergence as a word in Tolai Tok Pisin acts as an 'index of social change' (Volosinov 1973:19). This case, in which the emergence of new terms acts to both mark and to make new forms of social stratification and new moral critiques of inequality is not limited in its relevance to the case of contemporary Papua New Guinea, but can be seen as an example of a long standing wider global trend.

Big Shots may be a new kind of person in Melanesia, but in the picture of them drawn by their critics they bear some striking resemblances to other kinds of persons that we are familiar with elsewhere in the world. The Big Shot is a person who is considered to have placed themselves outside of their moral obligations to others. They act as if they owed nothing of themselves to other people. The very term 'Big Shot' with its contemptuous connotation of the tall poppy waiting to be cut down to size, acts as a grassroots critique of the kind of individual subject whose existence and ontology has been so problematic for modern social theory since its inception. In particular, the popular portrayal of the Big Shot has much in common with Macpherson's description of the 'Possessive Individual' who emerged with the dawning of the early modern age in seventeenth-century England, embodying a 'conception of the individual as essentially the proprietor of his own person or capacities, owing nothing to society for them' (1962:3). Something like this conception of personhood is what is being subjected to grassroots critique every time the term 'Big Shot' is muttered behind the backs of the emerging indigenous elite.

Macpherson's analysis of Possessive Individualism is essentially an analysis of moral obligation, or its denial, as the quotation above makes abundantly clear. It is also a theory that links that obligation with the nature of exchange relations. Possessive individualism is a theory of the person's inherent moral obligations that Macpherson argues is particularly suited to a society in which the market, a system of commodity exchange, is the predominant form of economic exchange:

> The assumptions of possessive individualism are peculiarly appropriate to a possessive market society, for they state certain essential facts that are peculiar to that society. The individual in a possessive market society *is* human in his capacity as proprietor of his own person; his humanity does depend on his freedom from any but self-interested contractual relations with others; his society does consist of a series of market relations. (ibid.:271–72, emphasis in the original)

Macpherson was not the first person to stress the ways in which the very nature of the individual person is intimately tied in exchange relations. Adam Smith (1994:14) famously explained the historical evolution of the division of labour as 'the necessary . . . consequence of a certain propensity in human nature . . . the propensity to truck, barter, and exchange one thing for another'. For Smith, this exchange was synonymous with commodity exchange; hence market exchange became the outcome of the nature of the individual human, rather than, as Macpherson argues, market exchange encouraging a theory of possessive individualism.

Marx, by contrast, links exchange with the nature of the individual person in a manner more reminiscent of Macpherson. Because for Marx, commodity exchange was not the universally predominant form of economic transaction, commodity exchange could not be seen as an outgrowth of a propensity in human nature. Instead, the particular forms of exchange that predominated in any given social context had an immense impact upon how the moral status of the individual person and the nature of their inherent obligations to others was presented and theorised. For example, he states in *Capital* that 'For a society of commodity producers . . . Christianity with its religious cult of man in the abstract, more particularly in its bourgeois development, i.e. in Protestantism, Deism, etc., is the most fitting form of religion' (Marx 1976:172). Marx's concern to undermine the naturalisation of the individual is even clearer in his unpublished notes on political economy that were to become the basis of *Capital*, as in the following extended passage:

The solitary and isolated hunter or fisherman, who serves Adam Smith and Ricardo as a starting point, is one of the unimaginative fantasies of eighteenth-century romances a la Robinson Crusoe . . . No more is Rousseau's *contrat social*, which by means of a contract establishes a relationship and connection between subjects that are by nature independent, based on this kind of naturalism. This is an illusion and nothing but the aesthetic illusion of the small and big Robinsonades. It is, on the contrary, the anticipation of 'bourgeois society', which began to evolve in the sixteenth century and in the eighteenth century made giant strides towards maturity. The individual in this society of free competition seems to be rid of natural ties, etc . . . The prophets of the eighteenth century, on whose shoulders Adam Smith and Ricardo were still wholly standing, envisaged this 18th-century individual – a product of the dissolution of feudal society on the one hand and of the new productive forces evolved since the sixteenth century on the other – as an ideal whose existence belonged to the past. They saw this individual not as an historical result, but as the starting point of history; not as something evolving in the course of history, but posited by nature, because for them this individual was in conformity with nature, in keeping with their idea of human nature. (Marx 1970:188)

Although there are clear differences between Marx and Macpherson's political philosophy, they do share a concern to stress the way in which the kind of conceptions of individuality that underpin the theories of the likes of Smith, are not the starting point of history, but are conceptions that are themselves historically evolving. I share that concern and that perspective, and it has been one of my aims in this book to explore the insights that anthropology can bring to an understanding of the historical evolution of such concepts.

The Historical Evolution of Individualism in East New Britain and Beyond

One obvious criticism of the position outlined above is that it seems to advocate a crude material and economic determinism, in which once we reach a certain stage of historical development, all exchanges become commodity exchanges and some form of bourgeois individualism becomes the only way in which we can conceive of our personhood. Such a view is easily undermined by pointing out the instances in ostensibly capitalist societies in which exchanges and persons are differently presented and theorised. It is true that Marx, in particular, often formulates the relationship between different historical eras or kinds of technology on the one hand, and social relations on the other, in a manner that suggests a crude and simple determinism, such as his famous statement that '[t]he hand-mill gives you society with the feudal lord; the steam-mill, society with the industrial capitalist' (Marx 1956:122). It is easy to find exceptions to such associations, so that if such formulations are taken in isolation as statements of immutable and universal empirical fact, they are demonstrably false. This approach mischaracterises the nature of such formulations, however. Marx's intention here is not to describe universal empirical fact, but to draw out the broadest historical tendencies of certain kinds of technology to be associated with certain kinds of social relations; tendencies that are of course not iron laws of inescapable causality. Likewise with the relationship between different historical epochs on the one hand, and types of exchange and conceptions of the person on the other, the emphasis is on tendencies. Just because capitalism, as analysed by Marx is a society in which the generalised exchange of commodities predominates does not mean that every exchange is unambiguously a commodity exchange, or that the moral legitimacy of commodity relations is universally accepted in every context. Far from it; it is the potential for the rejection of the commodification of social relations that underpins Marx's hope for the revolutionary transformation of capitalist society. And it is therefore not the case that the bourgeois or possessive individual is the only way in which the person is capable of being configured in capitalist society. Marx and Macpherson's case is rather that it is a conception of the person and obligation that it makes increasing sense for particular social groups in particular social contexts as new forms of exchange acquire increasing importance. It is of course not the case that it is a conception of the person that is simply given by economic circumstances and is never challenged, contested or complicated.

That those propagating historical explanations of the roots of differing conceptions of individualism have to guard themselves against this danger is something that Marx's lifelong collaborator, Engels, was acutely aware of. Towards the end of his life, in a consideration of the philosophy of historical materialism that he and Marx had developed, he wrote:

> [O]nly one point has been omitted, a point which, however, was never given sufficient weight by Marx and myself in our work, and in regard to which we are all equally at fault. For we all of us began, *as we were bound to do*, by placing the main emphasis on the *derivation* of political, legal and other ideological conceptions, as of the actions induced by those conceptions, from economic fundamentals. In doing so we neglected the formal in favour of the substantial aspect, i.e., the manner in which the said conceptions, etc., arise. This provided our opponents with a welcome pretext for misinterpretation, not to say distortion. (Engels in Marx and Engels 2004:164, emphasis in the original)[2]

It is this gap, the 'substantial aspect', the manner in which 'conceptions' such as possessive individualism are put forward, that ethnography is uniquely qualified to fill. Ethnography can examine the relationships between different 'conceptions' of the person, and the changing 'economic fundamentals' of exchange, be they the rise of mercantile capitalism in seventeenth-century England, or integration into a global capitalist economy in twentieth-century New Guinea. And by examining Engels' 'substantial' aspect it can do so in a manner that does not reify economic relations, giving them a mysterious and inexplicable agency that forces people into certain kinds of relations and ways of thinking. Such a reification is evident in some of Marx's own broader descriptions of general tendencies, and indeed in contemporary accounts that present an image of neo-liberal globalisation as tidal waves that 'impact' upon pre-existing cultures. Rather, ethnography provides the opportunity to examine the contexts in which people assert or reject different kinds of characterisations of economic transactions, or the individual's nature and inherent obligations, freeing us from a simplistic cause and effect mechanical determinism, but also freeing us from a kind of disembodied idealism in which conceptions of the individual are free floating notions with no relation to the ever changing social relations of a global political economy within which their progenitors are entwined.

It is not enough to state that the Big Shot, as a concept, is the outcome of postcolonial PNG's position in a global political economy. Rather, the task is to ethnographically examine the processes by which conceptions make sense of and help to constitute new kinds of social relations in contemporary PNG. The Big Shot is seen as being a person who at certain moments denies any inherent obligation or entailment to kin or others, and instead, like Macpherson's possessive individual presents themselves as proprietor of their own self. It is not my contention that PNG has abandoned a sense of essential collectivism to replace it with a Western individualism in the face of waves of capitalist 'penetration'. But I do argue that changing circumstances mean that for some people it makes sense to partially deny inherent mutual obligation in certain contexts, and hence to constitute themselves as Melanesian Possessive Individuals in contexts where this may not have been possible in the past. As circumstances change, the conditions in which people acknowledge or reject the legitimacy of claims made on the basis of mutual reciprocal obligation also change, and the moral contest over the extent of such obligations is part of the process by which people change the social circumstances in which they find themselves. In this book I have examined some instances of the ways in which people contest the extent of such claims. Does buying land remove you from relations of mutual obligation to the vendors? To what extent can the section of a clan constitute itself as a collective individual owner of a plot of land without reference to wider related clan section? Do 'customary' landholders whose land was alienated by the colonial regimes still have legitimate claims that they can make upon the postcolonial state on the basis of an ongoing obligation? To what extent does customary wealth bought with money satisfactorily discharge reciprocal obligations? Indeed is 'custom' truly customary anymore? I have aimed to show that all of these issues are instances of disputes in which the central moral dilemma is the extent to which claims made on the basis of reciprocal obligation can legitimately be made, or denied, thus, in this context at least, constituting the persons or groups involved as individuals with no inherent obligation to others beyond those that they choose to contract. The Big Shot, as the negatively evaluated modern leader, is perhaps the most striking example of this tendency. In order to understand the Big Shot as the morally ambiguous prophet of possessive individualism it is necessary to examine the idealised leader of the past, against whom the Big Shot is negatively defined: the Big Man.

Not only is the term 'Big Man' in common day-to-day use amongst Papua New Guineans, but the Big Man has long been the most recognisable figure in Melanesian anthropology, helping to define the ethnographic culture area by virtue of his perceived contrast as a leader with Polynesian 'chiefs' (Sahlins 1963:285). Two linked characteristics tend to define the Big Man, as an 'abstracted sociological type' (ibid.), in the ethnography of the region. The first is that the Big Man is a self-made leader, who does not inherit or even assume a fixed office, but is constantly having to prove his suitability as an organiser of social relations (Sahlins 1963:289). Ultimately a man becomes 'Big' by extending the number of people who are indebted to him (Gregory 1980:638), and thereby building an army of followers (Sahlins 1963:290–91), who rely on him in order to organise necessary events such as sponsoring marriage payments (Sahlins 1963:292, Martin 2006, Burridge 1975:101). These people in turn become a potential source of support in the organisation of larger exchange relations, such as marking the death of the Big Man of another clan.

This social character of the Big Man, as someone who makes himself Big by extending and drawing upon gift-debt relations is linked into his second fundamental characteristic: namely a moral ambiguity. Big Men are described as having to 'tread a delicate path' (Burridge 1975:96). Unlike the Polynesian chief, they constantly have to prove their ability to organise the relations and transactions that make them valuable to their followers. The Big Man is only able to organise such activities by virtue of his own history of respecting the reciprocities of day-to-day village life (Sahlins 1963:292). The Big Man may occupy a particular position within the network of debts and obligations that make up village life, but like everyone else he is enmeshed within them. His authority, such as it is, is an outcome of the special position that he has made for himself within those networks, not the result of an independence from them (Sahlins 1963:290, Burridge 1975:96).

Because the Big Man's power is reliant upon the support of followers who are not bound to him by virtue of an office, he has to be careful not to antagonise them too much in the course of organising them into the productive and exchange activities that enable him to be 'Big' (Sahlins 1963:292–93). In many parts of PNG the relationship between Big Man and followers is described in terms of extreme flexibility, with people deciding to move from one settlement and Big Man to another almost regardless of ties of kinship (e.g. Robbins 2004:201–3). Hence his authority was to a large extent subject to wider community approval. For example, in a typical portrayal of the Melanesian Big Man as dispute settler, Reay writes of the situation in the Minj area of the Western Highlands that '[A] dispute settler had to be absolutely certain that his pronouncement would find common acceptance . . . He was dependent upon public opinion and, judging by traditional leaders hearing disputes in 1953–5, usually very sensitive to it' (Reay 1974:202).

In PNG the category of Big Man that is so familiar to anthropologists is most frequently spoken of by the Tok Pisin phrase *bikman*. The Tok Pisin term *bikman*, like its English counterpart 'Big Man', is nearly always a term of respect, as is evidenced by its most familiar opposite, the 'rubbish man' (Tok Pisin: *rabisman* or *pipiaman*), a man who is unable to place himself in a position where his words carry any weight.

Beyond this, however, it is not easy to unambiguously state exactly what is referred to by the term *bikman*. I have argued in this book that the term *bikman* is far from unique in this regard, and that the shifting and contested meanings of words, depending on context, are a key tool in the moral struggle over the extent of reciprocal obligation and interdependence in contemporary PNG. For example, as mentioned previously, A.L. Epstein (1969:164) observes that 'the term *vunatarai* has a built-in ambiguity which . . . provides the Matupi with a language of argument and social controversy'. Other examples spring to mind of which the most obvious is *kastom*, a term whose built-in ambiguity has already been analysed at length in this book.

One way in which to illustrate the ambiguity of the Tok Pisin term *bikman* is to examine the overlapping, yet distinct concepts in local vernaculars that the term is used to gloss. The term is not easily translatable from Tok Pisin into Kuanua, although there is more than one term that would instantly be rendered as *bikman* if the translation was going in the other direction. Sack (1974:73–74) provides a summary of some of the terms traditionally used to refer to leaders in Tolai society. He reports that the most important type of leader was the *lualua*. 'The basic political leadership was provided by the *lualua* of the various (territoriless) clans or lineages' (Sack 1974:73). The *lualua* tended to be the most senior male member of a clan or lineage, although a less senior man, or even a particularly knowledgeable woman, could take his place if the most senior male member was unsuitable for reasons of temperament, lack of community esteem, or insufficient knowledge (K. *varvateten*) of the correct conduct of ritual, and histories of residence necessary to protect his clan's landholding interests. Sack (1974:73) sums up the role of the *lualua* in the following words:

> The *lualua* could be the leader of his group in all its affairs, in peace and war, in internal and external matters. The primary source of his political power, the constitutional basis of his office, was his control over the scattered landholdings of his group (within and outside of the district in which he resided). Of equal importance was his control over the group's shell money . . . funds, but this source of power was less secure because shell money, in contrast to land, was personal and not group property. The role of the *lualua* in this field was that of a manager rather than a trustee.

Shell wealth provided the basis for other positions of leadership that sometimes sat uneasily with that of the *lualua*. Others could amass *tabu* for themselves and become known as *uviana* (K. rich men), and 'begin to manage shell money for themselves and their personal followers' (Sack 1974:74). Other men could become war leaders or *luluai* (ibid.), although A.L. Epstein (1969:251) claims that while this was the meaning of the term in other Tolai villages, at Matupit it merely meant 'wealthy man'. Successful men competed to become *a ngala*, or *a ngala na tutana*, or literally a 'big man'. Sack claims that it was almost essential for a man to be a *lualua* before he could become recognised as an *ngala*, because '*a ngala* needed not only the support of personal followers, but the backing of a corporate group' (Sack 1974:74). Although *a ngala na tutana* is the phrase that translates literally into English as 'big man', all the above terms would be glossed in Tok Pisin as *bikman* in discussions about village level leadership, despite the significant differences in their vernacular meanings.

Simet (1991:153–54), a native of Matupit who conducted fieldwork in his own home village in the early 1980s, describes the vernacular terms used to describe big man in a slightly different manner to Sack, at times seeming to suggest that the terms are, in certain contexts, largely interchangeable. A.L. Epstein (1969:14–15) describes the terms in a manner more reminiscent of Sack, describing the *lualua* as the leader of a local matrilineage (ibid.:14; see also T.S. Epstein 1968:6). By contrast, within each local area:

> there were usually one or two persons marked out by their possession of large stocks of shell-money who were known as 'big men' (*ngala*). Such men served as bankers to the group, and were able to bind their supporters to them by maintaining an elaborate series of debt-relationships . . . Having access to large resources of *tambu* they alone were in a position to initiate large-scale mortuary rites and ceremonial dances or to sponsor the activities associated with the cult of the *tubuan* and *dukduk*, all of which involved the participation of, and competition between individuals and groups, from a number of different parishes, and so served to extend the effective range of social relationships. (ibid.:15; see also T.S. Epstein 1968:27)

In his fieldnotes, A.L. Epstein describes the following interchange with one of his elderly informants: 'I asked then how one became a luluai: and he said by hard work – *i uvia ma ra papalum upi ra tambu* ["it comes with working for *tabu*" –KM] – and he had accumulated two or three loloi then he would be recognized as a <u>luluai</u>' (A.L. Epstein n.d.).[3]

Even from this short summary it should be clear that, just as the Tok Pisin term <u>bikman</u> can translate a variety of vernacular terms in Kuanua, so these terms themselves have a shifting range of referents. This context-dependent reference may promote 'a built-in ambiguity which . . . provides . . . a language of argument and social controversy', as far as the Tolai are concerned, but for the anthropologist it creates the problem of how to gloss such terms for the reader in a coherent yet flexible manner. In other words, the differences in defining terms such as *lualua* or *ngala* between the writers cited above should not be taken as a sign that one or other of them got the definition 'right' or 'wrong', but as another sign of the difficulty of defining the meaning of terms in a context in which referential meaning shifts depending on the social context of specific speech acts. As Volosinov points out, translation may be indispensable, but it tends to rely on a strategy of constructing living contested creative languages as if they were fixed systems of meaning making that could be decoded. As far as possible in this book, I have sought to highlight such shifting and contested meanings where they occur. Rather than seeking to find a basic referential meaning for such terms, and then attempt to explain away those meanings that contradict that meaning, I take the very contradictory and contested meaning of such terms as their most salient feature. It is the contradiction that gives meaning and importance to such terms, rather than complicating or obscuring it.

Big Man and Big Shot as Self–Made Men

Perhaps the most important feature of the varying definitions of the different Kuanua terms glossed by the Tok Pisin term *bikman*, is the fact that they are all terms that describe someone who achieved their position of leadership 'through merit'. Rather than inheriting their position, they are self-made men. The question is what kind of 'self' is made by these Big Men, and is it a kind of self-making still available in the present day?

For some writers, there is a ready-made model of the self-made man in Western societies on which the Tolai Big Man can be modelled – the entrepreneur. The entrepreneur is the Bourgeois Individual *par excellence*. He enters into exchanges with others in the interest of accumulating wealth, owes nothing to others for the capacity to enter into those exchanges, and most crucially owes others none of the wealth he makes from them. The Tolai Big Man appears to have much in common with the entrepreneur, specifically with regard to his desire to accumulate *tabu*. According to A.L. Epstein (1969:249): 'The skills of the "big man" in the past were essentially entrepreneurial. Discussing the "raising" of the *tubuan*, my informants would frequently proffer the comment that it was a "business" (using the English word) from which the sponsor hoped to see a handsome profit'.

T.S. Epstein (1968:26–31) makes this argument in more detail in a section of her monograph *Capitalism, Primitive and Modern*, entitled '"Big Men" as "Primitive Capitalists"'. She analyses the Tolai institution of the *vuvue*, as described by contact era observers in the following terms:

> '[B]ig men' in an attempt to increase their wealth often distributed presents such as different kinds of crops, spears, clubs and ornaments among their kin and neighbours who then had to pay for these gifts

on the occasion of a special feast, *vuvue*, arranged for the purpose. For the *vuvue* the 'big man' organised the erection of a special hut, which was decorated with colourful feathers. Many people turned up for the feast, dressed for the occasion. A number of them performed dances. Afterwards each man who had received a present paid for it in tambu, usually a little more than its worth. The *ngala* remembered exactly the value of each of the presents he had previously distributed and made sure the return gift exceeded the value of the original present. Then there was a big feast for all guests. On one such occasion expenses amounted to 300 fathoms tambu whereas the return totalled as much as 420 fathoms (Parkinson, 1907: 93), involving a profit of approximately 30 per cent. *The vuvue was not simply an arrangement of reciprocity but represented the investment by one 'big man'* in the form of the distribution of articles which were then generally desired by the Tolai *with the knowledge of the risk involved and the intention of making a profit.* (T.S. Epstein 1968:28, emphasis added)

From specific examples such as these, T.S. Epstein extrapolates the general conclusion that '[t]he Tolai "big man", like a true capitalist, invested his resources in order to increase his wealth' (ibid.). On a wider scale, '[p]re-contact Tolai, like modern capitalist society, was pre-occupied with the accumulation of wealth . . . people were keen to accumulate as much as possible' (1968:28–29).

This view of the Melanesian Big Man in general, and the Tolai Big Man in particular, as 'primitive capitalist' has had its critics. Most notably, Gregory (1980) takes issue with a number of depictions of Melanesian Big Man politics that he claims analyse competitive gift exchange as if it were underpinned by a principle of 'interest-bearing investment of property', following Boas' (1966:77) analysis of potlatch. Gregory includes T.S. Epstein's analysis of the Tolai Big Man as 'primitive capitalist' among the accounts he criticises:

> The motivation of the gift transactor, some people believe (Epstein, 1968; Pospisil, 1963), is that of the capitalist, i.e. profit maximisation. This is a profound misunderstanding. The gift transactor's motivation is precisely opposite to the capitalist's: whereas the latter maximises net incomings, the former maximises net outgoings. The aim of the capitalist is to accumulate profit while the aim of the 'big-man' gift transactor is to acquire a large following of people (gift-debtors) who are obligated to him. (Gregory 1982:51; see also Gregory 1980:638)

There is plenty in the Tolai ethnographic record to support this rival picture of the Big Man, not as primitive capitalist, but as the entrepreneur's conceptual opposite. Take for example the definition provided by A.L. Epstein cited earlier: '"[B]ig men" ... were able to bind their supporters to them by maintaining an elaborate series of debt-relationships ... all of which ... served to extend the effective range of social relationships'. Or as he puts it elsewhere: '"Big man" leadership of the kind we have been considering here depends upon the presence of an institutionalised form of wealth, in this case *tambu*, which through the network of the exchange system, can be manipulated to create a following of political supporters' (op.cit.:250).

A.L. Epstein's fieldnotes contain a conversation that clearly demonstrates an indigenous analysis of how the Big Man uses *tabu* that explicitly eschews a commercial motivation, but instead concentrates on the Big Man's desire to maximise indebtedness, in language that could almost have been taken directly from Gregory: 'Labit denied that there was much in the way of borrowing: rather one who had much *tambu* helped those with a little. In this way *iau rang bat diat* [I make them indebted –KM], i.e. he explained his *varkurai* [K. jurisdiction –KM] would extend very far because many indeed were indebted to him' (A.L. Epstein n.d.).

Marriage provides a good example of the different ways in which the motivations for *tabu* transactions can be interpreted. The details of marriage transactions past and present have been more fully explored in Chapter Eight. Here it is sufficient to repeat that in the past it was largely considered the responsibility of the groom's *vunatarai* to arrange a *tabu* payment as a part of the exchange that constituted marriage. Anyone wishing to be considered seriously as a big man would have to play a central role in arranging that payment, whether as the trustee who looks after the group's *tabu*, or as the provider of a large share of the bridewealth payment. 'The "big man" paid the bridewealth for young men of his kin-group, who then had to work for him to pay off their debts. In this way, he used tambu as capital for productive investment' (T.S. Epstein 1968:29). Or, as A.L. Epstein elaborates at greater length:

> In the past a man began to make his mark as a future leader of his descent group when through his own efforts he started to accumulate wealth and then gradually came to contribute his share to various *vunatarai* undertakings. Thereafter, as *lualua* of his group, arranging the marriages of his uterine nephews and nieces was one of his most important tasks. This was an onerous responsibility; it was as the same time one of the chief means available to him of asserting control over the younger members of the groups, for a young man who showed himself indolent or in other ways earned the displeasure of his elders would find trouble in getting married. Assuming responsibility for the payment of bride-wealth was thus a way of creating dependents, and the stamp of the really 'big man' was that

he extended this responsibility to his sons and to his more distantly connected matrilateral kin. (A.L. Epstein 1969:223)

In the first description the Big Man does indeed extend obligations, but ultimately only as a means to increase his capital investment. In the second, the extension of obligations and dependents is itself the end. The implication is that these are debts that are not intended to be directly repaid; an implication backed up by my older interlocutors' recollections, and also by A.L. Epstein's fieldnotes: 'Turpui denied that a young man would work to pay off the tambu expended on his varkukul' (A.L. Epstein n.d.).

What sense are we to make of this contradiction? The Tolai Big Man clearly seemed to have his 'entrepreneurial' moments. During my fieldwork in East New Britain, the motives of customary leaders with regard to the organisation of *tubuan* initiation rituals were described in terms of 'business' and 'profit' almost identical to those reported by A.L. Epstein. However, the Big Man did not simply accumulate, but accumulated in order to disperse his wealth and build up obligations. In ethnographic accounts that pay attention to this aspect of 'Big Man-ship', the Big Man appears as the opposite of Marx's bourgeois entrepreneur, who is pushed by the pressure of competition to accumulate capital so that he can reinvest in his business to stay ahead of the competition: 'Accumulate, accumulate! That is Moses and the prophets! . . . Accumulation for the sake of accumulation . . . this was the formula in which classical economics expressed the historical mission of the bourgeoisie' (Marx 1976:742). This characterisation of the capitalist entrepreneur is remarkably similar to T.S. Epstein's characterisation of the Tolai Big Man as primitive capitalist, who focuses on the accumulation of wealth as the key to the Big Man's social position: 'From an economic point of view the accumulation of large amounts of tambu must be regarded as an aim in itself rather than a means to an end' (T.S. Epstein 1968:26).

However, as T.S. Epstein herself notes: 'The rich had hardly any greater or different range of commodities at their disposal than the poor. Yet *wealth did act as a means to an end in the social and political sphere*. It was associated with power and prestige' (ibid., emphasis added).

She goes on to cite the early German observer, Schneider:

A man did not go to all the trouble of collecting tambu just to be a miser or to have a more comfortable life, or to make his family richer; rather he did this so that his accumulated wealth would be distributed on his death in order that a lot of people would cry and speak of him with respect and arrange many feasts (Schneider, 1905: 36). (ibid.)

The Big Man would indeed try to ensure that alongside the relations of indebtedness that he built up over the course of a lifetime, he also wanted to ensure that there was a large amount of *tabu* ready to be distributed at his death, whether that be his own personal accumulated wealth or whether it be *tabu* belonging to kin or others who were indebted to him. 'During mortuary rites for a wealthy man almost all of his accumulated stock of tambu was distributed as well as some belonging to his next of kin' (ibid.).

> The distribution of the hoarded stocks at rituals and ceremonies appears to have been the only way in which the greater part of the accumulated wealth at any one time was actually used. There was no way open to a 'big man' to convert at least some part of his tambu wealth into some other durable asset; their technology was far too primitive for that. All he could do was translate his economic achievements into prestige and political influence. (T.S. Epstein 1968:30)

The implication here is clear, that the accumulation of *tabu* that did occur was directed towards an end; the end being the prestige that was gained through its dispersal. It is the giving away of *tabu*, not its accumulation per se. that is the source of its power. Whether by sponsoring marriages and *vunatarai* activities in life, or through distribution at death, the Big Man's orientation towards *tabu* was not simply 'accumulation for the sake of accumulation', but rather 'accumulation for the sake of distribution'. The situation is nicely summed up by the conclusion of the discussion between A.L. Epstein and one of his informants that I quoted earlier. After having told A.L. Epstein that accumulation of large amounts of *tabu* is what makes a Big Man:

> He went on to give another example: suppose that I am a luluai and I die, ToVauta will come in order to prepare the mortuary rites over me. Now in doing this *he will have expended his tambu in distributing it amongst the people . . . and thenceforth it would be said of ToVauta that he was luluai.* (A.L. Epstein n.d., emphasis added)

It may be the case that the Big Man's control over the *tabu* that made a young man's marriage possible provided 'a means of asserting control of the youngest members of the groups'. But it was equally the case that the expectation that the Big Man would make marriages possible was fundamental to his position. In cases in which a young man was not widely considered to be 'indolent' or big headed, a Big Man who consistently failed to arrange the *tabu* transactions that made marriage possible, quite simply ceased to be a Big Man.

Although the Big Man's control of *tabu* was central to his power to organise social relations, it was not a titanic power abstracted from social relations and often standing in opposition to the community's social morality, as the capitalist's power is often perceived. The position of Big Man was not inherited; the dispersal of accumulated *tabu* at a Big Man's death helped to see to that: 'During mortuary rites for a wealthy man almost all of his accumulated stock of tambu was distributed as well as some belonging to his next of kin, and hence the power arena was always left wide open for new and enterprising contestants to enter' (T.S. Epstein 1968:26).

An aspiring young man largely acquired *tabu* through his own efforts. However, as I have already described, this was not only a question of working hard in the gardens or the fish traps whilst others were indolent. Such work to acquire *tabu* was also the prerequisite for assistance from established elder men who had already acquired *tabu*. Men only acquired *tabu* that led to their emergence as Big Men through entry into the web of reciprocal obligation and interdependence of the village, and the power that their *tabu* gave them was tied into and reliant upon the continued observance and reconstitution of those obligations. Although Big Men were big because they could extend their 'gift-credit' (Gregory 1980:638) further than other men, they themselves were not free of obligation. The very accumulation of *tabu* that led to their emergence as Big Men was reliant on playing the game of reciprocal obligation, and in the course of doing so they inevitably gathered gift-debts to others. When T.S. Epstein (1964:65) reports that 'children grow up into a network of credits and debts from which they will find it very difficult to disentangle themselves', this is as true for the Big Man as it was for other villagers, even if the Big Man's position in the network of 'debts' and 'credits' is one in which he is in a position of greater authority.

In the past it was the Big Man who was responsible for the expeditions to trade with other groups for the shells from which *tabu* was made (Simet 1991:86). But the organisation of such expeditions would have inevitably involved the use of ties of reciprocal obligation in the village in which the 'entrepreneurial' Big Man was himself enmeshed. His power came from those ties in the village and was reliant upon people in the village recognising that he had respected those ties. This power was not an external force that can sweep away the opposition of a community, like the money that enables an American capitalist to buy an English football club, saddling it with his debt, against the wishes of the community of supporters who feel that something in which they had a stake has been ripped away from them against their wishes.

The Changing Political Economy of *Tabu* and the Ambivalence of Wealthy Men, Past and Present

The Tolai today are enmeshed in a very different kind of political economy from that of the early colonial era descriptions, when Big Men organised canoe trips to the Nakanai to collect *tabu* shells. Simet (1991:80–99) details the ways in which *tabu* collection and accumulation changed in the course of the twentieth century. At Matupit, in the years following World War II, there was an unprecedented shortage of *tabu*. The Japanese occupied the area during the war and they destroyed much of the *tabu* that had been accumulated. Most of the rest was spent on buying food at other villages that the Japanese paid less attention to (A.L. Epstein 1969:32). A.L. Epstein could already talk of *tabu*, and indeed the 'Big Man', as if they were dying species:

> Following the losses of the last war the older men have become poor in cash as well as shell-money, and the wealth of the community, measured in savings and personal property, is mostly in the hands of younger people who lack formal status within the village. Cash earnings are put to personal and private ends: building a permanent style house and furnishing it in the modern fashion, buying a motor-cycle or car and the like; unlike *tambu*, the new wealth is not invested in the sponsorship of ceremonies and other activities which in the past would have opened the way to prestige and influence. At Matupit therefore there has been a marked decline in ceremonial life, a tendency which the elders deplore but which they are powerless to stem, still less to reverse. The conditions for the emergence of 'big men' of the traditional type no longer exist. (A.L. Epstein 1969:308)

> At Matupit, as we have seen, loss of accumulated stocks of shell-money during the war, and increasing involvement in the wage and cash economy after the war, have seriously affected the capacity and interest of the islanders to accumulate shell-money and put it to work. Consequently, there has been a decline in their ceremonial life, accompanied by the virtual disappearance of 'big men' of the traditional type. (A.L. Epstein 1969:250)

In fact, during the 1970s and 1980s the Matupi restored their stocks of *tabu*, and ceremonies that had not been seen since the war reappeared. Men were once again able to organise impressive feasts such as the *balaguan* in which they gave away large amounts of *tabu*, and expressed their renown. Yet in the eyes of most Matupi, A.L. Epstein's most fundamental assertion has been proved correct. Most Matupi would agree that 'big men of the traditional type' had indeed disappeared. On my arrival at Matupit, like any good Melanesian ethnographer, I asked who the Big Men were, only to be answered with the same phrase time after time, 'all the Big Men are dead'. It was an answer that I found initially hard to understand. Big Men may die, but who took their place now? 'No one', seemed to be the universal response. As much as anything, this book has been an attempt to understand how the Matupi came to a place where such an answer seemed to be the most sensible response to my question.

A.L. Epstein predicted that the end of *tabu* would kill ceremonial ritual and the traditional Big Man at Matupit. Instead *tabu* and ritual have returned, but it is the ways in which *tabu* is acquired today that make its accumulation in large amounts, by some at least, morally dubious in the eyes of many. As we have seen, the Big Shot's *tabu* seems to have a different moral status from the *tabu* that was accumulated by the idealised Big Men of the past. Their involvement in commerce and government, and in particular their attempts to partially separate these activities from custom, lead to their commitment to the ethic of reciprocal interdependence being called into question.

Moral dilemmas such as this concerning the role of emerging elites in village life have a long pedigree. T.S. Epstein (1964) gives the example of ToDungan, a resident of the Tolai village of Rapitok. In the years after the war, many enterprises had been started on a *vunatarai* basis; clan members would pool their money to buy cars or copra dryers as a business investment. Unfortunately disputes over responsibility for repair and maintenance led to the collapse of most of these business ventures, leading ToDungan to take the unusual step of accumulating money in order to invest it in individually owned trucks and copra dryers. This made him 'one of the few Tolai to have succeeded in establishing individual ownership of capital assets' (T.S. Epstein 1964:61). T.S. Epstein describes ToDungan's standing in the community thus:

> The fact is that they are ambivalent towards him. On the one hand they admire his thrift and enterprise as well as his forceful personality; on the other, they are envious of his economic success and criticize his purely materialistic outlook. 'He cares more for money than for his people,' is a constant complaint levelled against him. Yet he is well-versed in most traditional activities, such as the *Tubuan* cult, the *Tabaran* dances, the making of *garamuts* (large drums), *kundus* (small drums) and so on. (T.S. Epstein 1964:64)

In this description we already see many of the negatively defining characteristics of the new popular term of disrespect, 'Big Shot'. ToDungan is characterised as greedy and obsessed with money at the expense of his people, despite that he is involved in customary activities. (T.S. Epstein clearly indicates that involvement in such activities should ideally protect him from such accusations, by starting her concluding sentence 'Yet he is well-versed in most traditional activities . . .'.) Especially notable is T.S. Epstein's depiction of how ToDungan's individual ownership of capital is widely seen as in conflict with the kind of village-based reciprocal obligations constituted through and symbolised by ritual circulation of *tabu*. Of all previous ethnographers of the Tolai, she is the most disposed to make the argument that Big Man *tabu* accumulation is a form of primitive capitalist accumulation.

The problematic figure of the Big Shot thus has his precedents in Tolai social life. But the situation today is in many ways different from that of nearly half a century ago, when the Epsteins were conducting their fieldwork. ToDungan still lived in the village, and despite his 'capital assets', his life was unlikely to have been materially different from his distrustful fellow villagers. He would have eaten similar food, and lived in a similar house. As T.S. Epstein states, 'there is little differentiation noticeable in the everyday standard of living' (T.S. Epstein 1964:65–66). Although well-educated Tolai might have had jobs as clerks in the colonial government, truly elite positions such as head of government department, university academic, parliamentarian or international diplomat were beyond imagining. Today's Big Shot, by contrast, may return to the village to participate in or lead a customary ritual, but unlike Big Men of earlier times he may return in his four wheel drive truck, from his office in town where the OBE presented to him by the Governor General is kept in a safe next to the title deeds of his property investments in Queensland and Canberra.

In the national election of 2002, Sir John Kaputin was defeated by the largest margin in the entire country. His defeat was notable as he had been a Member of Parliament for thirty years, was one of PNG's most respected elder statesmen and had previously enjoyed great popularity in the region as a result of his leading role in the Mataungan Association, a Tolai led anti-colonial movement in the early 1970s. In the course of the campaign what convinced me that his main challenger, Alan Marat, was likely to win handsomely was the way in which Kaputin's opponents increasingly succeeded in attaching the term 'Big Shot' to him in discussions in the village, even to the point that his supporters stopped objecting when the term was applied.

Every time the term Big Shot is attached to a particular individual as a moral critique of their distance from their kin in the villages it both reflects and reinforces an emergent grassroots ideology in which the separation of interests of 'grassroots' from 'Big Shots', and the moral culpability of the Big Shots, are accepted facts. When the security guard at the nightclub explicitly drew my attention to the distinction between how 'we' refer to these people as Big Shots, not Big Men, he was trying to shape a broad commonsense consensus concerning the existence of the negative category of persons known as Big Shots. The same is true every time the term is used. When someone refers to another as a Big Shot it means not only that they want to condemn that person, but that they are also relying upon and reinforcing the growing commonsense assumption that there is an 'incommensurate difference' (Gewertz and Errington 1991:56) between Big Shots and both contemporary grassroots villagers and the now idealised Big Men of the past. Even when someone uses the term reluctantly, as Kaputin's followers were increasingly forced to do during the campaign of 2002, it marks a grudging acknowledgement that this particular piece of rhetorical terrain has been lost.

Portraits of Three Big Shots

To convey a feeling of the kind of problem that existence as a Big Shot presents, both to the Big Shot and to those that he has dealings with, I will present three portraits of Big Shots that seek to illuminate the kinds of contradiction at the very heart of their being. These portraits are composites, not descriptions of particular individuals. But based upon my fieldwork in East New Britain, I believe that they accurately depict the kind of dilemmas at the heart of the Big Shot's existence.

The first Big Shot is a government minister. He comes from a Tolai village on the North Coast. His father was a renowned Big Man in custom, but was, even by standards of the 1950s, financially poor, his *tabu* having been accumulated through careful attention to the give and take of everyday village life. The minister was from the generation of young men who were picked out for success at school during the 1960s, as the Australians sought to train an indigenous educational elite capable of assuming more senior bureaucratic duties in preparation for independence. As the political struggles that hastened independence erupted in the late 1960s and early 1970s, the future minister, like many of his peers, dropped out of university education and used the academic skills he had acquired from the Australian regime against it. The prominence that he achieved in the course of those struggles led to his eventual election to the PNG national parliament in the 1980s. Since then he has held various ministerial positions as coalition governments have been formed and then fallen apart. Currently he holds a senior cabinet position. On the afternoon that we encounter him, he is flying back into East New Britain's regional airport at Tokua, in order to resolve a dispute. A new road into the new provincial capital at Kokopo is being built, but angry villagers in his constituency are blocking access for the contractors, claiming that they are true customary landholders, whose land was alienated under previous colonial regimes. Their demands include compensation for the building of the road, and also that members of their *vunatarai* should be given priority when it comes to contracting for manual work that does not require capital intensive equipment. As someone who comes from a similar background to the villagers and who therefore knows the feeling behind their claims, and also as someone who has learnt the value of pragmatism over the course of three decades in politics, perhaps he feels that the best thing to do would be to cut a deal enabling the work to go ahead without a long delay. However, the current mood in the capital city Port Moresby is to be hard on customary compensation claims.

The feeling among top political circles is that they are one of the main disincentives to the outside capital investment that is felt to be essential if PNG is to halt and reverse the economic decline that it has suffered over the past two decades. This feeling has been wholeheartedly and pointedly endorsed in a recent public speech by the High Commissioner of Australia, PNG's major aid donor. The High Commissioner has warned that his government and people's patience with their 'generous' aid package being 'wasted' on corruption and unfounded opportunistic compensation claims is rapidly coming to an end. On top of this, competitive tendering for contracts is a condition attached to funding of the redevelopment programme by donors such as the World Bank. Thus, even if a deal with customary landholders was pragmatically desirable, it cannot even be contemplated. The returning Big Shot cannot lose sight of these imperatives.

However, his position is complicated by his history. Land disputes focused on alleged unjust colonial alienation were central to the political struggles that led both to early independence and the launch of the Big Shot's career. His current position may give him no choice but to stick to the government line that the legal validity of such land transfers can now no longer be questioned, but it is not hard for grassroots critics living in the villages that he has left behind to point to his hypocrisy, and to imply that he has been bought off with power and money. His position is even more complicated by his relations to the protesters. Although he is not from the village concerned, his father was born in that village and was a member of the *vunatarai* that is involved in the current protests. As a child of the clan, he has provided assistance at customary events involving his father's *vunatarai* on many occasions in the past, in particular at mortuary feasts for deceased members of his father's clan. There he distributed large amounts of *tabu* in recognition of their contribution to 'fathering' him. Now, as he stands in his father's village, explaining the government's position to assembled members of his father's clan, he is met by the sullen stares of men with whom he has previously distributed *tabu*. They are not yet angry enough to publicly attack such a prominent visitor to their village, especially one to whom they are so closely related. However, he makes no headway in convincing them to moderate their demands, and as he steps back into his four wheel drive land cruiser, he hears the word <u>biksot</u> muttered with contempt behind him. As he drives to his hotel in town, he reflects that this standoff holds long-term dangers for him. He has several hundred cocoa trees planted on land given by his father's *vunatarai* to one of his brothers. If the resentment towards him strengthens, then it will not be long before they find an excuse to claim that the gift was only ever intended to be temporary, and start removing his trees. On the other hand, a combination of his high salary, and the contacts that he has built up over the years has enabled him to acquire a couple of property investments in Australia. If he can keep his career going for another decade, he may be able to add to these. This is a much more secure retirement plan than a few hundred cocoa trees planted on land that will never be entirely free of claims from his 'fathers'.

The second Big Shot does not travel in quite such exalted circles as the first. He is still based in East New Britain, and has never dined in Canberra with the Australian Prime Minister. Nonetheless in the eyes of most Tolai he clearly qualifies as a Big Shot. He runs a construction company building homes and offices in the new provincial capital of Kokopo. He began his career working for an Australian road maintenance contractor after leaving technical college in the mid-1960s. Since then he has built up his business to the point where his is one of the few locally owned companies capable of tendering for large-scale infrastructure projects. Today, as on most days, he is driving back from town, where he has been overseeing work, to his new house. The house is a large four bedroomed building, with running water, a satellite dish, and other mod cons that would be the envy of many expatriates. It is certainly beyond the imagination of almost any of his relatives still living in his home village. The most striking feature of his new house is not its relative luxury, however, but its location. Rather than build it in his home village, he has built it on land that he has bought from another *vunatarai* in a village on the other side of Kokopo. The reason that he cites in public for this is that it is closer to most of his work, and this is undoubtedly true. However, many at his home village suspect another reason. The distance makes it hard for members of his clan and other relatives to place demands on him. If he lived in his home village, he would be subject to a host of requests for financial assistance every day. He is certainly not immune to requests for assistance even now. He has to go back to the village on occasion, he may bump into a relative in town, and sometimes one of them may make the journey to his new home and wait at his gate, while the security guard that he has hired from one of the squatter camps on the edge of town goes to check the visitor's credentials. But the distance and the inconvenience do significantly increase the amount of peace that he is able to get. He is aware of the problems caused by the distance that he has put between himself and some of his relatives, even if discontent is rarely expressed publicly. He knows about the muttering to the effect that he only helps when he has to, that his involvement in <u>kastom</u> is a series of token minimum gestures, and that he does not employ enough of his relatives. But he is also aware that such distance and the rejection of many claims placed on his person was vital to the establishment and survival of his business.

The final Big Shot cuts a different kind of figure. His involvement in customary practices can hardly be described as minimal. Indeed, he is one of the best recognised customary leaders at his own home village. Although, he observes all of the traditions for the conducting of custom as rigorously as possible, he is still caught in the horns of a contradiction. His money is largely what has enabled him to take such a leading role in custom. It takes money to sponsor feasts and even to amass large amounts of *tabu*. Yet, it is precisely the actions that he has had to take to amass that money that have led others to dismiss him as not being a customary leader. Like the second Big Shot he has made his money in business. Also in a similar manner, he has had to build barriers, both physical and social, between his business and his relatives in order for his business to survive. This has led to suspicion of his motives. The distribution of *tabu* at rituals is considered by many to be a kind of fakery, when it is accompanied by a protection of individual interest in other contexts. Today large amounts of money seem to be the only way to accumulate enough *tabu* to become a customary leader. But the actions necessary to acquire large amounts of money seem to be precisely the actions that prevent the Big Shot from being evaluated in a morally positive light in the same way as the Big Men of before. It is not that people choose to become Big Shots or Big Men, or that a man's actions lead to him being assessed as one or the other. Rather, as A.L. Epstein predicted, the Tolai Big Man no longer exists. Or if he does, he exists as an archetype: a memory of a kind of person who can no longer exist, because the social relations that made him possible no longer exist, and an ideal figure against whom the Big Shot is negatively defined.

The Emergence of the Big Shot as the Marker of Grassroots Discontent

The emergence of the category of the Big Shot marks a growing awareness that there are new possibilities in social relations for elite Papua New Guineans and these are possibilities that many grassroots villagers find morally repugnant, such as by becoming 'big' in <u>kastom</u> through the use of *tabu* bought in bulk.[4] It is a rhetorical trope that builds on and innovates upon the older category of the Big Man by isolating the negative elements within that category, in particular the resentment evoked by the Big Man's character as a bighead who ordered people around and sometimes overstepped the mark, suggesting that he had forgotten the extent of his obligation to them.

Volosinov's analysis of the word as index of social struggle concentrates mostly on the 'multiaccentuality' of words. Volosinov pays less attention to the emergence of new words, yet it is clear that the emergence of a new term can mark a shift in the social context within which meaning is constituted just as surely as shifts in meaning within existing terms. There are a number of strategies that speakers can use to attempt to mark these shifts linguistically without the creation of a new word. In particular the 'evaluative accent' (Volosinov 1973:22) that speakers put on a word could, in certain contexts, make clear their moral evaluation of that which their words refer to. So, the term 'Big

Man' could be expressed in an ironic, sarcastic or contemptuous tone in order to clearly demonstrate that the member of the new elite being referred to did not live up to the speaker's ideal of a Big Man, and this is a strategy that I have heard used on occasion. Or on other occasions, I have heard the Big Men of previous generations referred to in Tok Pisin, as *ol bikman tru tru* ('real Big Men'), with the implicit contrast with today's leaders not even needing to be made explicit in the context of the conversation.[5]

The emergence of the term 'Big Shot' is likewise a rhetorical innovation on the term 'Big Man', but of a qualitatively different type. According to Volosinov (1973:79–80): '[T]here are as many meanings of a word as there are contexts of its usage. At the same time, however, the word does not cease to be a single entity; it does not, so to speak, break apart into as many separate units as there are contexts of its usage'.

But clearly there are times when words can no longer carry the weight of increasing and emerging contradictions that they are expected to carry. Or to put it another way, there will be times when changes in the social context within which these words carry some kind of meaning, make it an appropriate rhetorical strategy to express new evaluations not simply by placing new accents on old words, but also by attempting to express meaning by coining new terms that innovate upon commonly understood old ones. This is clearly not simply a matter of individual choice but rather a matter of intersubjective creativity in which the new term being expressed has to make sense to the community of listeners that the speaker is expressing it to, both in terms of the older terms that it innovates upon and in terms of the changes in social context that make that innovation meaningful. It does me no good to repeatedly use the term 'Big Shot' if no-one else acknowledges that the differences between Big Shots and Big Men are striking enough to justify the new terminology. Only terms that can be seen to refer to something that it is important to distinguish from other categories for those who are communicating with each other:

> will achieve sign formation and become objects in semiotic communication ... The sign is a creation between individuals, a creation within a social milieu. Therefore the item in question must first acquire interindividual significance, and only then can it become an object for sign formation. In other words, *only that which has acquired social value can enter the world of ideology, take shape and establish itself there.* (Volosinov 1973:22, emphasis in the original)

The emergence of the term Big Shot in East New Britain Tok Pisin marks a widespread acceptance of an evaluation that there is such a qualitative difference between Big Men and Big Shots that there is a social value in rhetorically acknowledging the fact in language. It is this process of *evaluation* that underpins referential meaning. As Volosinov puts it: '[W]ith respect to changes of meaning, it is precisely evaluation that plays the creative role. A change in meaning is, essentially, always a *reevaluation*' (Volosinov 1973:105, emphasis in the original).

Again Volosinov's main emphasis is on 'changes of meaning' in already existing signs. But it is clear that the same general principle applies to new meanings embodied in new signs; that they too are 'molded by evaluation,' an intersubjective sense that there is something socially and morally significant enough to have its own linguistic signifier. As I have argued above, conceptually the 'Big Shot' arises out of the contradictions embedded within the 'Big Man', the former carrying in concentrated form most of the negative aspects of the moral ambiguity that that the latter contained. The 'Big Shot' thus only exists as a categorisation by virtue of this contrast with its progenitor, the 'Big Man' and in doing so also leaves the 'Big Man' altered as a concept, retrospectively idealised by contrast with the new figure who carries the Big Man's negative potential to new previously unimagined extremes, thus demonstrating Volosinov's (1973:106), general point that: 'A new significance emanates from an old one, and does so with its help, but this happens so that the new significance can enter into contradiction with the old one and restructure it'.

Thus the term 'Big Shot' carries both similarities and differences with another contemporary key term of moral evaluation in East New Britain; _kastom_. It is similar in that both are means of passing judgement on the extent to which other people adequately fulfil demands of reciprocal obligation. That which they refer to is context-dependent and subject to conflicting context-dependent evaluations. Likewise, whether or not a grassroots villager refers to a member of the new elite as a 'Big Shot' or not is equally a matter of moral evaluation. A person is less likely to be referred to as a 'Big Shot' if people have memories of them at least attempting to recognise relations and obligations to others, even if they appear to be 'objectively' of a similar socio-economic standing to someone else who is commonly referred to as such. There can even be a degree of sympathy for the individual concerned and expressions of understanding of how hard their position must be trying to balance the need to spend time in the village with the demands of their 'modern' position.

Sir John Kaputin provides an example of the ways in which different moral evaluations of the same personal behaviour are possible from a grassroots perspective. In the mid-1990s Kaputin returned to Matupit to undertake an important customary initiation. The fact that he underwent this initiation in his fifties is itself significant, as previous generations of village Big Men, such as his well-respected father, Daniel Kaputin would have undergone the process at a much younger age. However, it was understood that Sir John had had to spend time away from the village as part of his work, and there was broad sympathy for the delay. Many people nevertheless felt compelled to repeat to me the allegation that whilst undergoing initiation Kaputin had expensive 'white' food sent to him from a hotel in Rabaul Town twice a day, rather than eat the local foods that other initiands had to consume. As I have made clear in previous cases where I have discussed grassroots accusations made against Big Shots (e.g. Martin 2007b), it is not my intention to make any claim as to the veracity or falsity of the accusations. What is of most interest is not whether the claims are true or not, but what the widespread nature and belief in the truth of these claims tells us about emerging social stratification in contemporary PNG.

The hotel in question was run by two Australian expatriates with whom Sir John was known to be on friendly terms, despite the militant anti-Australianism of his early career, and despite this couple's reputation, amongst some Matupi at least, for being contemptuous towards local people. For most people who relayed this story to me it was a perfect illustration of the hypocrisy of the 'Big Shots' and the 'pastiche nature' of their involvement in _kastom_. Even when they did come back to the village to perform _kastom_ they did not really partake in village life. Likewise, when Kaputin 'returned' to Matupit, he was roundly criticised, behind his back, for staying in the hotel in town rather than with his kin in the village. Air-conditioned, mosquito-free comfort was seemingly more important to him, so his critics implied, than showing the real respect for his kin that would give his distribution of money-bought _tabu_ at customary ritual some kind of sincerity. Indeed, Kaputin was often (behind his back again) referred to as the 'Member for the "Kaivara" Hotel'.[6] But there was also an alternative evaluation of this story. Some grassroots supporters of Kaputin would admit to me that the story was true, but would then claim that after years away at university and then in politics that Kaputin could no longer stomach native foods in the way that people used to eating them year after year could. They would point to my own experience as proof. Didn't I find it hard to stomach too much taro or bananas because my stomach was used to white man's foods?

This is more a difference of evaluation than it is of fact or interpretation. Kaputin's opponents would latch onto this interpretation as proof of their position. It proved their point that Kaputin had become so separate from ordinary villagers and their interests that he was no longer even able to eat as they did. The difference is in whether or not one views that distance with sympathy or contempt, whether one views Kaputin as the victim of circumstances beyond his control or morally culpable for cultivating the white man's tastes that characterise the new elite. For every grassroots villager willing to give Kaputin some leeway, by 2002, there were plenty more willing to condemn him, as the election result that year demonstrated. As one quip often repeated amongst his opponents put it, 'JK used to be interested in us. Now he's only interested in two things: red wine and white women'.

'Big Shot' differs from *kastom* as a term of moral evaluation, however. Whereas *kastom* carries the kind of ambiguity that Volosinov (1973:23) refers to when he says that any 'current curse word can become a word of praise', 'Big Shot' by contrast – for the time being at least – seems to be unambiguously negative with little scope to be used for positive evaluation. *Kastom* is commonly used as positive evaluator. To say something is *kastom* is more often than not a mark of approval, and to deny it that status is more often than not a condemnation. However, *kastom* can be used as a negative evaluator. Sometimes when Tolai contrast the state of PNG with what they imagine the white world to be like, they can blame the very aspects of their social life that they often positively evaluate, such as the effort that goes into maintaining kinship ties and the expectation that one will share one's wealth with one's kin, and these aspects that can often be glossed under *kastom* can lead the term to be negatively evaluated. 'It is *kastom* that holds us back', I was repeatedly told – often by the same people who in other conversations would express great pride in the concept (see also Bashkow 2006:227). 'Big Shot' by contrast seems to be ambiguous only by virtue of divergences over whom the term should be used to negatively evaluate. No-one uses the term 'Big Shot' admiringly to describe someone who has managed to successfully loosen some of the negatively perceived ties of *kastom*.

The most sympathetically viewed member of the elite from Matupit was ToLanger, who lived and worked in Port Moresby. Although distanced from everyday village life, and often having to limit the demands placed on him by distant kin, ToLanger was well-respected for having an ongoing interest in *kastom*, for making the effort to return to the village as often as possible and for devoting large amounts of his time when there to visiting his extended grassroots kin. In over a year of fieldwork, I had never heard him referred to as a 'Big Shot' despite the fact that he was probably wealthier than many others who were referred to as such. One afternoon, I was sat chatting with Philip, who was describing many of the ways in which he perceived that Tolai *kastom* had changed over the decades, an account with which I was by now familiar: *kastom* today relied on money and that a lot of contemporary *kastom* 'had no meaning'. I mentioned ToLanger's opinion that despite surface changes, *kastom* remained fundamentally unchanged from the 1960s and would continue to remain so. Philip's response was one of anger and incredulity.

> What does he know? He sits in *Mosbi* [TP. Port Moresby]. He doesn't know how we live. He's eating in restaurants in Waigani [the area of Port Moresby where most senior public servants work] while we eat taro . . . while we suffer on the ground. These Big Shots don't know what life is like on the ground. They don't know how life has changed.

If you haven't got 10,000K don't talk to me about *kastom.* You have to scale, 'do I have the *tabu* and money I need?'

In common with most other villagers, Philip was usually very positive about the way in which ToLanger tried as hard as possible to 'remember' his grassroots kin. But in this conversational context, ToLanger's distance from Philip's position seemed more pertinent than ToLanger's attempts to acknowledge and ameliorate that distance. Hence it felt appropriate to Philip to denounce ToLanger as a 'Big Shot', a denunciation that he would normally reserve for other members of the elite. A member of the elite who is more sensitive than others to potential criticism may well act in a manner that makes them less susceptible to that critique. Nonetheless, the reality of the difference in social position between themselves and grassroots villagers means that there is always potentially a context from which that critique will appear pertinent.

The idealisation of Big Men of the past, in a time when their negative aspects have been distilled into the new rhetorical construction of the Big Shot, is not absolute. Older Tolai would happily tell me stories of the old Big Men, and their tendency to anger, sometimes approvingly, sometimes with disapproval, depending on the context.[7] But such themes are not commonly highlighted. In the perceived absence of 'Big Men of the traditional type', the figure's main purpose is to act as a foil against which Big Shots are negatively defined. The nuances of their behaviour are not so much forgotten, as no longer so important to recall.

Nor is the distinction absolute between the Big Man as a leader whose power is absolutely internal and accountable to the local community versus the Big Shot whose power is absolutely external and unaccountable. First, the distinction between internal and external is itself a socially constructed, and therefore a shifting and contested one. People who most villagers would label as Big Shots may in fact think that their performance of *kastom* marks them as still existing within the moral community of the village, but grassroots villagers may not be so sure. And even if we feel confident in asserting that purchase of *tabu* shells with foreign dollars is an example of an external power qualitatively different from the trading parties to the Nakanai organised by Big Men in the past, 'external' unaccountable sources of power are themselves not something completely new. Foreign colonialism and occupation in the past provided one such source of power by which some villagers gained authority over others.[8] The *luluais* and *tultuls* that Australian administrators appointed to administer villages in their absence were very different figures from today's Big Shots in most respects. But like Big Shots, they are an example of how a new source of social power led to the creation of new social categories. The categories *luluai* and *tultul* involved Australians taking two terms from

Kuanua and adapting their meaning to describe their native lieutenants, while the category Big Shot involves Papua New Guineans taking a Tok Pisin term and innovating on it in order to describe their new masters.

The Relevance of the Shifting Evaluations of Big Men and Big Shots

Just because people move between romanticising and denigrating Big Men in different contexts does not necessarily mean that the contrasts they draw between then and now are unreliable. Like the ambivalence that Bashkow (2006:209–10) observes in Orakaiva people's evaluations of White Men, these different moral evaluations represent different moments or perspectives taken on differences in the social relations of power. The radical difference in these two moral evaluations does not suggest that Tolai or Orakaiva are wrong to believe that a change has occurred. Far from it: it merely suggests that the same distinction is capable of different kinds of moral evaluation depending upon the context (see also Thompson 1991:23–24).

The impossibility of old style Big Man-ship can be seen from both angles. The Big Shot may have the wealth and customary knowledge to become a customary leader who can sponsor events, but the means by which one acquires financial wealth in postcolonial PNG rules him out of being considered by many of the grassroots villagers to be a 'real' Big Man. Even if he still lives near the village it is as inherent to his position to remove himself from elements of the give and take of everyday village life, as it was inherent to the position of the Big Man to make himself central to them. Likewise it is possible for some grassroots villagers to acquire large amounts of customary expertise through hard work. But they can never become customary leaders in the same way as the Big Shot, because they do not have the money to sponsor feasts or accumulate *tabu* in large quantities. One man from a Tolai village some distance from Matupit that I became acquainted with explained his situation to me. His elder brother once asked him to become the 'manager' of their *vunatarai tubuan* (K. *a bit na tubuan*). This man was in many respects an ideal candidate. He had dedicated much of his youth to bush knowledge while many of his brothers had pursued careers in government or business, such that he had a customary expertise they lacked. Yet, he told me, such a role was an impossibility for him. He made the international hand signal for money, and ruefully raised his eyebrows.

Sponsorship of large-scale customary events, such as a *balaguan*, has always required large amounts of *tabu* that were beyond the reach of most Tolai. A.L. Epstein (1969:239) notes that: '[P]restige was assessed in terms of the number of dances put on, the beauty of the decorations, the amount of *tambu* distributed etc. Staging such a *balaguan* might be conceived as a large-scale exercise in building up prestige; the effect of a successful sponsorship was to proclaim the emergence of a new "big man" on the scene'.

In the 1960s the main routes to gaining *tabu*, such as selling at the market would not amass any individual the amount of *tabu* required to sponsor a *balaguan*. As a result, 'sponsorship rested therefore in the hands of political entrepreneurs who amassed the necessary resources by persuading other to contribute to their enterprises' (1969:240–41). Such leadership therefore rested on the ability of the would-be Big Man to mobilise others to work with him. His power was reliant on their support. Today the main route to acquire large amounts of *tabu* is to buy it with cash. Sponsorship of such events today largely relies upon a successful career in government or business. Although A.L. Epstein (1969:240) may have inaccurately predicted that 'social forces working against the islanders' accumulation of large stocks of *tambu*' would lead to the end of *tabu* and customary ritual at Matupit, he was correct to predict that social forces were leading to the end of *tabu*'s role in making the kind of political leadership with which shell money was previously associated. Even if the rituals are formally conducted in a manner identical with that observed by A.L. Epstein, the Big Shot's purchase of *tabu* means that the money is often perceived as symbolising a different kind of leadership. To this extent A.L. Epstein was correct to argue that 'matrilineage elders may survive, or wholly new kinds of leader emerge, but there can be no more "big men" cast in the traditional mould' (1969:245).

What is striking is the degree of variation in the amount of involvement that Big Shots have in organising such large-scale customary ritual. Although most are involved to some extent, a heavy involvement in this kind of *kastom* is not a necessary precondition for success as a Big Shot or even necessarily an advantage in that respect. Although heavy involvement in *kastom* might be imagined to be a precondition for success in politics, the shocking result of the 2002 Rabaul Open Election demonstrates that this is not necessarily the case. The successful challenger, Alan Marat, was a member of an evangelical denomination that eschewed involvement in *kastom* and he was known to keep to his church's prescriptions on involvement in practices such as the *tubuan*. Although it was pointed out to me on a handful of occasions that he had close relatives who were heavily involved in *kastom*, as if that might 'cover his back' in this respect, for most people that I spoke to, both supporters and opponents, this was not an issue. In fact for many grassroots Tolai that I spoke to at Matupit and Sikut his lack of involvement in *kastom* seemed to be a positive advantage, compared to the incumbent, Sir John Kaputin, who doubtless did see his involvement in *kastom* as a political card to be played. Talking to the same Sikut resident whom I quoted in the previous chapter dismissing Kaputin and other Big Shots for not having a 'fish trap for *kastom*', I asked the man why he thought that these men wanted so much *tabu*. He replied that it was: 'to butter people up for his campaign. We used to say JK was the member for dead people. When they were alive he did nothing for them. There's still some stupid people in the village, they don't know what's going on and they say "JK helps with *tabu* . . . he eats shit, so we'll eat shit too"'.

The distribution of *tabu* at events like *minamai* was seen by some supporters of JK as a sign of his power and generosity and by some of his opponents as a cynical attempt to buy votes from the gullible. What was apparent in 2002, however, was a growing sense amongst some Matupi that they were getting too sophisticated to fall for this trick anymore. As one elderly grassroots Matupit man who was heavily involved in <u>kastom</u> put it to me shortly after my arrival: 'By getting a pocket full of money, they forgot everything, they forgot the people . . . The money makes them big . . . Big men are only big men now because they have the money. Some have got degrees and because we thought they were clever we elected them'. This man had been a supporter of the Mataungan in the 1970s and was even briefly imprisoned by the Australians for his pro-Mataungan activity. Consequently, he had voted for Kaputin in every election since 1972, but in 2002, he along with hundreds of other Matupi switched his vote to rival candidates, including the <u>kastom</u> rejecting victor, Alan Marat.

Involvement in <u>kastom</u> can certainly be thought of as a way of building a political base. Through such involvement, elites can demonstrate a degree of generosity and attentiveness to the grassroots that makes a Big Shot a potentially desirable candidate. The ability to sponsor large-scale ceremonial that pulls a large number of people can help to demonstrate that the Big Shot in question is a potentially serious candidate capable of marshalling significant support. On my last visit to East New Britain in 2010, I was still meeting Big Shots who talked openly to me in such terms. But with the emergence of a growing cynicism about the involvement of Big Shots in <u>kastom</u> it is a potentially dangerous strategy, as Kaputin's defeat in 2002 demonstrates. If the candidate is becoming tarnished owing to an alleged lack of concern for his grassroots kin, then an involvement in <u>kastom</u> can backfire, with the ways he allegedly jets back to conduct <u>kastom</u> from a hotel room or the source of his *tabu* being rhetorically turned against him.

I have often been asked, when presenting some of this material in anthropological circles since my return from fieldwork, what is the interest of other Tolai Big Shots who are not building a political career, in taking part in <u>kastom</u>, and in particular activities that involve the purchase and circulation of *tabu*. It is hard to see what they get out of it, beyond a drain on their financial resources. There does seem little immediate material benefit. For some, it is at least in part a long-term insurance strategy. Not all Big Shots will be able to retire away from the village and it is good to have at least some well-disposed neighbours when one comes back down to earth in old age. This is not true for all Big Shots, however. And as anthropologists, we are surely aware that conscious strategising only accounts for some of how and why we act as we do. The vast majority of us take part in the reproduction and reconstitution of a variety of social networks with varying degrees of involvement and willingness, from reluctantly attending family Thanksgiving Dinners and weddings to buying Christmas cards and leaving presents for work colleagues that we are not desperately fond of. The fact that we do not attend as often as some of our relatives or colleagues would like does not necessarily mean that we are being hypocritical or strategic in attending. (Nonetheless, we may be characterised as such: the person whose first attendance at a wealthy grandmother's birthday for a decade coincides with her being on her deathbed can be accused of being strategic, just as the Big Shot who remembers to fly back to do *kastom* in the run-up to an election can be also accused.) Instead we do many of things because they are important to our sense of who we are. Certainly, on the occasions when I asked Big Shots why they took part in *kastom*, they gave me answers very similar to grassroots villagers: to show respect, because we have to help our relatives and so on. And if I tried to quiz them more closely, they would become slightly confused as to what I was asking, rather in the manner that I suspect that the CEO of a major corporation might become confused if I asked them why they were attending their child's wedding when there was no financial return to it. To ask the question of why they are involved in terms of 'what's in it for them?' is to miss the point, not in the sense of imposing a 'Western' cultural value on a 'Melanesian' cultural perspective, but rather in terms of imposing a limited instrumentality on human motivation. The fact that they are fully aware that their involvement might be denigrated behind their back does not necessarily imply that they do not have motivations beyond material gain. Indeed, the denigration may spur them on, to prove to themselves at least, that they are good people who do what they should do, even if it is not appreciated.[9]

There are clear similarities between the Big Shot and other morally ambiguous figures from the past, such as entrepreneurs like ToDungan. The moral dilemma of deciding in which contexts one respects reciprocal obligations and in which contexts one insists on one's individual proprietary rights is fundamentally the same. However, as I have also tried to illustrate, the extent of the Big Shot's separation from the grassroots has massively increased. ToDungan was never going to receive a knighthood or buy a property on the Gold Coast. He may have made tentative steps towards buying *tabu* in bulk with money (T.S. Epstein 1964:64), but he was never going to be able to do so at the level of today's Big Shots. Perhaps the strongest evidence of this increased separation is the emergence of the concept of the Big Shot itself. If Volosinov (1973:19, emphasis in the original) is correct in arguing that the evolving meaning of words is 'the *most sensitive index of social changes*', then the emergence of this new category is clearly significant. It signifies a grudging acceptance that the tendencies towards morally ambiguous behaviour pioneered by the likes of ToDungan has now become institutionalised, in a manner that makes the Big Man-ship of the past obsolete, and represents the emergence of a new kind of person.

The emergence of the category of the 'Big Shot' marks the emergence of a particularly Melanesian version of a developing global discourse of the failings of postcolonial neo-liberal leadership. The Big Shot is 'particularly Melanesian', as the category only makes sense in the context of the previously well-understood category of the Big Man, and the rhetorical removal of the positive elements of that ambiguous figure in order to create a new folk-devil. It is, however, also 'global' in the sense that the 'Big Shot' has strong resonances with other rhetorical figures who have emerged in recent decades around the world, at times when large numbers of people sensed a change in the nature of the relations that tied them to their leaders, and tied their leaders to them. In some African settings, for example, a similar process by which the integration of local leaders into global political economic networks of commodity exchange changes their perception amongst the poor is also well-established (Berman 1998). The postcolonial African elite is caught in the same double-bind as PNG's emerging 'Big Shots': 'Access to the state and its patronage resources became the key to the accumulation of wealth. At the same time, the wealthy used their surplus to invest in social networks, building their own clientage and positioning themselves for access to the wider patronage networks of the state' (Berman 1998:330).

To be 'traditional', Big Men they have to become business or political leaders in a way that invalidates their Big-Manship, and to become business or political leaders, they have to build local patron-client relations in a way that corrupts their 'modern' leadership positions. The distinction between traditional Big Men and modern political leaders is not an absolute empirical distinction. Neither of the ideal types that Big Shots are denigrated for failing to live up to – the 'traditional' Big Man or the 'corruption' free political leader – exist in reality. The whole social essence of Big Shots is that they carry throughout their lives their own historically specific set of contradictions and paradoxes. But they are judged from different perspectives according to particular 'ideal types' of behaviour (Sahlins 1963:285). In this case the ideal types are ones established not by social scientists but by the elites' increasingly cynical grassroots clients, and by those who deal with them and police them on a global level such as foreign governments or 'anti-corruption' agencies like 'Transparency International'. The paradox that these figures have to straddle is that in order to live up to the expectations of one group they have to satisfy the demands of the other in a manner that leaves them morally suspect in the eyes of the first.

Globalised neo-liberalism and the consequent shrinking of the ability of the postcolonial state in the developing world to provide welfare or resources for its citizens has contributed to a growing cynicism towards the postcolonial governing class and a growing nostalgia for colonialism in PNG and Africa.[10] Despite the Tolai history of being one of PNG's most pro-independence ethnic groups in the run-up to independence, and the continuing pride of many Tolai of their role in the establishment of the Mataugnan Association, I was struck by the frequency with which grassroots villagers expressed a sense that things were better under the Australians. As one old woman asked me plaintively, 'when are the Australians coming back to look after us again?' In a neo-liberal global political economy, the postcolonial state is frequently unable to provide the kind of educational, social or infrastructural services that were provided in the colonial era, and the political elite have a shrinking pot of resources to access in order to play Big Man politics at home. As Berman (1998:337) puts it for Africa: 'Declining and contracting states are incapable of creating new programmes and positions or even paying existing officials, while patrons with declining resources become increasingly unwilling and unable to sustain distributions to their clients . . . the relations of trust underpinning patronage networks are threatened by growing cynicism and corruption'.

Such tensions are also reflected in linguistic innovations that have emerged in Africa in recent years. Take the Swahili term *wabenzi* that is apparently in common use in East African countries such as Kenya (Brown, personal correspondence). The term innovates on existing Swahili, taking the prefix *wa* that signifies 'people' and then adding *benzi* in reference to the Mercedes-Benz cars that the new elite are supposed to drive, giving a new term that literally translates as 'the Mercedes-Benz people'. The kinds of processes that have led to the linguistic innovation of 'Big Shot' are far from unique to East New Britain.

Likewise, the ambiguous coexistence of different terms to evaluate the same person (such as the man who might be described as 'Big Man' or 'Big Shot' depending on the speaker's perspective) or the coexistence of different evaluative accents on the same term (such as the occasional ironic use of 'Big Man' as an insult) is far from being a purely contemporary phenomenon. Blok (1975:151) described how in the mid-twentieth century patrons and clients in the Sicilian village that he conducted fieldwork still referred to each other as *amici* (friends) as had been done for centuries. Yet this term coexisted with a more recent term, *mafiosi*, that marked the shifting nature of that relationship within a wider changing political economic restructuring that occurred in the mid-nineteenth century. Although Blok does not go into details, it is not hard to imagine that a careful examination of the contexts in which one term was preferred to the other would be as revealing in its own way as a comparison of the contexts in which Big Shot is preferred to Big Man. And Blok

(1975:11–12) contends, the new term *mafia* itself carries 'a variety of meanings' which indicate 'the extent to which it has changed over the past hundred years', in a manner reminiscent of Volosinov's argument about the power of the linguistic sign to index social change.

Naturally it would be a mistake to dismiss the specific ethnographic details of 'Big Shots' – to simply proclaim them to be identical to *wabenzi* or *mafiosi* and leave it at that. There is no doubt that there are radical differences between sociality in Papua New Guinea and sociality in the U.K. or East Africa or Sicily. But those differences are precisely the result of PNG's unique historical position within a global political economy and network of social relations rather than the result of a kind of cultural quarantine.

It is the indigenous critique of this new kind of person that is the major concern of the final chapter of this book. My argument does not start from the premise of either unchanging cultural systems on the one hand or culture clash and radical cultural change on the other. Instead I aim to understand the grassroots critique in terms of an understanding of the social relations that Big Shots are embedded within, such as the large-scale contemporary direct purchase of *tabu* with money. I view the critique of the Big Shot as a historically particular example of the critique of a historically specific example of Bourgeois Subjectivity. The needs of capital accumulation and the kind of social relations that one has to constitute to make it possible are not identical at Matupit and Manchester. Nonetheless it is always ultimately a process that entails the forging of social relations that are often morally ambiguous and contestable. And in particular it is in disputes over the appropriate boundaries of claims on the person that can be made by virtue of an asserted history of reciprocal interdependence that sociality is constantly reinvented.

Notes

1. See also Strathern (1988:81).
2. Or as Keesing (1981:170) observes, 'Marx himself was better at applying his method than at summarising it: so that some of his own general statements of his theoretical tenets have served as texts for crude and one-dimensional materialist interpretations'.
3. A *loloi* is a large wheel of *tabu* that is usually displayed publicly on ceremonial occasions.
4. See Martin (2008a, 2008b, 2008c, 2007a, 2007b, 2006a) for different examples of this trend.
5. See White and Lindstrom (1997:1) for a discussion of the ways in which 'chiefs' have become 'the subject of contestation and transformation, especially in postcolonial states' across the South Pacific, and the ways in which these 'controversies and contestations provide a window onto the course of social and political transformation in the Pacific today' (op cit.:3).

6. This quip is itself a reference back to a previous celebrated occasion when a political opponent in the PNG parliament referred to Kaputin as the 'Honourable Member for Cairns'; a reference to Kaputin's alleged preference for spending his time in the North Australian tourist resort rather than in parliament or in his constituency.

7. See Robbins (2004:198–200) for a discussion of ambiguous responses to the Big Men's anger amongst Urapmin of PNG's West Sepik Province, and A.L. Epstein (1999:155–57) for a similar discussion at Matupit.

8. See Hogbin (1951:151–63) for an example from Busama village in New Guinea's Huon Gulf, and Bashkow (2006:38) for an example from Orakaiva. See Epstein (1969:187) for an example from Matupit.

9. Carrier and Carrier's (1989:13–14) warning against explanations 'of variation in entrepreneurial innovation' that are 'reduce[d] to social psychology', although perfectly understandable in its desire to avoid the pitfalls of methodological individualism perhaps marks an example of the danger of this kind of thinking.

10. For a discussion of postcolonial nostalgia as a response to neo-liberalism in Africa, see Bissel (2008).

Your Own _Buai_ You Must Buy

The Big Shot as Contemporary Melanesian Possessive Individual

In the previous chapter I discussed the similarities between contemporary uses of the term 'Big Shot' at Matupit, and Macpherson's analysis of the political theory of 'Possessive Individualism'. The theory of Possessive Individualism stresses the 'conception of the individual as essentially the proprietor of his own person or capacities, owing nothing to society for them' (Macpherson 1962: 3). This autonomy grants the individual the moral right to assert agency in various social spheres. Macpherson (1962:107–59) cites the Putney Debates over the extent of the franchise between the Independents and the Levellers after the English Civil War as an example. Macpherson claims that both sides to the debate share a common starting point: that of the individual who is born as the innate owner of his human capacities, and who then 'chooses' to live in ways that either maintains that natural autonomy, or alienates it to others. The debate between the Independents and the Levellers revolved around the point at which people could be considered to have ceded their natural autonomy through living lives that made them dependent on others.

It is my argument that something akin to Macpherson's description of Possessive Individualism is being asserted in postcolonial Papua New Guinea (PNG), but as in seventeenth-century England it is a contested vision, whose hegemonic scope is not readily accepted by everyone in every social context. How this ideology of the person is contested in the two contexts differ significantly, however. For the opposing sides at Putney, Possessive Individualism was taken as being a legitimate basis to morally evaluate persons within the social sphere of electoral politics. In PNG, rather than being accepted by two sides of a debate as a common good within a particular social context, the contest is over which social contexts (if any) it is appropriate to present oneself as a Possessive Individual. In the course of criticising the attitude towards customary obligations allegedly held by grassroots villagers, those elite individuals widely disparaged as 'Big Shots' seek to create contexts in which they can constitute themselves as Possessive Individuals. In the preceding chapters, I have discussed _kastom_ as a contested linguistic sign that marks out the appropriate limits of reciprocal obligation and interdependence in contemporary PNG. I return to that analysis here, arguing that different evaluations of _kastom_ are part of the way in which the emerging indigenous elite attempt to constitute themselves as Possessive Individuals, and are also part of the way in which grassroots villagers denigrate those same elites as Big Shots.

The Importance of Differences between Big Shot and Grassroots Evaluations of _Kastom_

I was struck during the course of my fieldwork by the differences in attitudes towards customary ceremonial obligations and day-to-day demands for sharing and material assistance that tended to be expressed by Big Shots and by grassroots villagers. Many Big Shots took a leading part in the promotion of customary events and rituals, often because they were the only ones with the money to sponsor such events. They therefore tended to see themselves as having a major role in preserving _kastom_, and took it upon themselves to protect it from corrupting modernising influences. Some Big Shots disparaged the attitude of grassroots villagers towards _kastom_, arguing that their lack of respect threatened its very survival. The problem extended beyond customary ritual, however. The attitude that the grassroots were felt to display towards _kastom_ was taken by elites as symptomatic of a cultural malaise that afflicted PNG, and that made it hard for those political elite to deliver development. The perceived problem was well summarised by Isaac ToLanger. He complained to me that the problem with PNG was 'a culture of consumption'. 'We don't produce anything', he told me. 'We don't create anything. The only thing that people _do_ is church', he concluded despairingly. Knowing that ToLanger had devoted much of his life to the preservation and promotion of traditional culture, I suggested that maybe there was _kastom_ as well. His reply was that _kastom_ was just part of this consumption culture as well, with people 'sitting around waiting to be spoon-fed'.[1]

His reply fascinated me, because I knew him to be a keen proponent of the importance of preserving _kastom_, and unlike many Big Shots, his involvement in _kastom_ tended not to be disparaged by grassroots villagers. It was a sign of the unusual degree of respect in which he was held that he was in fact never referred to as a Big Shot, despite that his privileged economic position meant he fulfilled all of the criteria to be described as such. I had heard this sentiment expressed many times by other men in elite positions. For these men the demands of grassroots villagers for assistance with school fees, preparation for customary rituals, travel expenses etc., are felt not just as a constant irritation, but as a threat to their position (see Gewertz and Errington 1999:29). Customary events, at which hundreds of people expect to be fed largely at the Big Shots' expense, can become archetypes of this frustrating inability of the grassroots villagers to take care of themselves. Just as the grassroots villagers contrast the behaviour of present-day Big Shots unfavourably with the idealised Big Men of the past, so the Big Shots bemoan the lack of effort that the grassroots put into *kastom*, allegedly seeing it as a chance, as one Big Shot contemptuously put it to me, to, *kaikai nating* (TP. eat for free).

Perhaps the archetypal representative of the figure of the 'Big Shot' in the Matupit social imagination was ToNgala. ToNgala was in his late sixties at the time of my fieldwork and was living in Rabaul Town near the office of his tourist business. He had gained business experience working for an oil company in the 1960s and had gone on to run his own petrol station in town in the 1980s. This had apparently been a very profitable business until the eruption ruined the local economy. ToNgala had a personal commitment to Tolai custom that was much stronger than most other Big Shots, many of whom would return to the village only to take part in what was absolutely necessary given their position. ToNgala, by contrast, had thrown himself into *kastom* from an early age. At the time of my fieldwork, the performance of almost any customary performance at Matupit, particularly anything involving the *tubuan*, was almost unthinkable without his involvement. He lived only a couple of miles from Matupit in Rabaul Town, which meant that he could be involved more closely in day-to-day village life than other Big Shots. Ironically this strong personal commitment to *kastom* was part of the reason that he was denigrated more than any other Big Shot. ToLanger, who as noted above was hardly ever criticised by grassroots villagers, was one of the few people to defend ToNgala. ToLanger argued that unlike other Big Shots, ToNgala was at least trying to behave like a proper Big Man from the past, taking an interest in day-to-day village life, and that it was very sad that this involvement led to his unpopularity.

One evening I had a chance encounter with ToNgala at a Chinese restaurant in Rabaul Town located on the ground floor of the building where he had his offices. He apologised to me for the way that the villagers were 'messing up' the *kastom* that I had come to PNG to see. He complained that they did not show respectful demeanour and were often drunk during customary events. It was down to people like him to try to convince them to behave properly but he was aware that people did not listen to him as they had listened to the Big Men of his father's generation. Here we see much the same concern that *kastom* is being 'messed up' that Solomon Islander Jonathan Fifi'i reported to anthropologist Roger Keesing (Keesing 1992:122). In this case, though, rather than the desire to 'straighten out' *kastom* being part of a struggle to resist colonial hegemony, this desire is part of a postcolonial elite's struggle to straighten out the behaviour of their grassroots kin who have been corrupted by an imperfect modernisation.

Such views are not limited to discussions of <u>*kastom*</u> in its grandest sense of costly rituals that bring together hundreds of people. These sentiments also often arise in discussions of acts of everyday village reciprocity, acts that are sometimes described as *kastom* and on other occasions described using the Tok Pisin word <u>*pasin*</u> (also a term meaning 'custom, fashion, way'). On another occasion I interviewed ToNgala about his role in business and <u>*kastom*</u>. At the end of the interview, sitting in his business office near his town house, I jokingly mentioned one of the men in the village who always asked me for cigarettes, until I eventually grew so tired of it that I had told him to go to the store to buy his own. ToNgala suddenly grew very serious, and told me a story of about a music festival in Rabaul Town, many years ago, before the eruption. The story concerned another Matupi and one of the local white expatriates. This expatriate was well known for his fluency in Tok Pisin and his consumption of betel nut (<u>*buai*</u>), a habit looked down on by most other expatriates as being unspeakably disgusting. The villager approached the expatriate and demanded betel nut. The expatriate's response was to say, 'old man, the store's over there, and the road isn't closed' (<u>*lapun, stoa i stap long hap, na rot em i no pas*</u>). It was clear that ToNgala wholeheartedly approved of the expatriate's actions and the point it made to the villager. ToNgala then dismissed the villager's actions with a sigh; 'that's just the culture here', he said. He told me that while in the past he thought it was alright to constantly ask other people for betel nut, now he realised that 'you white people are right about this sort of thing, and now I don't like it when I see someone just walk up to someone else's basket and put their hand in'. When his wife's relatives came around, he got angry and upset when she asked them for betel nut. 'It's all right for them to ask us for <u>*buai*</u>, but I don't want us to be the sort of people who ask other people for <u>*buai*</u>.'

This statement well summed up ToNgala's horror of dependency. During the interview, while stressing how he had not forgotten his 'customary' obligations to certain relatives, he also emphasised how he had struggled to carve out a niche for himself in business, even if that meant that he had not been as constantly generous to others as he would have liked. He described how when he was a young man in the 1960s, his father had often counselled him against being too individualistic and ambitious. His father was worried that the jealousy of others would lead to gossip, or worse, sorcery. His father had said: 'why are you doing this . . . this is a new concept for our people, it doesn't look good for our people . . . if you make money, people will be jealous'. ToNglala replied that it was a new era, it was development and he was making money for them to live: 'My father was a poor man. I told him, "I would not like to live like you. You were lucky the things you eat came from the garden and the sea. I had to live the modern life with a bit of the community life which I put together as my strength".'

What is of interest here is the way in which he 'put together' what he saw as being these two opposed 'lives', the modern and the community. In this interview, the 'community' life largely referred to customary ritual obligations to kin, such as mortuary feasts or wedding exchanges. Often I had found that the practical blurring of this conceptual distinction was acknowledged by Matupi in conversations concerning village *kastom*. As we have seen, discussions of how money had changed or corrupted *kastom* often marked *kastom* as being, in many respects, a 'modern' cultural phenomenon. Here, however, ToNgala felt the need to sharply distinguish the 'modern' and 'community' lives, in order to describe to me how he put them together again. The 'community life' as he described it was a cycle of ongoing customary ritual obligations:

> I still go back to the village life, throughout this week I have contributed a lot of *tabu* for dead people. Last Saturday it was a woman at Raluana. I'm committed automatically. . . . Of course ToAn is not related to me, but the understanding at the village level is there, in terms of *tubuan*, and *singsing* [TP 'customary ritual songs and dances']. He's got relatives at Matupit. The people he was married to [i.e. his wife's *vunatarai* –KM] like ToBeni at Matupit would go. This is the kind of traditional tie that you must keep to. So it will never stop. My activity with the people is never ending. I attended ToAnselm's *namata* [initiation] as I have a traditional tie. David and ToPatuana are the sons of my uncle, so I can't avoid it, so I have to be there with ToAnselm who is the nephew. The traditional tie must always be there, pulling me out of the office.

For ToNgala this kind of reciprocal interdependence performed through *kastom* was the essence of 'village' or 'community' life as opposed to 'modern' or 'town' life. He was second to none in its observation, and in public proclamation of its continued importance. However, in proclaiming its importance he also delimits it and stresses its separation from his town and business life. He was, as his father had predicted, the object of much jealousy and bitter accusations. He described how after the volcano, he had been accused of not doing enough to help evacuate the victims from Matupit. After relating what he had done to help, he added that he had demanded of his accusers: 'Who am I? Is the volcano mine?' It is clear that it is not just responsibility for the volcano that he is denying, but responsibility for the care of its victims; or at least the level of responsibility that they would like to demand of him. In stressing the extent to which he is mindful of what he considers to be his customary obligations or 'traditional ties' in ritual contexts, he simultaneously claims legitimacy for his denial of claims made by grassroots villagers on the basis of those ties in other contexts.

What does this attempted delimitation of *kastom* tell us about the ideology of Possessive Individualism in East New Britain today? In drawing a distinction between these two lives, Big Shots such as ToNgala in effect claim that different moral personae are appropriate in different social contexts. When he goes 'back to the village' to perform *kastom*, ToNgala is keen to acknowledge his relationships to others, whether based on blood or a previous history of exchange. As we have seen, Tolai customary exchanges, in particular those concerning mortuary rituals, often do make explicit a history of relations in a manner that acknowledges the debt persons owe to those who made them. A good example takes place at the *minamai* mortuary feast, when *tabu* are distributed to a deceased man's clan by children of that clan in order to 'reimburse the members of the deceased's clan who had gave them life and reared them' (Simet 1991:279–80). As we have seen, these distributions are not always accepted as living up to this ideal. The relational person is a moment of personhood that is kept within the bounds of a delimited social sphere, namely 'village life', which from the Big Shot's point of view primarily means customary ritual.[2] In delimiting *kastom*, or the 'village life', the Big Shot is simultaneously attempting to fence in the relational person, which entails attempting to set boundaries around the social contexts in which claims upon his own person and autonomy can be made. ToNgala, as a customary leader, could easily describe to me the ways in which different people were mutually obliged to exchange in certain ways in *kastom*. But he was also keen to at least partially keep those claims boxed up by the word *kastom*. He may not always have been successful in this demarcation, but the struggle to do so is simultaneously a struggle to constitute a particular kind of moral person.

The Possessive Individual Big Shot as Non-Fractal Big Man

Discussing the famous Highland *moka* exchanges as part of his larger account of Melanesian relational personhood, or what he refers to as the 'fractal person', Wagner (1991:162) claims that it is 'difficult or impossible to define the successful or unsuccessful maker of *moka* as either individual or group, because the big man aspires to something that is both at once'. This may also be true for large-scale customary exchanges among the Tolai such as *balaguan*, but only to an extent. On my last visit to the Gazelle Peninsula in 2010, many people were keen to talk to me about a large-scale customary exchange that ToNgala had recently arranged to honour the dead of his *vunatarai* and that would also be his own *minamai* mortuary feast that he was organising before his death. This was in and of itself a controversial decision. Some persons claimed there was no precedent for this at Matupit and that it was typical of ToNgala's arrogance and disrespect for *kastom* to organise such a thing before his own death. Others, including ToNgala himself, told me a history of Big Men of previous generations who had organised events of this type and that it marked an ignorance of customary history on the part of his opponents to make such accusations. I cannot untangle all of the implications of this debate here. The salient point is that many grassroots Tolai were keen to tell me that while ToNgala claimed to be organising the event on behalf of his *vunatarai*, he was really organising it for himself and in fact many members of his own *vunatarai* were highly reluctant to take part. Some people said that ToNgala, knowing he had neglected to acknowledge the supporters who made him successful over the years, feared they would not honour him properly with a large-scale distribution of *tabu* after his death. As a consequence, he was organising it now to make sure that they could not avoid doing it properly. The importance of these reports is the sentiment of distrust towards contemporary leaders that they display. Their literal accuracy is hard to ascertain and is not the issue. Many persons would dispute this representation. When I talked to ToNgala himself about this event, it was very clear that he identified making his own name big by organising this event, with successfully honouring members of his *vunatarai*. There was no opposition between the two; they were synonymous for him. In this respect at least, Tolai patterns match Wagner's observations about the organisation of the *moka*. However, from the point of view of many grassroots Tolai it was possible to draw an opposition between the individual and the group he claimed to embody or represent in this context. Such a contradiction in perspectives may be an inherent potential in the relationship of Big Man and follower, as described by Sahlins (1963) for example. However, as I have argued, what the emergence of the figure of the Big Shot marks is a kind of purification of the ambiguity at the heart of Big-Manship and a concentration of all its negative aspects in the figure of the Big Shot. As a consequence, from the grassroots perspective, the distinction between individual (Big Shot) and group (*vunatarai*) can at times be stated in a very stark, even oppositional tone. The Big Shot might want to rhetorically separate <u>kastom</u> from other spheres of life in which his Possessive Individualism can operate unimpeded, but many grassroots respond by questioning his ability to do so, not only by attempting to extend the reciprocal claims of customary relations into spheres he finds uncomfortable, but also by angrily implying that his customary persona is corrupted by the taint of Possessive Individualism that he carries with him, even into the realm of *kastom*.[3]

Big Shots use the ideology of Possessive Individualism ambiguously. On the one hand it is held up as a universal ideal for all to aspire to. The grassroots should get beyond the 'culture of consumption' and acknowledge their moral responsibility to be proprietors of their own selves. In this sense the ideology of Possessive Individualism becomes a stick with which to beat the grassroots;

they are held responsible for their failures to live up to the ideal (see also Gewertz and Errington 1999:46, 58). On the other hand, it is asserted that they never will live up to the ideal: 'that's just the culture here', as ToNgala put it. An elite accepts the grassroots villagers' inability to live up to the ideal, an inability that illuminates by contrast the elite's own decision to take moral responsibility for proprietorship of the self. So ToNgala does not mind other people asking his wife for betel nut, but gets angry if she does likewise, because it threatens his family's identity as Possessive Individuals: 'I don't want us to be the sort of people who ask other people for *buai*'. Possessive Individualism is an ideal that only the Big Shot seems willing to strive for, thus explaining his separation from the grassroots, and his right to take a leading role in village life, whether in politics or even in the customary rituals in which the importance of relationality is reaffirmed.

Betel nut is significant because it marks the separation of _kastom_ from the 'modern' world of business and individual responsibility. Whereas the patterns of reciprocal exchange established in customary ritual ideally demonstrate mutual interdependence, and the collective effort that goes into enabling each person's capacities, ToNgala wishes to deny that this extends too far into the 'modern' life. Other people are not responsible for the enabling of his capacities; what he has achieved in this sphere of life, he has largely achieved himself. Conversely, since he alone is responsible for these capacities, they cannot make a claim upon him on that basis. Hence he does not automatically bear the responsibility for their care that they may like to claim. The grassroots villagers fail to understand that demands to a share of other people's things are illegitimate outside of certain customary contexts where the 'traditional ties' make one's obligations clear. By dipping their hands into other people's baskets without asking, to search for betel nut, they surrender responsibility for themselves. Hence ToNgala is not so much concerned with being asked for betel nut as he is with asking for it. By not asking for betel nut, he hopes to preserve autonomy. Crucially, if he is not reliant on others, he is not obliged to them either, giving him the self-possessive autonomy to act as a rational agent. When other people give and take betel nut it is because they are tied into never-ending cycles of everyday reciprocity ('that's just the culture here'), upon which they depend.

There are certain contexts in which expectations of being given betel nut are legitimate. Some customary rituals (such as the *namata*), incorporate large-scale distribution of betel nut as one of their stages. In these contexts there are clear guidelines about who is responsible for giving betel nut and who should be expecting it, according to the relations being played out by the event. ToNgala, as a strong proponent of this kind of _kastom_, would always acknowledge such claims, but sees these claims as having a different legitimacy from day-to-day reciprocity. By asserting that the grassroots villagers are incapable of following his example he draws a distinction between himself, as a rational agent able to draw a distinction between these two spheres of sociality, and the grassroots who are not. This social distinction is a mirror-image of the distinction they themselves draw, when they refer to him as a 'Big Shot'.

The Big Shot's assertion of autonomy is of course contested. For example, it was frequently complained to me that in the early days of setting up his business, ToNgala had relied upon the cheap or free labour of those to whom he had a customary relation, and even that much of the initial capital had come from community development schemes, often organised along the lines of customary relations. These claims were hotly denied by ToNgala and his supporters, who said that such claims were the jealous lies of persons put out by ToNgala's necessary hard-headedness in putting the welfare of the business over requests for assistance. The truth of the allegations is again not the point. In such cases, I found that the competing histories being told were often quite similar. What differed was interpretation. What one person presented as a fair wage, another presented as subsidised labour given on the basis of a history and expected future of ongoing reciprocal assistance. The point is that in these kind of cases, a reason is nearly always found to explain how the Big Shot's success is not purely his own responsibility, and that a large cast of grassroots villagers had a hand in that success that has not yet been properly acknowledged. In other words, critics claim that *all* of Big Shots' innate and acquired capacities are as much the result of their entanglement in reciprocal relations as are the relational capacities that they are willing to acknowledge in *kastom*. For example, maybe the school-fees that enabled the Big Shot to get his education were paid by a supplicant's uncle, or his first truck was paid for in a similar manner.

Sometimes the Big Shot accepts arguments supporting such claims for assistance that inevitably blur the distinction between customary and modern spheres of life. However, the claims are inevitably pushed too far for the Big Shot to sustain, and often he is forced back upon the conceptual separation of the two social spheres, and the contest begins again. Even the example of the betel nut is recognised by others for what it is and contested. I recounted this story to a group of Tolai from another village. They had jobs and were thus subject to a degree of pressure to share money from relatives and others, but could by no means be described as Big Shots. They were happy to describe their strategies to keep bits of money for themselves and their families, but they protested strongly when I told them the story of the expatriate man refusing betel nut to a villager. It is always wrong to refuse to share betel nut, they claimed. One even told me, 'that's Tolai *kastom*'. They understood very well the symbolic significance of betel nut as the archetypal day-to-day exchange object, and they saw that in telling this story that ToNgala was implicitly criticising village culture, and seeking to separate himself from it to an extent that they could not accept. Nor was the symbolic significance of approvingly quoting a white man's dismissal of demands for the sharing of betel nut was not lost on these villagers.[4]

I was struck by the large economic gap in living standards between Big Shots and the close kin whom they occasionally assisted, a gap that contrasts with earlier situations reported by T.S. Epstein. Clearly Big Shots felt capable of resisting many of the claims that were made upon their person. And the attempts made to present those moments when the Big Shot does give to kin in certain ways are themselves of great importance. ToNgala acknowledges the pull that *kastom* has on his business ('The traditional tie must always be there, pulling me out of the office'). But in the very act of acknowledging that pull, he again asserts a separation, according to which he is not automatically responsible for things that fall outside of the remit of *kastom*. A public official responsible for training villagers in how to start up small businesses once discussed with me the common problem of the '*wantok* system', or relatives killing small businesses with demands for credit and assistance: he told me, 'You have to tell them, that you are one thing and your business is another'. He seemed to suggest that it is legitimate to blur the boundaries of individual responsibility in the village, but once one establishes a business it is necessary to establish boundaries more firmly. This of course implies being a different type of person in one context, and fighting to treat other people in a more individual manner in that context. Matupit is home to some of the most successful small businessmen in East New Britain. Their businesses have developed well beyond the scale of the small village-based trade store owner who has to face his own relatives, demanding credit, as customers every day. Instead these businesses are on a par with many of the major expatriate owned businesses in the province. Most of the owners' day-to-day business is conducted in this social sphere set apart from village life, rather than in the village where they would be more vulnerable to a blurring of the 'modern' and 'community' lives (as these were distinguished by my earlier-quoted interviewee). In this respect the business owners have reached something approaching the degree of *relative* independence achieved by Big Shot bureaucrats living in Port Moresby who are often successful at preventing or rebuffing claims upon their pay cheques. Significantly, the two most notable businessmen from Matupit, although they 'return' to the village for *kastom*, both live in houses elsewhere in the province, even though they have built houses at 'home'. Grassroots villagers are in no doubt about the main reason for this decision: to lessen the ability of villagers to pester them with constant requests for assistance. Such a tactic is not open to the small-scale trade store owner. In pursuing such a course, the Big Shot entrepreneur marks out his difference from such small-scale traders, and claims an affinity with the Big Shot holding a position in the government bureaucracy.

15. Alois' Trade Store, the biggest store at Matupit

Strathern (1999:206–12) argues that in Melanesian custom, what is valued is the publicly displayed ability to handle certain valued capacities. The grassroots villagers are clear that the 'capacities' being handled by today's Big Shots are very different from those that were handled in the course of the same rituals by a previous generation of Big Men. Take for example Matthew, who summed up the difference between the Big Shots of today and the Big Men of before as being that in the case of the 'money power' of the Big Shots, 'you hold it by yourself' (*yu yet yu holim*). Or as one elderly man at Matupit contemptuously dismissed today's generation of political and customary leaders, 'the money makes them big'. Although money is incorporated into customary exchange, at Matupit today people clearly see power as having a different source than before, as thus being the measure of a different capacity. Power is not reliant on an intimate involvement in the reciprocal obligations of day-to-day village life, but is held by Big Shots individually. From a grassroots perspective, money-power separates the Big Shot from the grassroots by embodying capacities and aspects of his personhood that they are not a part of constituting and that he is not accountable to them for.

Both grassroots and Big Shots clearly understand that this money-power implies a different way of seeing one's obligations to others, and hence of seeing one's own person. Big Shots are portrayed as being less reliant on others for their capacity for social action than the Big Men of before who are described as having influence by virtue of consent. As Matthew put it, you can be someone's nephew, but they can still fire you from a job. The right of a business owner to fire a young man from his own clan would perhaps be contested by other relatives, but it was certainly a possibility, in a way that a Big

Man firing an awkward nephew from the clan was not. In fact one of the most common behind the scenes complaints made against Big Shots was that they refused to employ their close relatives. These kinds of complaints illustrate that the current situation is not one of Possessive Individualism displacing more Melanesian relational models of moral personhood, nor of those earlier models retaining their fundamental cultural integrity in the face of colonialism and globalisation. Instead, what is going on is an ongoing struggle over the applicability of different moral visions of the person in different social contexts. The Big Shot instantiates Possessive Individualism in the context of his business dealings, that as proprietor of the self he has a moral obligation to look out for himself and his possessions. Many grassroots villagers make claims upon him that challenge that assumption. They demand forms of assistance that suggest that they believe that they have a claim upon him; that he is in some manner fundamentally and intrinsically obliged to them.

Macpherson points out that the English property holders who saw their care of the self in such terms of moral obligation, believed that in doing so they safeguarded the wider social good.[5] The Melanesian Big Shot follows their example, as is made clear by all their discussions of defending business against the rapacious claims of the *wantok* system. Without their hardness in protecting their businesses against these claims, there would be no business or development at all, and everyone would suffer. Or so the story goes. They are the only ones with the strength to act rationally in the face of constant demands that would destroy business and development, thus giving their self-interest a moral virtue. As Macpherson (1962:99) notes, Possessive Individualism posits that the 'rational is he who labours and appropriates. Such behaviour is rational in the moral sense . . . as well as in the expedient sense'. The Big Shot has to enforce this rationality in the face of demands based on reciprocal obligation. Relatives should not expect to keep jobs purely on the basis of being *wantoks*; they have a responsibility to act in such a way that they prove their merit and they have a responsibility to look after themselves. However, as with the sharing of betel nut, the Big Shots are resigned to the fact that the grassroots are often 'culturally' incapable of fully facing up to these responsibilities, to constitute themselves as properly individual moral persons in these contexts. And so the struggle goes on, a struggle simultaneously over the specifics of whether a particular relative should expect a job with the company, and a over the general remit of the ideology of Possessive Individualism in postcolonial PNG.

It is not just the grassroots, but the emerging elite as well, who view the Big Shots' 'money-power' as being of a very different order from the Big Men of the past. The world has changed, as ToNgala suggested in recounting the earlier-quoted conversation with his father, who had been a noted Big Man of the traditional type. One evening I was at Matupit with Isaac ToLanger at a mortuary ritual for one of his close relatives, and he expressed fear that kastom had become part of a culture of consumption. He told me that he had paid brideprice for at least 25 people at Matupit. He went on to explain that this was something different from the custom of the past, when the Big Man of the clan would organise a young man's bridewealth payment. In the past the Big Man would use *tabu* belonging to the clan held under his trusteeship in the clan '*tabu* house' (K. *pal na tabu*). His *tabu* on the other hand was his own 'individual' *tabu*, presumably bought with money that he had earned at work.

The importance of this became clear a few days later at the final mortuary event, the *minamai*, where a large-scale distribution of *tabu* to some relatives of the deceased and other villagers took place. On this occasion there were a number of small but significant differences from the routine that I was used to. In particular, ToLanger made sure that all of the *tabu* that was to be distributed by family and clanspeople was assembled in separate piles and then the names of the clan members who were to distribute it were publicly called out. This caused much discussion after the event, and people generally agreed that ToLanger had done this to shame his fellow clan members because he was unhappy with what he felt had been a lack of care for the deceased in the last few months of his life. His way of doing this was to publicly demonstrate that the *tabu* that they were to distribute was not the clan's (i.e. that they had no stake in it), but that it was his and his alone. But while he may well have been publicly condemning them for failing to live up to their clan responsibilities, the power that he used to do so was his money-power, a power that was not reliant on clan consent for its exercise. Much of the *tabu* that was distributed had been brought to the *minamai* in the form of a large wheel. Rather than get a member of his clan to cut the wheel prior to distribution, ToLanger chose a distantly related associate. This man looked very reluctant to perform the task, and afterwards confirmed to me that ToLanger had to get angry with him to make him do it. He had not wanted to do it himself, because he was not a member of the clan. He told me that ToLanger had said to him: 'it's my *tabu*, what are you ashamed of?' (*yu sem olsem wanem*). ToLanger's motivation for having this man cut the wheel was the same as for the public assembly of the piles of *tabu* to be distributed: to demonstrate that the *tabu* was his and not the clan's. By demonstrating that it was 'his' *tabu*, he was seeking to demonstrate that his clanspeople were incapable of fulfilling their reciprocal obligations to fellow clan members in death. In doing so he was also thought to be passing comment on their alleged inability to fulfil these obligations in life too.

Shifting Combinations of Relationality and Individualism in Twenty-First-Century Tolai *Kastom*

What this example illustrates is that the situation at Matupit today is not as simple as the assertion of either Possessive Individualism or a kind of relational personhood based on reciprocal obligation and interdependence. Rather in the current era, the two often are often placed together in different combinations depending on the needs of the situation. ToLanger was a man who sought to enforce reciprocal obligations and preserve *kastom*. Yet both he and the grassroots Matupi were well aware that the power by which he attempted to encourage them was very different from that of the Big Men of before. Traditional Big Men are often described as being 'big heads', who paradoxically flout norms and conventions in order to give themselves the individual power to strengthen those conventions. For example Robbins (2004:200) discusses the way that Urapmin Big Men are described as 'angry men', a phrase that is normally an insult, but applied to Big Men often reflects admiration for their abilities to organise social relations. ToLanger's behaviour could legitimately be seen as a continuation of that pattern. But it is more than simply a continuation. The Big Man's individual power to break conventions of respectful behaviour in order to enforce them relies upon the respect that he has built up in attending to the give-and-take of village sociality over the years. He walks a tightrope in this respect (see Robbins op cit.:206). Hence Matthew's comment that: 'You had to be chosen by the community. You had to have the respect of the community. With "money-power", *yu yet yu holim pawa'*. By having to use money-power to enforce an ethic of reciprocal obligation through the performance of *kastom*, ToLanger simultaneously and paradoxically marks himself as standing outside of those relations at that moment, and constitutes himself as someone who in his capacity to shape social relations is beholden to no-one as a person. Rather than the traditional Melanesian Big Man whose power in ritual measures capacities outside of himself that he is able to handle, just as he handles the give-and-take of everyday life in the village, instead he is, as Macpherson describes the Possessive Individual, 'proprietor of his person and his capacities', including in this case displaying his capacity to use his money-power to shame others into appropriate behaviour through *kastom*.

Similarly, we know that concern with the sharing of betel nut is far from being a new concern amongst Melanesian customary leaders. Malinowski (1979:46) describes the trouble that the Trobriand Chief has to go to in order to conserve some of his betel nut from his fellow villagers, illustrating the pattern that leadership places one under even greater obligation to show constant generosity. But ToNgala's concern is different. He is not concerned with preserving his betel nut. In fact, he claims not to mind sharing it out.

But he is concerned to present himself as not being 'the kind of person' who inhabits a 'culture' of continually expected sharing. Maybe his concerns are ultimately to hold on to some of his own possessions, such as his car or his satellite dish, in parallel to the concerns of a Trobriand Chief. And in claiming to be a different kind of person, maybe ToNgala attempts to lessen the force of claims upon himself. But clearly this kind of assertion of Possessive Individual personhood is not a strategy that was open to or being pursued by the Trobriand Chief, hiding his betel nut at the bottom of his basket. Both the Big Shot and the Trobriand Chief at various points want to limit claims upon themselves and at other points want to stress their generosity. The difference is the contexts within which they stress these different tendencies. More fundamentally, the Big Man (or 'Chief') relies upon displays of generously acknowledging reciprocal interdependence as being basic to his identity as relational leader. The Big Shot relies on *limitation* of claims made on the basis of reciprocal interdependence, for his identity as big shot and bourgeois individual. His capacities as bureaucrat or business leader depend on his ability to protect the source of his leadership capacities (his money-power) from such claims. The problem is that successfully pursuing this strategy lessens his effectiveness at those moments when he wishes to stress his customary generosity.

The heart of the problem for the Big Shots is what ToLanger described as people expecting to be 'spoon-fed'. Descriptions of PNG's grassroots as people who expect spoon-feeding are frequent. Sir John Kaputin had become famous in the early 1970s as a leader of the Mataugnan Association, appealing to resentment against negative stereotypes of Papua New Guineans held by Australian colonisers. By 2002, however, I was told that at a meeting at Matupit he had denounced the villagers for expecting to be 'spoon-fed' when they asked for assistance in replacing the schools and electricity supply that had been destroyed in the eruption and its aftermath. This story was frequently repeated to me with great resentment, and I have no doubt that it was one of the reasons why JK went from being one of PNG's best known and longest serving MPs, to being defeated by the biggest electoral margin in the country in 2002. For the Big Shots it is this 'hand-out mentality' that hinders the nation's development as the grassroots sullenly make unreasonable requests and use their inevitable refusal as an excuse to stagnate. Both sides blame each other for the failure of the Papua New Guinea state.[6]

In discussing the distribution of betel nut, ToNgala seeks to demonstrate that he is not the kind of person who makes such requests. Given the central importance of the sharing of betel nut in day-to-day village social life, it is not surprising that it should come to be used as the archetypal illustration of this problem. In telling the story of the expatriate refusing to give someone betel nut, ToNgala implies that he has partially removed himself this culture of consumption, and that this makes him the kind of person who can take a moral responsibility for leadership. Just as business requires the kind of person who can separate his obligated self from his business self, so too community and political leadership requires a similar ability. The story ToNgala tells of his father's warnings of village jealousy is designed to highlight the obstacles that he overcame, and to illustrate that it was by his own efforts that he reached the position he has attained today. His capacities, both inherent and achieved, are his alone. Hence the volcano is not his responsibility. He is aware that whatever he offers will never be enough, and he wants to stress that the grassroots have no right to make demands on his person and the property that he gained through his own efforts, beyond those that he chooses to acknowledge. As Macpherson (1962:221) puts it: 'If it is labour, a man's absolute property, which justifies appropriation and creates value, the individual right of appropriation overrides any moral claims of the society. The traditional view that property and labour were social functions, and that ownership of property involved social obligations, is thereby undermined'.

Knauft (2002), writing of Gebusi of PNG's Western Province, describes their relationship to the postcolonial state and other vehicles of expected development and modernisation as being characterised by 'recessive agency'. This involves the hopeful expectation that if they constantly make the effort to adopt the appropriate demeanour of quiet listening submission then they will somehow prove themselves worthy of receiving their share of the fruits of development. This endeavour that Knauft (op cit.:40) describes with the beautiful oxymoron 'active passivity' does not sound so far from the position that Tolai Big Shots often disparage as 'waiting to be spoon-fed' or a 'hand out mentality'. Whereas for Knauft, whose empathy for Gebusi shines through strongly, this is a particular and paradoxical form of agency, Tolai Big Shots in their less empathic moments view this stance as a morally repugnant abrogation of agency. The infantilising insult of 'spoon feeding' says it all. By demanding to be spoon fed you give up your right to be treated as an adult worthy of respect. And grassroots Tolai are well aware of this attitude on the part of elites. Hence the sense that Knauft (ibid.) picked up that Gebusi 'tend on the whole to be appreciative rather than resentful of those in power', contrasts greatly with my experience of Tolai attitudes towards their new masters. Rather than an appreciative and expectant silence that marks a kind of subordination, grassroots Tolai attitudes tended to be marked by an increasing truculence, expressed in phenomena from JK's election defeat to the growing tendency for the young men to shout abuse in public at councillors and leaders who they say have delivered them nothing but blame and demonise them for the village's ills. For Tolai and Gebusi (indeed probably for all of us) 'desire for modern wealth informs altered modes of subjectivity and new forms of subservience' (op cit.:6). But the ways that it does so and the sense that people make of the altered subjectivities they ascribe to others vary wildly from place to place.

The Big Shot versus grassroots dynamic may not be the only context in which something akin to a Possessive Individualist self-proprietorship is being asserted in the face of opposition in contemporary PNG. Another example would be the young women from Matupit frequenting night clubs in the face of opposition from relatives, who allegedly justify their actions by claiming, 'it's my life not the clan's'. Likewise, Gewertz and Errington (1991:108) report the statement of a young Chambri man who prefers to live in town rather than the village, in order to get away from the control of elderly Big Men: 'You are free to walk about; you are the master of yourself'. Such claims are doubtless as context dependent as the claims for autonomy of the Big Shots, but they do show an awareness that there is more than one way to constitute a person in contemporary PNG.

Like the seventeenth-century English property holders, the Big Shots are convinced that those beneath them are too dependent on others to take the responsibility of leadership. Their lack of autonomy and reliance on 'spoon-feeding' leaves them incapable of the disinterested rational decision-making that true leadership requires. The moral contempt of the English property holder for beggars is matched by the Big Shot's contempt, in moments of frustration, for grassroots villagers and their habit of relying on others. Both are held to have failed to preserve or assert their independence and by relying on claims on the property of others they have proved themselves incapable of rational agency. By asserting 'traditional' claims of customary reciprocal interdependence in a modern world, they betray both tradition and modernity, at least from a Big Shot perspective. As Keane (2007:8) observes, 'those who seem to persist in displacing their own agency onto . . . traditions, or fetishes, are out of step with the times'. Possessive Individualism is an ideology of the person that inevitably has a role to play in an increasingly socially stratified postcolonial Papua New Guinea.

Notes

1. See also Gewertz and Errington (1999:49, 58) for a discussion of how the emerging PNG middle-class comes to see dependence on 'handouts' as the cause of poverty.
2. As Foster (1995:19) observes, the Possessive Individual as a 'particular construction of the subject potentially competes and clashes with other constructions, realised in other practices, that posit subjects not as bounded, self-contained proprietary individuals but, rather, as "relational persons," nodes in a matrix of social relations'. It is worth restating that this is often best conceptualised not as the clash of two discrete self-contained cultural systems, but rather as a struggle over deciding in what contexts particular idioms and constructions are appropriate and what are the social implications of allowing them in certain contexts and not in others.

3. Although I was not present for this event, I have seen a large number of photos and video recordings of it. It is striking for a number of reasons, not least the large number of pigs piled up one on top of the other in a style reminiscent of large-scale customary events in New Ireland. I was reminded at this point of my informant that I mentioned in Chapter Seven who distinguished New Ireland *kastom* from Tolai *kastom* and pointed to the use of corned beef in Tolai *kastom* as a sign of what had gone wrong with Tolai *kastom* as opposed to the large-scale use of pigs in New Ireland. Many of my older informants told me that it had been a long time since they had seen such a display of pigs at a customary event around Rabaul, and they were willing to grudgingly admit that it was a major achievement on the part of the organiser. I doubt that the presence of pigs gave the event extra customary legitimacy in the eyes of the Big Shots' critics. If anything the large amount of money and resources necessary to organise such a display, totally out of the reach of the vast majority of grassroots Tolai, would simply further underline the increasingly incommensurate differences between the two groups.

4. As the most common example of day-to-day sharing and requests amongst Tolai villagers, it is perhaps unsurprising that *buai* is sometimes emblematic of this 'culture', as ToNgala puts it. The SDA is widely regarded as the most 'Westernised' and 'individual' of the three major denominations at Matupit and the refusal of their most devout members to indulge in *buai* was often mentioned to me as a sign of these traits by critics. See also Keane (2007:108) for a discussion of the antipathy of some missionaries in Sumba, Indonesia towards betel nut as it was 'profoundly implicated in concepts of soul, reciprocity, and identity' (see also op cit.:140).

5. See, for example, his discussion of Locke's views on individual ownership of land and the increase in the national wealth (Macpherson 1962:204–11).

6. It is worth mentioning at this point the widespread, if not universal feeling that was expressed to me around the Gazelle Peninsula that the Papua New Guinea state had indeed been a failure. It is worth mentioning because the orthodoxy in Melanesian anthropology seems to be that to point out how new postcolonial states often appear to fail to live up to the templates that they inherited from the colonial powers is somehow a bad thing that should be replaced by a more 'generous' (Foster 2002:12) understanding of how nation-making is inherently flexible and dependent on differing circumstances. It may well be the case that much of the criticism of so called 'failed states' depends on and justifies a kind of neo-colonial politics that most anthropologists would find problematic. But when the people that we work with insistently tell us that their nation-state is 'rubbish', we have to take this problem seriously as well. During my fieldwork there was a long standoff between the PNG government and its major aid donor, Australia, over the conditions placed on continued support. In particular the Australian government insisted that Australian civil servants be placed in PNG government departments to check alleged rampant corruption. The PNG government vociferously protested but eventually backed down. On the day after the PNG government's climb down, I met an English long-term resident of the area in Rabaul Town. He waved a copy of the *Post Courier* newspaper at me and jubilantly exclaimed: 'It's rampant neo-colonialism. And about bloody time too!' Most anthropologists will not have much sympathy for this position. Several months earlier, I clearly remember meeting a very elderly lady from Matupit who was trying to eke out a living for herself with great difficulty at Sikut. She pointed to the poor state of the roads, the health

aid post and other government services, contrasting them with the situation in the years prior to independence. She then plaintively asked me, 'when are the Australians coming back to look after us again?' I was struck by the number of times that I heard this sentiment or something like it during my time at Matupit (the home village of the anti-colonial Mataungan Association only a generation previously), predominantly from grassroots villagers (see also Martin 2007a). The point that is important to make is that just because accusations of 'failure' are often motivated by expatriate or neo-colonial politics does not mean they are always motivated by such politics – much as George Orwell once famously reminded British socialists that something is not necessarily untrue just because it is said to be true in the pages of the *Daily Telegraph* (Orwell 1968:207). Indeed the fact that most of the expressions of failure come from grassroots villagers, whereas as most of the claims of partial success or justification for failure come from political elites, suggests that claims of failure might just as commonly be expressing a growing subaltern contempt for their new masters and that by presuming that claims to failure are always politically problematic as we only see them through the lens of (post)colonial relations, we silence those voices and implicitly line up with the local elites who agree with us that we should be more generous in how we judge failure or success. A similar problem is clear in the work of those who presume that invoking 'specters of inauthenticity' is inherently bad, colonial, Othering or whatever (e.g. Jolly 1992). This presumption silences the ways in which subaltern claims as to the inauthenticity of elite performances of *kastom* act as a grassroots critique of growing socio-economic inequality (see also Martin 2008a, 2008b, 2010).

Conclusions

The emergence of the category of the Big Shot and the contests around its use and meaning are perhaps the starkest illustrations of the ongoing contest over the appropriate limits of reciprocal interdependence that characterises contemporary Tolai sociality. But the ways in which the limits of reciprocity are contested in this context have parallels in other contexts. ToNgala's attempts to keep the claims of his extended kin within a box marked _kastom_ in order to protect his own individual household are of a similar order to Philip's desire to remove _kastom_ from the land at Sikut in order to protect his children's interests from their cousins. Although ToNgala has a broadly positive view of _kastom_ and Philip a broadly negative one, for both of them delimiting the claims of _kastom_ provides a rhetorical mechanism by which they attempt to guard against some of the claims that might be made on the basis of extended ties of reciprocal interdependence. Neither of these men is impoverished, but they are of very different socio-economic standings. The uneasy tension that they both display between asserting and denying claims made on bases of reciprocal interdependence is one that engages all Tolai right down to the grassroots.

Nor is such a tension simply limited to the dimension of individual/ household versus clan, although this is one appearance that it often takes, and one that attracts a great deal of attention in debates about land tenure and economic development. Rather it is a question of the extent to which any single human being or group can stand as an individual self-contained entity prior to their relations with others. Hence the 'clan' can in some contexts be the location of the extended networks of obligation that threaten the discrete individual/household and its interests in land or other economic interests.[1] In other contexts the clan can be the corporate individual whose discrete identity and interests need protecting against others that it is entangled with, such as its relatives, exchange partners or 'children'. The boundaries of the discrete unit and the extent of its ability to constitute itself, like Smith's 'Man in Nature', as being prior to the relations that it enters into may vary, and the contexts in which the boundaries are negotiated also may vary. But this battle illuminates many of the key controversies of contemporary Tolai social life, from land disputes to the contested politics of _kastom_.

This struggle is one that takes place both in bitter face to face disputes between those contesting the meaning of their relationship and also at the level of village, provincial and national politics in debates over the future of land tenure. Provincial Government policy makers see efforts to remove *kastom* from the land at Sikut as desirable attempts to loosen some of the ties of reciprocal obligation that hinder 'development' by cramping the emergence of individuals and individual households with an interest in economic accumulation.

The struggle over *kulia* is an example of how these processes can be seen simultaneously from either end of the social scale. The ongoing contest over the meaning of *kulia*, and the extent to which it is a stand-alone transaction between two individuals that does not imply an ongoing relationship of reciprocal obligation, is not a process instigated by government decree. It is the unplanned outcome of hundreds of specific disputes and debates over ownership and meaning. But it is a process that state policy makers and legal officials feel that they have to play a central part in directing through their attempts to codify *kulia* in the context of national legislation that allows for 'customary' land transfers, or through the regulation and recording of the semi-official practice of registering *kulia* transactions.

The category of *kastom* provides us with the perhaps the signifier par excellence of the contested boundaries of reciprocal interdependence. If we were to attempt to systematise Tolai culture, we would find its very essence in paradox and contest. Contradiction is its defining feature, rather than a problem to be explained away. Likewise, *kastom* as a concept carries such power precisely *because of* its contested and contradictory meanings, not despite them. As Lindstrom (2008:165) observes, '*Kastom* was, and is, a rhetoric based on the selective recognition of some, though not all, elements of what anthropologists like to call "culture"'. As a word it is deployed in attempts to fix the boundaries of reciprocal obligation in a number of different contexts. As a practice, particularly in the form of the large-scale ceremonial exchanges, *kastom* is the site of some of the most bitterly contested battles over these boundaries. We are now very familiar with the falsity of assumptions that integration into a global commodity economy would lead to the death of such practices. Indeed they often lead to their efflorescence (Gregory 1982:166). But what ethnographic analysis of the different positions held on these events (as opposed to simply taking for granted the 'official' cultural description of a few powerful figures or culture brokers) reveals is that it is a mistake to automatically confuse the efflorescence of such practices for an essential cultural continuity.[2] Rather, as the site of the contest between different value systems, or more accurately contests over the appropriate contexts for different value systems, the efflorescence of customary ritual perhaps reflects a deepening of conceptual disputes and dilemmas. Such disputes have perhaps always been a feature of Melanesian social life, as in the famous *kula/gimwali* distinction analysed by writers as distinguished and varied as Malinowski, Mauss and Sahlins (1972:200–1). But maybe the lesson gained through the ethnographic analysis of competing evaluations of *kastom* is that the most fundamental tendency of the past hundred years of engagement with a global commodity-based economy has not been a eruption of commodification destroying culture in its wake, or an efflorescence and continuation of underlying culture but rather an intensification of such disputes between different ways of valuing relations and transactions in different contexts.[3]

That the relations of respect for reciprocal obligation underpin a certain definition of _kastom_ is made clear by Matupi discussions of the relationship between fishing technologies and the types of marriages that young people today enter into. The social relations made through fish traps that previously made marriage possible are seen as ones that inherently tied young men into relations of respect and reciprocal interdependence. The marriages that ensued were likewise seen as having been anchored in such respectful relations. Contemporary marriages are seen by many as not embodying such a customary ethic. To an extent, perhaps older generations do everywhere bemoan their children and grandchildren's disobedience and fall from grace. But what is striking is the way in which in this instance it is the loosening of reciprocal ties, a loosening made possible at least, by the introduction of commodified new technologies, that is held to be at fault. If nothing else, the case demonstrates that Tolai themselves often feel a keen sense that the problems of contemporary _kastom_ and the contradictions that it embodies are part and parcel of their position within much wider networks of global political economics.

The widely proclaimed 'death' of the 'Big Men' and the negative evaluation of contemporary 'Big Shots' in contrast with their idealised predecessors could equally well be dismissed as a romantic harking back for a past that never existed. But again what is truly interesting about this controversy is the way in which it is a perceived loosening of ties of reciprocal interdependence that is at the heart of the unease with new developments. Grassroots Tolai are able to very precisely illustrate examples of the perceived differences in the lifestyle and behaviour of these two different categories of leaders. Even if we were to assume that all of these stories were the completely fantastic products of rose tinted spectacles (which I would argue is an assumption that we have no reason to make), then the very fact of the stories would still tell us something important about the ways in which grassroots Tolai morally evaluate the demands of competing value systems. This is parallel to how 'cargo cult' beliefs demand to be taken seriously as expressions of a negative moral evaluation of Europeans' denial of reciprocity, even if we do not literally believe in the existence of underground caves full of cargo being hidden from Melanesians by the Whites.

Evaluations of Social Change in Early Twenty-First-Century Melanesian Ethnography and the Contested Limits of Reciprocity in the Twenty-First-Century Neo-Liberal World

The issue of changing valuations of social relations is one that has recently returned to the fore of Melanesian ethnography. In particular, the publication of Joel Robbins' 2004 book *Becoming Sinners* marked a major attempt to describe a situation in which Melanesians themselves were describing a radical shift in their value system with their adoption of a fervently anti-customary form of Evangelical Christianity. Drawing on Dumont's (1970) earlier contrast between Western individualism and Indian hierarchical holism, Robbins describes the situation of Urapmin people of highland PNG as one in which a Melanesian culture with paramount value of relationality comes into conflict with an introduced culture of Western origin having individualism as its paramount value. Urapmin were until recently extremely isolated, but in the late 1970s they converted almost en masse to a new belief system that was radically in contradiction to their old ones. Thus Robbins' case study seems to fit very well an analytical frame of the replacement of one cultural system with another, leaving the people themselves caught in a kind of limbo, like Ruth Benedict's (1934:22) famous American Indian Digger Chief of nearly a century ago, who 'straddled two cultures'.[4] The Tolai case, however, with its long history of local involvement with colonialism and a global capitalist economy, the retention of *kastom* side by side with the widespread acceptance of forms of Christianity that are happy to accommodate *kastom*'s continuation, and a more ambiguous attitude towards the past than outright rejection and devaluation of their own history, does not perhaps fit this model so well.[5]

Where there is a similarity between the analysis of early twenty-first-century Tolai advanced in this book and the analytical frame that Dumont developed to make sense of Indian society, it is in the central role given in both cases to axiomatic contradictions between opposed categories in making sense of social life. For India in Dumont's analysis, the opposition between purity and impurity is key. For my analysis of East New Britain, it is the opposition between reciprocal interdependence and non-reciprocal independence that is central. The main difference between the two frameworks of analysis is that Dumont starts from the construction of a fixed underlying system in which purity is preferable to impurity. Although Tolai will often validate reciprocity over non-reciprocity in abstract conversations, particularly ones in which they compare their culture or *kastom* to those of the whites and find the latter wanting, in day-to-day life there is much more ambiguity. As we have seen, there are many contexts in which people can be criticised for an inappropriate extension of the value of reciprocal interdependence into situations where other values are felt to be more appropriate. Rather than starting from an opposition between a systemically determining paramount value[6] and its axiomatic opposite, I have found it more useful to start from an analysis of the ways in which people contest the appropriateness of evaluating relations by specific moral standards in different concrete contexts.

Hence in this analysis, there is no underlying 'cultural grammar' (Rio and Smedal 2009:19), in which relations, obligations or substance are necessarily passed on 'in certain directions' which cause the 'reproduction' of that very system.[7] Of course one could see the very opposition itself as the basis of a kind of underlying cultural grammar: the fact that both sides of most of the disputes described in this account are perfectly capable of understanding each other's positions could be taken as proof of that. But such mutually comprehensible disagreement should not be taken for granted as a starting point. The opposition or tension between reciprocal interdependence and non-reciprocal independence may well be a universal one. That certainly seems to have been Mauss's perspective in his original essay on 'The Gift'. But how that opposition plays itself out for other people is not always immediately apparent. And this is not a simple 'culture area' distinction, in which the opposition works itself out in certain ways in the West and in other ways in Melanesia, so that the different workings of that universal opposition could in and of themselves be taken as the basis for yet another reworking of regional-based cultural relativism. It is possible to imagine many cases where I would not immediately 'get' how this tension over the limits of reciprocal obligation worked in my own hometown of Manchester.

A few years ago, 'my' football club, Manchester United was bought in a hostile takeover by an American businessman, Malcolm Glazer, using the club's own assets as security to finance the deal. In an instant 'we' had gone from being the richest sporting organisation on earth to the most indebted. To thousands of us it was morally repugnant that the club's financial assets, which ultimately came from our support at the turnstiles, could be used to rip the club away from us without our consent. To service the debt, ticket prices have risen dramatically in the years since, pricing out many working class locals for whom support for the club is a generations' old tradition. Our distaste was not shared by all football fans, however. For more pragmatic supporters, football was a 'business' like any other and that was just how the world was. The attitude of the new middle-class football fan is well summed up in Nick Hornby's (1992:222) book *Fever Pitch*, a book that more than any other cultural artefact came to represent the emergence of this new demographic in the 1990s:

'What about the supporters who have followed the club through thick and thin, paid the players' wages? How can clubs really contemplate selling them down the river?' This is an argument that goes right to the heart of football consumption . . . Football clubs are not hospitals or schools, with a duty to admit us regardless of our financial wherewithal. It is interesting and revealing that opposition to . . . bond schemes has taken on the tone of a crusade, as if the clubs had a moral obligation to their supporters. What do clubs owe us, any of us, really? I have stumped up thousands of pounds to watch Arsenal over the last twenty years; but each time money has changed hands, I have received something in return: admission to a game, a train ticket, a programme. Why is football any different from the cinema, say, or a record shop? The difference is that all of us feel these astonishingly deep allegiances, and that until recently we had all anticipated being able to go to watch every game that our team plays for the rest of our lives; now it is beginning to appear as though that will not be possible for some of us. But that won't be the end of the world.

Hornby's narrator expresses one position on the meaning of a supporter's transactions with a club, and it is a position that is also shared by English commercial law. This position stresses the stand-alone alienable nature of the transaction ('each time money has changed hands, I have received something in return'), and hence a position that sees no room for any enduring 'moral obligation' beyond that simple commodity transaction. But it is not the way in which all supporters see the relationship and its constitutive transactions. It is equally possible to see transactions over the years as building up just such a moral obligation (we after all 'paid the players' wages'). The idea that Hornby seems to subscribe to, that it is always clear cut in which contexts institutions have a moral obligation to meet demands regardless of income, is undermined by his own examples. It might be axiomatic to his British readers that hospitals have such a moral obligation. To readers in the United States or to Britons who remember how difficult it was to access healthcare before the establishment of the National Health Service in the 1940s, this assumption might not be so readily made. Hence the allegiance and loyalty built up over years of exchanges can demand reciprocal recognition. David Gill, the Chief Executive of Manchester United both before and after the takeover and the man most hated by fans for his role in the affair, understands this better than most:

> 'The passions run high,' Gill told me in August, when I asked him about the hostile action to Glazer. 'That is one of strengths of any football club, and Manchester United in particular. *The fans think it is their club.* They passionately believe that. You don't have to agree with that sentiment, but you have to respect it'. (Cassidy 2006, emphasis added)

To understand many of the conversations and arguments through which this debate over reciprocity and non-reciprocity unfolds, one would need to understand how key terms in that debate such as 'business', 'club' or 'fan' subtly shifted their meaning within the context of the variety of overlapping speech communities participating in the debate, much as an understanding of how this opposition plays itself out in East New Britain requires a similar understanding of the shifting accents and meanings carried by key terms such as <u>kastom</u>. And to really understand many instances of the playing out of this contradiction, one would have to gain an understanding of even more eso-teric terms such as 'Top Red' or 'muppet', whose shifting meanings would be instantly clear to those involved in those particular conversations, but would need explaining to many of their neighbours and workmates who were not so closely involved. Of course, it would be entirely possible and legitimate to try to make sense of this situation using a concept such as a 'subculture', thereby simply moving the analytical problem down to a smaller level. The point is that it is easy to imagine conversations in Manchester in which the ways in which the opposition between reciprocity and non-reciprocity was being worked out at a particular moment were not immediately understood by all. In other words there are situations where even the alleged 'cultural grammar' would not be recognised or even does not exist. And the same is true in Papua New Guinea. Although in most of the cases that I have analysed there is broad mutual comprehension of the opposing positions in the dis-putes in question (or at least there is a widely imagined ability to understood what one's opponent truly means or is truly motivated by), that does not mean that we should *always* assume such mutual comprehension. And therefore it is perhaps wisest not to always take that assumption of an underlying cultural grammar as our analytical starting point.

This is not to say that analytically constructing such a grammar is always a mistake or some kind of totalitarian imposition, as many of us were taught at graduate school during the heyday of the master narrative of anti-master narrativity. It merely means constantly reminding ourselves of what we have long known: that every grammar that we construct to make sense of the mess of social life is a partial perspective of our own making that occludes whilst it reveals and partially freezes a process that it is itself a part of (see for example Wagner 1981:50–60). As Volosinov observes, language as system does not exist outside of the linguist or translator's construction of it as an abstrac-tion: a construction that is totally legitimate for the purposes of the linguist or translator provided that they remember that that is what it is. Wagner (1974:119) observes that concepts such as 'Society' form a kind of modern shorthand for particular social phenomena and processes. There is nothing inherently wrong with the use of such shorthands, as long as one remains constantly vigilant to their reifying potential.

The reason that I choose to finish with this example, a long way from Melanesia but very close to my heart, is to emphasise what I consider to be the most important point of this book. Although this book is clearly an ethnography geographically based in the part of the world known as Melanesia, I hope to have described an instance of a tendency towards a certain tension in social relations whose relevance transcends this particular time and place. From Matupit to Manchester the battle over the meaning of transactions and the obligations that they entail is central to how all of us make our way in a paradoxical world. As Mauss (1970:65) put it during the last period that the world's population faced the misery caused by global economic meltdown:

> A considerable part of our morality and our lives themselves are still permeated with this same atmosphere of the gift, where obligation and liberty intermingle. Fortunately, everything is still not wholly categorized in terms of buying and selling. Things still have sentimental as well as venal value, assuming values merely of this kind exist. We possess more than a tradesman morality.

As we again face the negative consequences of a refusal to acknowledge the importance of any morality other than that of the tradesman, an understanding of the ways in which people attempt to balance the values of 'buying and selling' with other equally socially important values is, if anything, more important now than it has been at any previous point in our history.

Notes

1. There is something of this contradiction expressed in Rio's description of the ways in which the acknowledgement of maternal nurture at life-cycle ceremonies creates 'a tension between the endogamous and exogamous perspectives' on the patrilineage on Ambrym Island. The same expression (with the terms reversed) could easily express the situation at Matupit. Rio's focus is on the how this tension expresses different perspectival moments within the reproduction of Ambrym customary sociality as a total system. My focus is on the ways in which this tension can be seen as reproductive on the one hand or as a motor of fundamental transformation on the other, depending on perspective. As mentioned in Chapter Two, the tension between a *vunatarai* and its 'children' is of long pedigree, but today it seems clear that in certain contexts, such as ownership of land, the balance tends to be shifted much more towards the 'endogamous' self-contained perspective. And this shift is itself a result and part of how Tolai people create a position for themselves within a global capitalist political economy, such as by seeking land rights for the purposes of securing investments such as cash crops or permanent houses. Hence the shifting nature of the 'tension' can be seen as evidence of radical social change, not just continuity.

2. Or as Launay (1982:11) puts it in his description of Dyula on the Ivory Coast of Africa: 'the very features which seem loudest to proclaim the continuity turn out, on closer inspection, to exhibit subtle but hardly inconsequential changes with the way things were'. See Leach (2004:12) for a surprisingly recent example of an approach taking brokers' descriptions at face value.

3. Interestingly the opposing sides in such a debate often rely on the same distinction between a Melanesian cultural system based on the Gift and a Western cultural system based upon the commodity. For example Strathern (1988) bases her distinction between the Melanesian relational sociality and Western idioms of the individual and society centrally on this distinction. Carrier and Carrier (1989) are sceptical about what could be considered as the ahistorical and essentialising claims of Strathern and the so-called 'New Melanesian Ethnography', but these authors also base their claims on the argument that 'The cultural logic and sociological order of the encroaching capitalist system revolve around class and the production relations that are a part of it, the realm of commodity relations. Alternatively the cultural logic and sociological order of precapitalist Melanesian societies are quite different, revolving around kinship and the exchange relationships that are a part of it, the realm of gift relation' (ibid.:14). Both positions draw heavily upon Gregory's (1980, 1982) original theoretical juxtaposition of Marx's analysis of the Commodity and Mauss's analysis of the Gift, leaving Gregory to subsequently complain (to seemingly little effect) that it was never his intention to assert that 'we are to Commodities as they are to Gifts' (Gregory 1997:47). As Keane (1997:12) observes: 'The point is not to abolish difference in the name of universals, but to thwart the inclination to turn all differences into versions of one big opposition, that is, into inversions of ourselves.'

4. Robbins analyses Urapmin cultural change using Sahlins' model of 'humiliation' according to which an enabling condition of radical cultural change is that a people come to view 'their culture-as something shameful and debased' (Robbins 2005:4). Or as Sahlins (2005:38) puts it, in order to modernise, they 'have to despise what they are, to hold their own existence in contempt – and want, then, to be someone else.' Whilst this model seems to fit well with the outright complete rejection of their own past that Robbins found amongst Urpamin, such an experience has not occurred amongst Tolai, many of whom have a much more ambiguous and sometimes extremely positive view of their own cultural heritage. Most Tolai, although they may want to change many aspects of their social lives, do not want to be 'someone else.' Yet if we were to take 'humiliation' as the essential precondition of cultural change, as many of the contributors to Robbins and Wardlow (2005) seem to imply, then the absence of such unambiguous 'humiliation' amongst Tolai would have to be taken as evidence for some sort of essential cultural continuity, which I hope I have demonstrated would also not be a useful description of their situation. Sahlins' 'humiliation' thesis rests upon the theoretical starting point of separate discrete cultural systems that come into contact and either subsume or change each other. Assuming the continuity and reproduction of fixed cultural systems of meaning, and assuming that indigenous people try to 'encompass what is happening to them in terms of their own world system' (Sahlins 2000:10), lead to the logical conclusion that it takes the destruction or denigration of that total system in order for new meanings to be possible. Even when Sahlins is concerned with 'history', which as Robbins accurately points out is clearly central to his reading of Levi-Straussian structuralism, the starting point is always 'the explication of the work of history in its most powerful form, the *persistence of structure* by means of event' (Sahlins 1976:23 cited in Robbins 2005:6, emphasis added). Hence the tendency for an either/or perspective on cultural change in which either the 'structure' persists or it is humiliated and destroyed.

5. See also Martin (2010). The long standing co-existence of Christianity and forms of ceremonial events that would today usually be glossed with the term *kastom* on the Gazelle suggests a situation that is very different from the one described by Tonkinson (1982) for Ambrym. There, people were largely negative towards ancestral practices, before the emergence of a pre-independence politically inspired re-evaluation during the 1970s, in which promotion of the category of *kastom* had a central part (Lindstrom 2007:166–67). Whatever the case might have been in Ambrym in the 1970s, Tolai *kastom* at the start of the twenty-first century was not primarily the political expression of a partial recovery from cultural 'humiliation'. For another example of a case from the South Pacific where *kastom* and Christianity are often viewed as mutually compatible, see Facey (1995). Tolai ambiguity towards the past not only contrasts with negative evaluations such as that described by Robbins for the Urapmin, but also with the opposite scenario in which people denigrate their inability to keep to ancestral customs in the face of colonialism and capitalism, such as the situation described by Akin (2004:299) for Kwaio people of the Solomon Islands.

6. Most typically, 'relationality' in the Melanesian context.

7. Likewise, this is not an analysis based upon the supposition, still very common in Melanesian anthropology, of a 'total system' (Mosko 1991:98) that 'reproduces' itself through exchange. Nor is my starting point the contrast between initial gift and return as perspectives that illuminate different stages in the circular motion of 'the system as a totality' (Rio 2007:450). Rio has performed a valuable service in re-drawing our attention to the importance of the distinction between prestation and counter-prestation in understanding the exchange of gifts, challenging many of received anthropological notions about the relationship between the Gift and reciprocity. My own concern is with the ways in which particular transactions can be characterised as initial free gifts or as returns. So the Big Shot who tries to keep reciprocal interdependence in the box called *kastom* will often present assistance that he gives to grassroots villagers as an expression of his individual generosity. The grassroots villagers in turn might present it as a partial and inadequate return for gifts that they have already given, as for example when construing ToNgala's establishment of a petrol station business as being the result of the labour that they gave as part of customary kinship ties outside of the sphere of *kastom*. Such differences of perspective are probably not best analysed as different stages in the reproduction of a shared total social system but instead as part of a wider conflict about the nature of the society that Big Shots and grassroots find themselves in. To the extent that there is a total system it is a total system that only appears from certain perspectives and is invisible or unpalatable from others.

Glossary

As in the rest of this book, in the following list, Kuanua words and expressions are given in *italics*, while Tok Pisin words are given in combined *italics and underlining*.

Word	Translation
a bit na tubuan	manager of *vunatarai tubuan*
a bobotoi	(time of) darkness
a ngala	literally 'a Big', but often used for 'Big Man'
a ngala na tutana	Big Man
a warwe takodo	a meeting to 'straighten instruction'
apik(tarai)	subdivision of *vunatarai*
apiktarai	see above
babau	fish trap
balaguan	impressive feast
bara	sign of the plural used only with words expressing relationship
bara talaina	friends
bara tamana	father and son (or sons)
bara tana or *nana*	mother and child or children
bara taulai	husband and wife
bara turana	brothers
bartamana	family
bikman	Big Man
biksot	Big Shot
bisnis	business
blut	blood
buai	betel nut
dinau	debts
famili	wider groups of relatives
famili	family
famili tru tru	real or proper family
halivim	literally 'help(ing)'
hausboi	boy's house
iap	fire
kaia	local spirits
kakalei	inalienable right
kastom	custom

kastom tasol	custom only
kulia	purchase or transfer
lualua	lineage leader
luluai	government-appointed village headman
malolo	relax
minamai	mortuary feast
mosbi	Port Moresby
motonoi	piece of beach reserved for fishing activities, only open to adult men
namata	a kind of initiation for the first-born son of a family
natugu	my child
ngala	big
pal na tabu	*tabu* house; house for storing shell money
pasin	way or lifestyle
pipiaman	rubbish man – a man who is unable to place himself in a position where his words carry any weight
popoai	culmination of launch of a new net
rabisman	rubbish man – a man who is unable to place himself in a position where his words carry any weight
raskols	criminals
savvy	know-how
singsing	customary ritual songs and dances
tabar	to give
tabu	customary shell wealth
tama	father
tamagu	my father
tamana	his or her father
tambu	in-law
tariau	the secret place in the bush of the male *tubuan* cult
tasol	only
tubuan	see Chapter Four
tultul	government-appointed deputy to the *luluai*
Turguvuai	standing together
umbene	fishing nets
uviana	rich man
variru	respect
varvateten	knowledge
vevedek	an occasion on which *tabu* is counted
vunatarai	a matrilineage often translated as clan
vuvue	special feast
waira	outsiders or 'strangers', i.e. non-Tolai Papua New Guineans

wantok	literally someone from the same language group, but can be used for 'friend', 'kinsmen', 'people to whom one has an obligation'
wariru	or _variru_, literally 'respect'
warwarngala na	child of the clan
wokboi	work boy

References

Akin, D. (2004). Ancestral Vigilance and the Corrective Conscience: Kastom as Culture in a Melanesian Society. *Anthropological Theory*, 4 (3), 299–324.

Appadurai, A. (1986). Introduction. Commodities and the Politics of Value. In A. Appadurai (ed.), *The Social Life of Things: Commodities in Cultural Perspective* (pp. 3–63). Cambridge. Cambridge University Press.

Bakan, J. (2004). *The Corporation: The Pathological Pursuit of Money and Power.* New York: Simon and Schuster.

Bashkow, I. (2006). *The Meaning of Whitemen: Race and Modernity in the Orokaiva Cultural World.* Chicago: The University of Chicago Press.

Berman, B. (1998). Ethnicity, Patronage and the African State: The Politics of Uncivil Nationalism. *African Affairs*, 97, 305–341.

Blok, A. (1975). *The Mafia of a Sicilian Village: A Study of Violent Peasant Entrepreneurs.* Oxford: Blackwell.

Boas, F. (1966). *Kwakiutl Ethnography.* Chicago: The University of Chicago Press.

Bradley, S.C. (1982). *Tolai Women and Development* (Ph.D thesis). London: University College London.

Briggs, C. (1998). You're a Liar – You're Just Like a Woman! Constructing Dominant Ideologies of Language in Warao Men's Gossip. In B. Schieffelin, K. Woolard, and P. Kroskrity (eds.), *Language Ideologies: Practice and Theory* (pp. 3–47). New York: Oxford University Press.

Burridge, K. (1975). The Melanesian Manager. In J. Beattie, and R. Lienhardt (eds.), *Studies in Social Anthropology: Essays in Memory of E.E. Evans-Pritchard* (pp. 86–104). Oxford: Clarendon Press.

Carrier, J., and Carrier, A. (1989). *Wage, Trade, and Exchange in Melanesia: A Manus Society in the Modern State.* Berkeley: University of California Press.

Cassidy, J. (2006, 6 February). The Red Devil. *The New Yorker* .

Dumont, L. (1970). *Homo Hierarchicus: An Essay on the Caste System.* Chicago: University of Chicago Press.

Epstein, A.L. (1963). The Economy of Modern Matupit: Continuity and Change on the Gazelle Peninsula. *Oceania*, 33, 182–215.

Epstein, A.L. (1964). Variation and Social Structure: Local Organization on the Island of Matupit. *Oceania*, 35, 1–25.

Epstein, A.L. (1969). *Matupit: Land, Politics and Change among the Tolai of New Britain.* Canberra: Australian National University Press.

Epstein, A.L. (1970). Autonomy and Identity: Aspects of Political Development on the Gazelle Peninsula. *Anthropological Forum*, 11, 427–443.

Epstein, A.L. (1988). Matupit Revisited: Local Organization, Change and the Sense of Place. *Journal de la Société des Océanistes*, 86, 21–40.

Epstein, A.L. (1991). Changing Patterns of Tolai Residence and Marital Choice. *Ethnology*, 31, 49–64.

Epstein, A.L. (1992). *In the Midst of Life: Affect and Ideation in the World of the Tolai.* Berkeley: University of California Press.

Epstein, A.L. (1999). *Gunantuna: Aspects of the Person, the Self and the Individual among the Tolai.* Bathurst: Crawford Publishing House.

Epstein, A.L. (n.d.). Unpublished Field Notes. University of California at San Diego: held at Special Collections.

Epstein, T.S. (1964). Personal Capital Formation among the Tolai of New Britain. In R. Firth, and B.S. Yamey (eds.), *Capital Saving and Credit in Peasant Societies* (pp. 53–68). London: George Allen and Unwin Ltd.

Epstein, T.S. (1968). *Capitalism, Primitive and Modern: Some Aspects of Tolai Economic Growth.* Manchester: Manchester University Press.

Epstein, T.S. (1970). The Mataungan Affair. *New Guinea,* 4, 8–14.

Evans-Pritchard, E.E. (1940). *The Nuer: A Description of the Modes of Livelihood and Political Institutions of a Nilotic People.* Oxford: Oxford University Press.

Eves, R. (2000). Sorcery's the Curse: Modernity, Envy and the Flow of Sociality in a Melanesian Society. *Journal of the Royal Anthropological Institute,* 6 (3), 453–468.

Fingleton, J. (1985). *Changing Land Tenure in Melanesia: The Tolai Experience* (Ph.D. thesis). Canberra: Australian National University.

Fingleton, J. (2005). Introduction. In J. Fingleton (ed.), *Privatising Land in the Pacific: A Defence of Customary Tenures* (pp. 1–5). Canberra: The Australia Institute.

Fitzpatrick, P. (1983). The Knowledge and Politics of Land Law. *Melanesian Law Journal,* 11, 14–34.

Foster, R. (1995). *Social Reproduction in Melanesia: Mortuary Ritual, Gift Exchange, and Custom in the Tanga Islands.* Cambridge: Cambridge University Press.

Foster, R. (2002). *Materializing the Nation: Commodities, Consumption and Media in Papua New Guinea.* Bloomington: Indiana University Press.

Gal, S. (1998). Multiplicity and Contention among Language Ideologies: A Commentary. In B. Schieffelin, K. Woolard, and P. Kroskrity (eds.), *Language Ideologies: Practice and Theory* (pp. 87–110). New York: Oxford University Press.

Gaywood, Patrol Officer. (1959). *Report on the Toma Case.* Located in Epstein Collection. Special Collections, Geisel Library: University of California at San Diego.

Gewertz, D.B., and Errington, F.K. (1991). *Twisted Histories, Altered Contexts; Representing the Chambri in a World System.* Cambridge: Cambridge University Press.

Gewertz, D.B., and Errington, F.K. (1999). *Emerging Class in Papua New Guinea: The Telling of Difference.* Cambridge: Cambridge University Press.

Gregory, C. (1980). Gifts to Men and Gifts to God: Gift Exchange and Capital Accumulation in Contemporary Papua. *Man,* 15 (4), 626–652.

Gregory, C. (1982). *Gifts and Commodities.* London: Academic Press.

Gregory, C. (1994). Exchange and Reciprocity. In T. Ingold (ed.), *Companion Encyclopedia of Anthropology* (pp. 911–939). London: Routledge.

Gregory, C. (1997). *Savage Money: The Anthropology and Politics of Commodity Exchange.* Amsterdam: Harwood.

Guha, R. (1983). The Prose of Counter-Insurgency. In R. Guha (ed.), *Subaltern Studies II: Writings on South Asian History and Society* (pp. 1–40). Delhi: Oxford University Press.

Hobsbawm, E. (1973). *The Age of Revolution: Europe 1789–1848.* London: Sphere Books Ltd.

Hogbin, I. (1951). *Transformation Scene: The Changing Culture of a New Guinea Village.* London: Routledge and Kegan Paul Ltd.

Hornby, N. (1992). *Fever Pitch.* London: Victor Gollanz.

Hughes, H. (2003). *Aid Has Failed the Pacific.* Retrieved March 12, 2006, from The Centre for Independent Studies: http://www.cis.org.au/IssueAnalysis/ia33/ia33.htm

Irvine, J. (2006). Speech and Language Community. In K. Brown (ed.), *Encyclopedia of Language and Linguistics,* 2nd edition (pp. 689–696). Oxford: Elsevier.

Jessep, O. (1980). Land Demarcation in New Ireland. *Melanesian Law Journal,* 8 (1 and 2), 112–133.

Jolly, M. (1992). Specters of Inauthenticity. *Contemporary Pacific,* 49 (1), 49–72.

Jolly, M. (1994). *Women of the Place: Kastom, Colonialism and Gender in Vanuatu.* Chur: Harwood Academic Publishers.

Jorgenson, D. (1997). Who or What is a Landowner? Mythology and Marking the Ground in a Papua New Guinea Mining Project. *Anthropological Forum,* 7 (4), 599–628.

Kahn, M. (1986). *Always Hungry, Never Greedy: Food and the Expression of Gender in Melanesian Society.* Cambridge: Cambridge University Press.

Keane, W. (2007). *Christian Moderns: Freedom and Fetish in the Mission Encounter.* Berkeley: University of California Press.

Keesing, R. (1981). *Cultural Anthropology: A Contemporary Perspective.* New York: Holt, Rinehart and Winston.

Keesing, R. (1991). *Custom and Confrontation: The Kwaio Struggle for Cultural Autonomy.* Chicago: University of Chicago Press.

Knauft, B. (2002). *Exchanging the Past: A Rainforest World of Before and After.* Chicago: The University of Chicago Press.

Kulick, D. (1998). Anger, Gender, Language Shift, and the Politics of Revelation in a Papua New Guinean Village. In B. Schieffelin, K. Woolard, and P. Kroskrity (eds.), *Language Ideologies: Practice and Theory* (pp. 87–110). New York: Oxford University Press.

Laidlaw, J. (2002). For an Anthropology of Ethics and Freedom. *Journal of the Royal Anthropological Institute,* 8 (2), 311–332.

Launay, R. (1982). *Traders without Trade: Responses to Change in Two Dyula Communities.* Cambridge: Cambridge University Press.

Lea, D. (1997). *Melanesian Land Tenure in a Contemporary and Philosophical Context.* Lanham: University Press of America.

Leach, J. (2003). *Creative Land: Place and Procreation on the Rai Coast of Papua New Guinea.* Oxford: Berghahn Books.

Lederman, R. (1986). *What Gifts Engender: Social Relations and Politics in Mendi, Highland Papua New Guinea.* Cambridge: Cambridge University Press.

Lederman, R. (1991). 'Interests' in Exchange: Increment, Equivalence and the Limits of Big-Manship. In M. Godelier, and M. Strathern (eds.), *Big Men and Great Men: Personifications of Power in Melanesia* (pp. 215–233). Cambridge: Cambridge University Press.

Lindstrom, L. (2008). Melanesian Kastom and Its Transformations. *Anthropological Forum,* 18 (2), 161–178.

Lindstrom, L., and White, G. (1997). Introduction: Chiefs Today. In G. White, and L. Lindstrom (eds.), *Chiefs Today: Traditional Leadership and the Postcolonial State* (pp. 1–18). Stanford: Stanford University Press.

Macpherson, C.B. (1962). *The Political Theory of Possessive Individualism: Hobbes to Locke.* Oxford: Oxford University Press.

Malinowski, B. (1979). *The Ethnography of Malinowski* (edited by M. Young). London: Routledge and Kegan Paul.

Mannering, C. (n.d.). *English Kuanua Dictionary.* Vunairima: Methodist Mission.

Martin, K. (2004). *Land, Custom and Conflict in East New Britain.* Retrieved 12 June, 2005, from Resource Management in Asia-Pacific. Working Paper No. 53. Canberra. Resource Management in Asia-Pacific Program. Resource School of Pacific Studies. The Australian National University: http://rspas.anu.edu.au/rmap/workingpapers.php

Martin, K. (2006a). Land, Customary and Non-Customary in East New Britain. In J. Weiner, and K. Glaskin (eds.), *Customary Land Tenure and Registration in Australia and Papua New Guinea: Anthropological Perspectives* (pp. 39–56). Canberra: The Australian National University Press.

Martin, K. (2006b). A Fish Trap for Custom; How Nets Work at Matupit. *Paideuma*, 52, 73–90.

Martin, K. (2007a). The Chairman of the Clan; Emerging Social Divisions in a Melanesian Social Movement. *Paideuma*, 53, 111–125.

Martin, K. (2007b). Your Own Buai You Must Buy: The Contested Ideology of Possessive Individualism in East New Britain. *Anthropological Forum*, 17 (3), 285–298.

Martin, K. (2008a). Tourism as Social Contest (Introduction for special edition). *Tourism, Culture and Communication*, 8 (2), 59–69.

Martin, K. (2008b). The Work of Tourism and the Fight for a New Economy; The Case of the Papua New Guinea Mask Festival. *Tourism, Culture and Communication*, 8 (2), 97–107.

Martin, K. (2008c). Custom: The Limits of Reciprocity in Village Redevelopment. In K. Sykes (ed.), *Ethnographies of Moral Reasoning: Living Paradox of a Global Age* (pp. 93–116). New York: Palgrave USA.

Martin, K. (2009, 26 August). Magic and the Myth of Rational Markets. *Financial Times.*

Martin, K. (2010). Living Pasts: Contested Tourism Authenticities. *Annals of Tourism Research*, 37 (2), 537–554.

Marx, K. (1956 [1847]). *The Poverty of Philosophy.* Moscow: Foreign Languages Publishing House.

Marx, K. (1970). *A Contribution to the Critique of Political Economy.* Moscow: Progress Publishers.

Marx, K. (1976 [1867]). *Capital: A Critique of Political Economy.* Volume One. Harmondsworth: Penguin Books Ltd.

Marx, K., and Engels, F. (2000). *Collected Works* Volume 50. London: Lawrence and Wishart.

Mauss, M. (1970). *The Gift: Forms and Functions of Exchange in Primitive Societies.* London: Cohen and West Ltd.

Merlan, F., and Rumsey, A. (1991). *Ku Waru: Language and Segmentary Politics in the Western Nebliyer Valley, Papua New Guinea.* Cambridge: Cambridge University Press.

Methodist Overseas Mission. (1964 [1939]). *A Kuanua Dictionary*. Rabaul: Methodist Mission Press.

Moran, M. (2003). *Beyond the Coral Sea: Travels in the Old Empires of the South-West Pacific*. London: HarperCollins.

Mosko, M. (1991). Great Men and Total Systems: North Mekeo Hereditary Authority and Social Reproduction. In M. Godelier, and M. Strathern (eds.), *Big Men and Great Men: Personifications of Power in Melanesia* (pp. 97–114). Cambridge: Cambridge University Press.

Moulik, T. (1973). Money, Motivation and Cash Cropping. *New Guinea Research Bulletin*, 53. Canberra. New Guinea Research Unit. The Australian National University.

Myers, F. (1986). *Pintupi Country, Pintupi Self: Sentiment, Place and Politics among Western Desert Aborigines*. Washington DC: Smithsonian Institution Press.

Narotzky, S. (1997). *New Directions in Economic Anthropology*. London: Pluto Press.

Neumann, K. (1992). *Not the Way It Really Was: Constructing the Tolai Past*. Honolulu: University of Hawaii Press.

Neumann, K. (1996). *Rabaul Yu Swit Moa Yet: Surviving the 1994 Volcanic Eruption*. Oxford: Oxford University Press.

Orwell, G. (1968). *Collected Essays*. London: Secker and Warburg.

Otto, T. (1992). The Ways of Kastam: Tradition as Category and Practice in a Manus Village. *Oceania*, 62 (2), 264–283.

Parkinson, R. (2000 [1907]). *Thirty Years in the South Seas*. Honolulu: University of Hawaii Press.

Petersen, N. (1993). Demand Sharing: Reciprocity and the Pressure for Generosity among Foragers. *American Anthropologist*, 95 (4), 860–874.

Popisil, L. (1963). *Kapauku Papuan Economy*. New Haven: Yale University Press.

Pullen-Burry, B. (1909). *In a German Colony*. London: Methuen and Co.

Radin, M. (1996). *Contested Commodities: The Trouble with Trade in Sex, Children, Body Parts, and Other Things*. Cambridge, MA: Harvard University Press.

Reay, M. (1974). Changing Conventions of Dispute Settlement in the Minj Area. In A.L. Epstein (ed.), *Contention and Dispute: Aspects of Law and Social Control in Melanesia* (pp. 198–239). Canberra: The Australian National University Press.

Rio, K. (2007). Denying the Gift: Aspects of Ceremonial Exchange and Sacrifice on Ambrym Island, Vanuatu. *Anthropological Theory*, 7 (4), 449–470.

Robbins, J. (2004). *Becoming Sinners: Christianity and Moral Torment in a Papua New Guinea Society*. Berkeley: University of California Press.

Robbins, J. (2005). Introduction: Humiliation and Transformation: Marshall Sahlins and the Study of Cultural Change in Melanesia. In J. Robbins, and H. Wardlow (eds.), *The Making of Global and Local Modernities in Melanesia: Humiliation, Transformation and the Nature of Cultural Change* (pp. 4–21). Aldershot: Ashgate Publishing Ltd.

Robbins, J. (2007). Between Reproduction and Freedom: Morality, Value and Radical Cultural Change. *Ethnos*, 72 (3), 293–314.

Robbins, J., and Wardlow, H. (2005). *The Making of Global and Local Modernities in Melanesia: Humiliation, Transformation and the Nature of Cultural Change*. Aldershot: Ashgate Publishing Ltd.

Rumsey, A. (1981). Kinship and Context among the Ngarinyin. *Oceania*, 51 (3), 181–192.

Sack, P. (1974). The Range of Traditional Tolai Remedies. In A.L. Epstein (ed.), *Contention and Dispute: Aspects of Law and Social Control in Melanesia* (pp. 67–92). Canberra: The Australian National University Press.

Sahlins, M. (1963). Poor Man, Rich Man, Big-Man, Chief: Political Types in Melanesia and Polynesia. *Comparative Studies in Society and History*, 5 (3), 285–303.

Sahlins, M. (1974). *Stone Age Economics*. London: Tavistock.

Sahlins, M. (2000). *Culture in Practice; Selected Essays*. New York: Zone Books.

Sahlins, M. (2005). The Economics of Develop-man in the Pacific. In J. Robbins, and H. Wardlow (eds.), *The Making of Global and Local Modernities in Melanesia* (pp. 23–42). Aldershot: Ashgate Publishing Limited.

Salisbury, R. (1966). Politics and Shell-Money Finance in New Britain. In M. Schwartz, and A. Tuden (eds.), *Political Anthropology* (pp. 113–128). Chicago: Aldine Press.

Salisbury, R. (1970). *Vunamami: Economic Transformation in a Traditional Society*. Berkeley: University of California Press.

Salzmann, Z. (1993). *Language, Culture, and Society: An Introduction to Linguistic Anthropology*. Boulder, CO: Westview Press.

Schneider, O. (1905). *Muschelgeldstudien*. Dresden: Verein für Erdkunde.

Scott, J. (1988). *Seeing Like a State: How Certain Schemes to Improve the Human Condition Have Failed*. New Haven: Yale University Press.

Scott, M. (2007). *The Severed Snake: Matrilineages, Making Place, and a Melanesian Christianity in Southeast Solomon Islands*. Durham: Carolina Academic Press.

Silverstein, M. (1976). Shifters, Linguistic Categories, and Cultural Description. In K. Basso, and H. Selby (eds.), *Meaning in Anthropology* (pp. 11–56). Albuquerque: University of New Mexico Press.

Silverstein, M. (2004). 'Cultural' Concepts and the Language-Culture Nexus. *Current Anthropology*, 45 (5), 621–652.

Simet, J. (1991). *Tabu: Analysis of a Tolai Ritual Object* (Ph.D. thesis). Canberra: Australian National University.

Smith, A. (1994 [1776]). *An Inquiry into the Nature and Causes of the Wealth of Nations*. New York: The Modern Library.

Smith, M.F. (1994). *Hard Times on Kariru Island: Poverty, Development, and Morality in a Papua New Guinea Village*. Honolulu: University of Hawaii Press.

Strathern, M. (1979). The Self in Self-Decoration. *Oceania*, 49 (4), 241–257.

Strathern, M. (1988). *The Gender of the Gift: Problems with Women and Problems with Society in Melanesia*. Berkeley: University of California Press.

Strathern, M. (1999). *Property, Substance, and Effect: Anthropological Essays on Persons and Things*. London: Athlone Press.

Sykes, K. (2001). Paying a School Fee is a Father's Duty: Critical Citizenship in Central New Ireland. *American Ethnologist*, 28 (1), 5–31.

Thompson, E.P. (1991). *Customs in Common*. London: Penguin.

Tonkinson, R. (1982). National Identity and the Problem of *Kastom* in Vanuatu. In R. Keesing and R. Tonkinson (eds.), *Reinventing Traditional Culture: The Politics of Kastom in Island Melanesia*. Special Issue *Mankind*, 13 (4), 305–315.

Tuzin, D. (1997). *The Cassowary's Revenge: The Life and Death of Masculinity in a New Guinea Society*. Chicago: The University of Chicago Press.

Volosinov, V. (1973). *Marxism and the Philosophy of Language*. New York: Seminar Press.

Wagner, R. (1974). Are There Social Groups in the New Guinea Highlands? In M. Leaf (ed.), *Frontiers of Anthropology – An Introduction to Anthropological Thinking* (pp. 95–122). New York: Nostrand Company.

Wagner, R. (1981). *The Invention of Culture*. Chicago: The University of Chicago Press.

Wagner, R. (1986). *Asinawarong: Ethos, Image and Social Power among the Usen Barok of New Ireland*. Princeton: Princeton University Press.

Wagner, R. (1988). Visible Sociality: The Daribi Community. In J. Weiner (ed.), *Mountain Papuans: Historical and Comparative Perspectives from New Guinea Fringe Highlands Societies* (pp. 39–72). Ann Arbor: University of Michigan Press.

Wagner, R. (1991). The Fractal Person. In M. Godelier, and M. Strathern (eds.), *Big Men and Great Men: Personifications of Power in Melanesia*. Cambridge: Cambridge University Press.

Woolard, K.A., and Schieffelin, B. (1994). Language Ideology. *Annual Review of Anthropology*, 23, 55–82.

World Bank. (2001). *Project Appraisal Document on the First Phase of a Proposed Loan in the Amoung of US$ 25.26 Millions Equivalent to the Independent State of Papua New Guinea for a Second Gazelle Restoration Project*. Retrieved 18 January, 2005, from Urban Development Sector Unit, Papua New Guinea and Pacific Islands Country Management Unit East Asia and Pacific Regional Office: http://www-wds.worldbank.org/external/default/main?pagePK=64193027andp.PK=64187937andtheSitePK=523679andmenuPK=64187510andsearchMenuPK=64187511andtheSitePK=523679andentityID=000094946_99112505311322andsearchMenuPK=64187511andtheSitePK=5236979.